THE I
HYPOTH
GREEK NAT

It has often been thought that the ancient Greeks did not take mechanics seriously as part of the workings of nature, and that this contributed to the marginalization of their natural philosophy. In this book Sylvia Berryman challenges that assumption, arguing that the idea that the world works 'like a machine' can be found in ancient Greek thought, predating the early modern philosophy with which it is most closely associated. Her discussion ranges over topics including balancing and equilibrium, lifting water, sphere-making and models of the heavens, and ancient Greek pneumatic theory, with detailed analysis of thinkers such as Aristotle, Archimedes and Hero of Alexandria. Her book shows scholars of ancient Greek philosophy why it is necessary to pay attention to mechanics, and shows historians of science why the differences between ancient and modern reactions to mechanics are not as great as was generally thought. Her historical treatment of the meaning of 'mechanistic' or 'mechanical' is of value to contemporary philosophical debates about explanation.

SYLVIA BERRYMAN is Associate Professor, Department of Philosophy, University of British Columbia.

THE MECHANICAL
HYPOTHESIS IN ANCIENT
GREEK NATURAL PHILOSOPHY

SYLVIA BERRYMAN

CAMBRIDGE
UNIVERSITY PRESS

CAMBRIDGE
UNIVERSITY PRESS

The Edinburgh Building, Cambridge CB2 8RU, UK

Published in the United States of America by Cambridge University Press, New York

Cambridge University Press is part of the University of Cambridge.

It furthers the University's mission by disseminating knowledge in the pursuit of education, learning and research at the highest international levels of excellence.

www.cambridge.org
Information on this title: www.cambridge.org/9781107657618

First published 2009
First paperback edition 2013

A catalogue record for this publication is available from the British Library

ISBN 978-0-521-76376-9 Hardback
ISBN 978-1-107-65761-8 Paperback

Cambridge University Press has no responsibility for the persistence or accuracy of URLs for external or third-party internet websites referred to in this publication, and does not guarantee that any content on such websites is, or will remain, accurate or appropriate.

Contents

Illustrations

Acknowledgements

Given the wide-ranging nature of this project, stretching over several years and two research leaves, I can only begin to acknowledge the advice, encouragement and support I have received. For invaluable advice, comments on chapters, encouragement and help in articulating my project at various stages, I am immensely grateful to Markus Asper, Bob Batterman, Tad Brennan, David Creese, Andrea Falcon, Monte Johnson, Sean Kelsey, Paul Keyser, Stephen Menn, John Murdoch, Tim O'Keefe, Georges Rey, Alan Richardson, Bob Sharples, Heinrich von Staden and Rob Wisnovsky. I owe a great ongoing debt to my teachers, Jim Hankinson, Alex Mourelatos, Richard Sorabji and Stephen White, who have shaped the way I approach the study of ancient Greek philosophy. This project has required going out of my field, and I particularly thank Daniel Garber and Michael Mahoney for allowing me to audit their graduate seminar on Galileo and Descartes; Alan Gabbey for helpful advice on More and Boyle; Alan Bowen for comments and references on the sections on astronomy; and Len Berggren and Jim Evans for instruction on astronomical devices.

For generous support during the academic year 2001–2, I would like to thank the Center for Hellenic Studies, the National Humanities Center and National Endowment for the Humanities, and the College of Humanities at The Ohio State University. For research funding during the academic year 2003–4, I am grateful to the Institute for Advanced Study, Princeton, and the National Science Foundation; this material is based on work supported by the National Science Foundation under Grant No. 0500100. I thank the Social Science and

Humanities Council of Canada for additional research support during the last year of revisions. I am grateful to the Department of Philosophy and College of Humanities at The Ohio State University and The University of British Columbia for granting me study leaves to undertake this project, and for lending moral support to work on a project that extends beyond a narrow view of the scope of philosophy. Not every department of philosophy would humour junior scholars looking for philosophical insight in catapult building manuals.

Earlier versions of some parts of chapters have appeared in other publications. I thank Brill for permission to use material from 'Ancient Automata and Mechanical Explanation', published in *Phronesis* 48.4 (2003), which appears in reworked form as part of Chapters 2 and 6, and Academic Printing and Publishing, for permission to reproduce parts of my article, 'Galen and the Mechanical Philosophy', *Apeiron: a Journal for Ancient Philosophy and Science* 35 (2002), included in revised form within Chapter 6. I also thank W. W. Fortenbaugh and Rutgers University Press for permission to use material within Chapter 5 from my article 'The Evidence for Strato from Hero of Alexandria's *Pneumatics*', forthcoming in the Rutgers University Series in the Classical Humanities volume on Strato of Lampsacus.

This tale grew in the telling. For discussion, ideas and encouragement, I particularly thank colleagues and audiences at the Center for Hellenic Studies, The University of Texas at Austin, Oberlin College, The Ohio State University, the University of Maryland at College Park, UNC-Greensboro, the University of South Carolina, the History of Science Department at Harvard University, the Stanford University conference on artificial life, The University of British Columbia, Columbia University, Northwestern University, the Friday Harbor History of Science Workshop, the History of Science Society, and Cambridge University History and Philosophy of Science Department. I benefitted greatly from comments by anonymous readers on an earlier draft of this manuscript; their generous and detailed observations allowed me to avoid many infelicities, mistakes and omissions. Roger Stanev and Max Weiss gave able assistance in checking references and editing; I am indebted to Jan Chapman's fine copy-editing suggestions and to Annette Coppings' proofreading. Abbreviations of the titles of ancient Greek works follow Liddell, Scott and Jones (1996), except for those of Galen, which follow Hankinson (1998b); Latin works follow Hornblower and Spawforth (2003). It hardly needs to be said that all errors are my own responsibility.

Introduction

Historians agree on the importance, both to natural philosophy and to the development of the modern sciences, of the emergence of a 'mechanical world picture': many have studied its history, defining features and governing motivations. One important reason for the development of this world picture in the early modern period seems to have been the reintroduction of a number of ancient Greek texts.[1] Rose and Drake suggest that it is no coincidence that the circulation of the Aristotelian *Mechanica* coincided with the formative period for modern science.[2]

Against this background, it might seem necessary to account for the absence of any comparable interest, amongst the ancient Greeks themselves, in the implications of their mechanics for natural philosophy. A number of classic explanations have been offered as to why ancient Greek thinkers might not have seen the applicability of ideas from mechanics to the understanding of the natural world. I suggest that these explanations are spurious, and moreover that there is evidence of a philosophical reception of ideas from mechanics, especially in late antiquity. The evidence is scattered and often only preserved in the criticisms of its detractors: the dominant figures in late antique philosophy rejected the 'mechanical hypothesis'. But its

[1] The Aristotelian *Mechanica*, works of Archimedes, Vitruvius and Hero of Alexandria all came into circulation in the sixteenth century, many of them acquiring considerable popularity.

[2] Rose and Drake (1971). The treatise gained currency after it was included in the Greek Aldine edition of 1495–8, the first printed edition of Aristotle's works. See the appendix for more on its history.

very existence is an interesting development that should not be overlooked.

Ancient Greek mechanics was a broad and diverse field, including a number of subfields concerned with different kinds of 'working artifacts' and the theory of their operation. Its branches include not only weightlifting technology, but also 'pneumatics', ballistics, sphere-making, and the making of automated theatrical displays. Its practitioners developed a number of theories and analytical techniques that were of interest to natural philosophers. The theory of weightlifting technology included analysis of circular motion as compound; the idea that causes of motion compounded mathematically; the use of weight as a way to measure effort or force; a distinction between weight and downward impetus; the notion that various parameters involved in the causes of motion co-vary, and that a given force can, ideally, be made to lift any given weight. The property of elasticity of matter was highlighted by third-century work on pneumatics and ballistics and seems to have been the inspiration for the idea of *eutonia* so important in Stoic physics. Pneumatics also discovered techniques for moving fluids intermittently, forcefully and uphill, providing the inspiration for a new approach to explanation in medical physiology and forcing philosophical reconsideration of the theory of void. The making of theatrical automata offered a new model of causal sequencing, showing how intended results could be preprogrammed to result by material means through a chain of events, and offering a new model for divine control of the natural world. The possibility that animals, the heavenly bodies, human beings – or even the whole cosmos – might work like mechanical devices merited consideration.

I suggest that there are a number of reasons why the reception of mechanics in Greek antiquity has not been taken more seriously. One is simply the practice of focusing on one branch of mechanics alone as definitive of the field: lever technology, because it played such a prominent role in the development of mathematical techniques for the new physics of the seventeenth century, is often treated by modern scholars as *constituting* the field of mechanics. This was not so in antiquity, nor, incidentally, in the eyes of figures such as Descartes and Boyle, who developed the idea of a 'mechanical philosophy'. Pneumatic technology, for example, played a signifi-cant – if sometimes overlooked – role in seventeenth-century texts articulating the idea that nature might work 'like a machine'.

Another prominent reason why scholars have not thought that there was much to say about the reception of mechanics in antiquity is a belief that the ancient Greeks regarded mechanics as working 'against nature', as an art rather than part of natural philosophy, or as associated with trickery and deception. Claims of this sort about the ancient attitude to mechanics are found especially amongst historians of science and are partly based on some remarks by Galileo. Galileo's bid to regard mechanics as material for natural philosophy depends on rejecting some misconceptions of the status of mechanics. However, these conceptions gained currency in the Middle Ages, not Greek antiquity.[3]

Historians of technology offer somewhat different analyses of the supposed indifference to mechanics amongst Greek intellectuals in general. They postulate a disinterest in the menial or practical disciplines, often attributed to a disdain for manual labour common to a slave-holding society. While there are Greek texts that show this dismissal of the practical – Plutarch's famous presentation of Archimedes as only turning to practical mechanics under royal command, and the claim that Plato was angry about the association of mathematics with instruments, for example – there is little evi-dence that such disdain dominated the intellectual reception of ancient mechanics. The field was not perceived as purely practical: it was grounded in mathematical techniques and interacted with natural philosophical theory.

A further barrier to the recognition of the ancient reception of mechanics exists in twentieth-century histories of philosophy. This is the tendency to classify natural philosophical systems in terms of a dichotomy between teleological and so-called 'mechanistic' schools of thought. Because ancient atomism is taken as the prime example of the latter, yet developed before there was much evidence of mechan-ics, we are left to conclude that the school called 'mechanistic' arose

[3] I argue this in detail in the appendix to this volume.

without the inspiration of mechanics. At the least, this framing of the ancient debate in seventeenth-century terms has tended to minimize or mask the extent of the impact of Hellenistic mechanics on natural philosophy.

It is often thought that – despite some 'eclectics' in the Hellenistic period – the dichotomous division into teleological and mechanistic schools aptly characterized the viable alternatives available through-out the remainder of the ancient Greek world. The idea that the emergence of modern science involved the rejection of teleological thinking in favour of mechanism too easily plays into a caricature in which the scientific advances of the mechanistic atomists were impeded by the teleological Aristotelians. A simplistic understanding of the dichotomy would suggest that only ancient atomism is worthy of serious philosophical consideration as a precursor to modern ideas on causal explanation, and much ancient natural philosophy would too readily be dismissed as naive, *ad hoc*, superseded, or philosophically uninteresting.

There are, of course, many problems with this caricature.[4] Aristotle's school, after all, produced the earliest surviving treatise on mechanics. It was Aristotle, rather than Democritus, who even considered the idea that animal functions could be understood by comparison to mechanical devices. It has long been noticed that some of those most interested in mechanical comparisons in explaining the functioning of organisms are also committed teleologists; labelling hard-to-classify views as 'eclectic' is unilluminating.[5]

The dangers inherent in the twentieth-century classifications of the 'mechanistic' are best illustrated by two important works from the early 1960s. Dijksterhuis' classic work, *The Mechanization of the World Picture*, traces the history of the emergence of a concept by looking for antecedents of a modern notion of the 'mechanistic' in antiquity. His work illustrates the ways in which focus on the different senses of the term 'mechanical' affects the questions that are considered. Taking as a given that atomism is a 'mechanistic'

---

[4] A point well made by De Groot (2008).
[5] For difficulties with the classification 'eclectic', see Donini (1988).

theory, Dijksterhuis traces the prehistory, in antiquity, of ideas contributing to what came to be called a 'mechanical' world-view – the development of mathematical physics and corpuscular materialism – and scarcely considers the contributions made by the discipline of mechanics.[6] Tellingly, he downplays the contribution of the machine analogy to the history he is writing, *because* of its incompatibility with atomism.[7]

This shows how the identification of atomism with mechanical can mislead, since it risks omitting a significant facet of the history of the reception of mechanics, and missing the opportunity to illuminate the process by which a particular *kind* of materialism – not that of the Stoics, for example – acquired an unparalleled authority in early modern science. The appeal to mechanics as a reference point played a role in the emergence of a consensus as to the properties that *should* be ascribed to matter, a consensus that did not exist in antiquity. Moreover, a history of the development of mathematical techniques for analysing motion and its causes would be lacking if it did not consider the contributions of mechanical theory.

Even an author as aware as Sambursky of the importance of mechanics to the natural philosophy of late antiquity is hampered by the use of the term 'mechanistic' to describe the atomists. Sambursky's *The Physical World of Late Antiquity* offers a rich and searching survey of the reception of mechanics in ancient natural philosophy. Avoiding some of the assumptions of Dijksterhuis' approach, he notes the importance of Hellenistic machinery in producing a 'mechanistic attitude'.[8] The debt the present work owes to Sambursky's synthetic knowledge of late antiquity will be apparent. Yet the association of the 'mechanical' with atomism prevents the importance of the ancient discipline of mechanics from coming through more clearly in his study.

Although the core of this work is a historical account of the emergence of mechanics and its impact on natural philosophy, I believe

---

[6] Dijksterhuis (1961), pp. 72–5, is dismissive of the ancient understanding of mechanics.
[7] Dijksterhuis (1961), p. 12.   [8] Sambursky (1962), p. xi.

that to fail to address the existing terminological confusions would inevitably lead to misunderstandings. Despite all the careful attention paid to the exact meaning of the term 'teleological', the term 'mechanical' is freely used in current scholarship in sometimes anachronistic or ill-defined – and certainly various – ways, as though it were a self-evident concept available to all. This obscures the historical development of ideas about mechanics, and the critical historical role played by the discipline of mechanics in *formulating* our notions of 'the mechanical' and of the natural world.

Contemporary notions of the 'mechanistic' are in fact quite various, despite a belief in its simplicity and perspicuity. Attention to the history of the term, and to the different ways 'the mechanical' can be used – to describe the genesis of a view, or our own perception of its systematic features – helps us disentangle its complex meanings and, with it, the origin of the belief in the perspicuity of the term.[9] This 'perspicuity thesis' is itself a historical artifact, important in understanding the contribution of mechanics to the history of natural philosophy.

Attention to the impact of ancient Greek mechanics on natural philosophy is merited. While ancient natural philosophy is typically understood as dividing into two contesting approaches, I argue that a third, independent approach emerged, principally in the post-Aristotelian period. Unlike atomism, this third approach is inspired by mechanics. I shall understand 'natural philosophy' broadly, not limiting its scope only to the systematic theories of the natural world formulated by schools of philosophy, but including the views of the natural world held by others of its students, including medical theorists, astronomers and the mechanics themselves. While philosophers proper tended to reject this approach, traces of a 'mechanical hypothesis' can be found in late antique discussions of the natural world. The evidence is vestigial, but it is there.

The understanding of mechanics, perhaps unsurprisingly, changed considerably between the time of Homer and late antiquity. There is little credible evidence before Aristotle's time that might

---

[9] I thank Max Weiss for noting a meaning–use distinction here.

count as the use of working artifacts in understanding the functioning of nature: stories in early literature are not, as some think, evidence of mechanical conceptions of organisms. Evidence from the fourth century is mixed. Some ideas important to mechanics can be found in Plato and Aristotle, used only in piecemeal fashion. It seems to be in the Hellenistic period that mechanics consolidated as a discipline. Unfortunately, some of the key texts are lost or survive only in part, and there are many gaps in our understanding. But this can be said: with the development of mechanical technology and mechanical theory in Hellenistic times, some ancient Greek thinkers made use of mechanical theories and drew analogies to mechanical devices as a guide to investigating the natural world.

In tracing the origins of mechanics and its development in the Hellenistic period, no attempt is made to provide a complete account of the field, nor to offer a technical history of ancient mechanics.[10] The intent is to do something rather different: to sketch a *philosophical* history of the discipline, that is, to consider the relationship of ancient Greek mechanics to the categories and concepts of ancient Greek natural philosophy. It is not the intent of this work to detail every piece of technology or to assess the technical significance of the devices or theories presented. Much remains to be said, nonetheless, about the impact of mechanics on theories of matter and void; of motion and its causes; of natural order and its transmission.

To write a thorough history of the impact of ancient Greek mechanics on the history of philosophy would require knowledge of ancient technology, archaeology, art history, literature, military history and medicine, as well as philosophy, mathematics, astronomy and practical engineering, Arabic, medieval and Renaissance mechanics, and seventeenth-century natural philosophy and science. Needless to say, I am not such an expert. Some will doubtless find this work inadequate in its attention to the social and economic context in which technology existed, in its lack of engagement with the technical proficiencies of the theories, or in its lack of detail on the

---

[10] The decision to use modern drawings, for example, is made for the convenience of the reader and not for the specialist.

devices themselves. While I am conscious of the many limitations of this work, I nonetheless hope to open a question. If we reject the implications behind our current, troublesome terminology and ask instead what effect ancient mechanics had on the history of ancient Greek philosophy, would there be a story to be told?

CHAPTER I

Mechanics and the mechanical: some problems of terminology

David Furley begins his work *The Greek Cosmologists* with a concise presentation of the differences between two main approaches to natural philosophy in antiquity. One of these, the teleological tradition, best represented by Aristotle, understands form to be explanatorily irreducible and holds that teleological explanations cannot be omitted from a complete account of the natural world. Philosophers in this tradition consider matter to be continuous and to have no imperceptible microstructure; they regard qualitative change as fundamental and not reducible to rearrangement of smallest parts; and they think of the material cosmos as structured and finite in extent. The atomists, by contrast, take all change to be fully explained by the spatial rearrangement of these smallest parts, without reference to any purposes these changes might be thought to serve. They take matter to be composed of indivisible smallest parts moving in a void, treat macroscopic structures as explanatorily reducible to the properties of the smallest parts and regard the universe as infinite and unstructured.[1]

It is important to notice that the contrast between two competing approaches is not presented as a logically exhaustive dichotomy: neither in the ancient nor the modern world are these the only possible explanatory options. Furley's point is not simply to segregate philosophical positions according to an exhaustive and exclusive dichotomy, but to note an interesting tendency of philosophical positions to cluster around certain key assumptions. Part of the

---

[1] Furley (1987), pp. 1–15.

fascination of Furley's account is that it raises a question why there should be an association between distinct ideas: why a certain view of matter should tend to align with a given view of the nature of explanation or of the form of the cosmos. Furley takes these two main explanatory alternatives to characterize ancient natural philosophy, even while he allows that some later figures forged so-called 'eclectic' or 'compromise' positions.[2]

I take his account to capture elegantly a consensus of contemporary scholarship as to the classification of ancient theories of the natural world, and to correctly identify two main trends in ancient natural philosophy in Aristotle's time, at the least.[3] It is an established usage in twentieth-century scholarship on ancient natural philosophy to describe this dichotomy as an opposition between teleological and 'mechanistic' views. Nonetheless, there is a legitimate question – as Furley himself recognizes – whether the term 'mechanistic' adequately and illuminatingly describes the non-teleological side of this divide. I suggest that some confusion might easily be avoided if we were to describe the opposition here as between teleological and materialist approaches, and I reserve the term 'mechanistic' for a third approach that later emerges, inspired by the mechanics of the Hellenistic period. At the very least, different senses of the term 'mechanistic' need to be clearly distinguished.

Despite the vast amount of attention in twentieth-century scholarship on ancient philosophy to the notion of teleology, there has been much less analysis and discussion of the notion of 'the mechanistic' or 'the mechanical'. As twentieth-century scholars apply this term to ancient philosophy, it is defined in a surprising number of different ways. Some of the attempts in the literature to define the 'mechanistic' are really definitions of a materialist or efficient-causal system and could better be relabelled to avoid potentially misleading associations that surround the complex term 'mechanistic'. Others

---

[2] Furley (1987), p. 8. The tradition of regarding deviations from this binary classification as compromises dates back to Diels (1893).

[3] See Hirsch (1990), Menn (in preparation), for discussion of the reasons why this dichotomy is not easy to formulate in Presocratic thought.

classify ancient natural philosophy in terms of the features of seventeenth-century debates.

To establish that there are problems and confusions inherent in current scholarly usage, first, I shall examine some criticisms that have already been raised of the practice of describing ancient philosophers as 'mechanistic'. Then I shall examine how scholars typically define the term 'mechanistic' in the context of ancient philosophy, and I shall indicate that the term is not as self-evident as sometimes thought. After identifying some potential problems with the usage of the term ahistorically as a description of systematic features of a world-view, I indicate why it might nonetheless be appropriate to describe ancient natural philosophies as 'mechanistic' if they are inspired by ideas from mechanics.

THE CRITICS OF PREVAILING USAGE

Several scholars have offered criticisms of some aspect of the current practice of applying the term 'mechanistic' to early ancient Greek philosophers. Some of these criticisms take the form of identifying a feature thought to be definitive of the mechanistic, and denying that particular ancient philosophers in fact exhibit that feature. Others are more general criticisms suggesting that we should not expect the term to be applicable to ancient thinkers at all.

Balme's classic criticisms are of the first variety. In two articles, published in 1939 and 1941, he assumes that there are certain criteria that, if satisfied, would qualify an ancient account as 'mechanistic', and he asks whether the atomists in fact meet those criteria.[4] At issue is whether, when Aristotle distinguishes his view from that of his materialist rivals – especially the early atomists – it is accurate to describe Aristotle as if he were staging a debate between mechanism and teleology. Balme notes several points on which the view Aristotle ascribes to the atomists differs from – what Balme takes to be – modern ideas about mechanism. In the companion piece, Balme looks more closely at the atomist position and denies that it is

---

[4] Balme (1939), p. 133.

accurately described as mechanistic. Although, he points out, some
commentators *assume* that the ancient atomists share modern ideas
about inertial motion – taking this as one of the definitive aspects of
modern 'mechanistic' thought – Balme raises doubts that Democritean
atoms move inertially.[5] This points to a serious problem: if we use
the term 'mechanistic' as a systematic description and forget that it
is a changing concept that evolves historically, it is easy to retroject
modern ideas onto the ancients as though they were self-evident.

However, Balme's caution about the term seems not to have been
widely accepted. The terms 'mechanical' and 'mechanistic' are still
frequently applied to ancient natural philosophers today.[6] Although
the terms are particularly applied to the ancient atomists, they are
also used of other Presocratics and medical writers, or even of some
aspects of Aristotle's system.[7]

---

[5] Balme (1941). See also Konstan (1979), (1982), on Epicurus.

[6] A sample of twentieth-century scholarship available in English using 'mechanistic' or
'mechanical' – or terms so translated – to describe ancient philosophers would include
classic accounts, such as Brumbaugh (1964), p. 84; Cherniss (1935), pp. 5, 10; Cornford
(1957), pp. 142, 157; Dijksterhuis (1961), p. 12; H. Gomperz (1943), p. 166; T. Gomperz
(1955); Heath (1913), p. 217; Heidel (1933), p. 14; Hesse (1962), p. 51; Jaeger (1948),
pp. 383ff.; Robinson (1968), p. 27; Ross (1923), pp. 79ff.; Sambursky (1962), pp. 21ff.;
Solmsen (1960), pp. 109, 315. The usage has not disappeared in works published since
1970: Asmis (1990); Barnes (1982), p. 415; Berryman (1997); Bobzien (2000), p. 299;
Caston (1999); Charlton (1970), p. 93; Cooper (1987), p. 273; Dicks (1970), pp. 94, 203;
Engberg-Pedersen (1990), p. 59; D. Frede (1985), p. 216; M. Frede (1992); Furley
(1987); Hahm (1977), p. 161; Hamlyn (1976); Hankinson (1998a); Hussey (1972),
pp. 139–40; Kahn (1985); Kirk, Raven and Schofield (1983), pp. 419–20; Lindberg
(1992), p. 31; G. E. R. Lloyd (1970), (1979); Long and Sedley (1987), p. 63; Longrigg
(1993), pp. 116ff.; Lonie (1981a), pp. 68, 180; Matthen (1989); McKirahan (1994), p. 321;
McPherran (1996), pp. 280ff.; Menn (1990), p. 221; Mourelatos (1991), p. 12; Nussbaum
(1978), pp. 65, 256; Pyle (1997); Sedley (1988), p. 318; Siorvanes (1996), p. 232;
C. C. W. Taylor (1999); Vlastos (1971), (1975); Wardy (1990), pp. 257–8; Waterlow
(1982), p. 35; Wieland (1975); Wright (1995), pp. 75ff. In scare quotes, also Gotthelf
(1976); M. B. Hall (1981), p. 434. Sorabji (1983), p. 351, talks of the 'mechanics of
atoms'. Others question its legitimacy in specific contexts, without challenging its
applicability to antiquity: Freeland (1991), p. 68; Grene (1963), p. 101; J. H. Randall
Jr. (1960), p. 126.

[7] E.g. Charlton (1970), p. 93; Dicks (1970), p. 203; Nussbaum (1978), pp. 65, 256;
Kahn (1985), p. 183; Matthen (1989), p. 168; Caston (1999), p. 220. See Chapter 3,
below, for the idea of a 'mechanics' in Aristotle.

I. M. Lonie's examination of the eighteenth-century application of the term 'mechanist' to 'Hippocrates' – to what we would now refer to as the Hippocratic corpus – notes the difficulty of determining precisely what is meant in applying this term to an ancient. Rather than treating the notion of the 'mechanistic' as univocal, Lonie identifies three different meanings:

In one sense, a mechanistic explanation is one which involves the mathematical application of the science of mechanics to bodies in motion; but in a second, equally valid sense, it is one which, without such application, is delivered in terms of the mutual contact and pressure of bodies, both solid and fluid. To these two senses we may add a third: we label "mechanistic" an explanation which is modelled upon the working of machines or automata.[8]

As Lonie notes, all three of these quite diverse ideas seem to capture some aspect of the way the term is used, in some contexts at least. His analysis of the different senses of the term raises a serious problem. Given this multiplicity of senses, the possibility of misunderstanding exists. If the term has several senses, we need to understand how they are interrelated and whether some are central, others peripheral. Lonie takes the first sense to be primary.[9] However, he does not defend this claim or explain how and on what authority the various senses came to be interrelated. Without some rationale for the ordering, others might take another sense to be the core meaning or indeed offer a different list of possible meanings. One might argue, for example, that the third sense – because it historically gave rise to and justifies the other two – should be regarded as primary.

In his authoritative exposition of the view that there is, broadly, a dichotomy between teleological and so-called 'mechanistic' approaches in early ancient natural philosophy, Furley also questions whether 'mechanistic' is the appropriate label for an ancient view, this time that espoused by the atomists. He takes a comparison to machinery to be central to the applicability of the term 'mechanistic', and notes that there is very little complex machinery around in Democritus' day to use as a point of comparison.[10] Furley suggests that 'automatic' or

---

[8] Lonie (1981b), p. 123.   [9] Lonie (1981b), p. 123   [10] Furley (1987), p. 13.

'necessary' functioning might be a more accurate label for the kind of explanation that avoids teleological reasoning.

Furley's discussion raises the possibility that the label 'mechanistic' is misleadingly anachronistic when applied to early ancient philosophers such as the atomists. Hirsch's criticism of the view that Democritus' approach is 'mechanistisch und antiteleologisch' centres on the concern about anachronism.[11] Some of her criticisms address specific issues in Democritean theory, such as whether Democritus espouses an irreducible – that is, not a 'mechanistic' – principle of attraction. Hirsch suggests that a 'mechanistic' world-view is one that would only be formulated in explicit opposition to a teleological world-view, and that there were at the time no developed teleological world systems – such as those of Plato and Aristotle – for Democritus to be reacting against.[12]

Hirsch's argument presupposes that there are a number of quite distinct ideas associated with the term 'mechanistic', but she offers no rationale for treating some features as essential, others accidental. Against the background of this plethora of competing intuitions, the question is whether the term 'mechanical' or 'mechanistic' has a meaning robust enough that it can be captured by any single definition, and if not, whether there is a convincing story to be found as to how the diverse senses of the term interrelate. Dijksterhuis is surely right that the meaning of the term also fluctuates through time.[13] I shall examine some proposed definitions of the 'mechanistic' found in the scholarly literature on ancient Greek philosophy, in order to illustrate the extent of the current confusion.

[11] Hirsch (1990).

[12] It is not clear that there was not a suitable foil available even in Democritus' day to motivate a restrictive ontology. I have elsewhere argued in favour of Mourelatos' suggestion that the principle of 'nothing from nothing' would suffice. See Mourelatos (1984); Berryman (2002b).

[13] Dijksterhuis (1961), p. 4. Fleury (1993), p. 16, also notes that the term 'mécanique' shifted meaning in the seventeenth century and asks whether we can talk of 'mécanique' in antiquity. His focus is on devices, however, not on the application of the term to a natural philosophy.

SOME CANDIDATE DEFINITIONS
OF THE 'MECHANISTIC'

Sometimes the term 'mechanistic' is treated as though it simply means the rejection of teleology.[14] I have suggested above that the two categories are not exhaustive, however, and that there are additional specific commitments required to qualify as 'mechanical' or 'mechanistic', as the term is typically used. Those classified as mechanists typically restrict themselves to specific kinds of efficient causes and do not employ, for example, occult powers or action at a distance: the 'mechanistic' is characterized by certain ontological commitments, as well as the direction of explanation.

Furley defines the mechanistic by its reliance on processes that happen necessarily or automatically.[15] The idea here seems to be that once certain conditions are in place, no further causal input or explanatory resources are needed to account for the unfolding of a process.[16] This might seem an apt way to characterize what we think to be peculiar about clockwork, perhaps, in contrast to the use of tools that merely augment human capabilities. This characterization focuses on the modality rather than the directionality of non-teleological processes. Cooper, perhaps motivated by a similar concern, coins the term 'Democritean necessity' for the view to which Aristotle opposes himself.[17] Yet one could certainly conceive of goal-directed processes that happen necessarily or automatically in certain circumstances, such as an Aristotelian conception of activities that occur once any impediment is removed.[18] Inevitability of the result, given the conditions, will not reliably distinguish teleological and mechanical accounts. A variant of this idea is that the term 'mechanical' is used to distinguish inanimate systems from those

---

[14] Hirsch (1990). [15] Furley (1987), p. 13.
[16] Cf. Nussbaum (1978), pp. 65, 155. [17] Cooper (1987), p. 259.
[18] E.g. *Ph.* 8.4, 255b23; *de An.* 2.5, 417a28; *EN* 10.4; *Metaph.* 9.8. See Mourelatos (1967). Some readings of Aristotle interpret his view of teleological explanation in a way that seems to allow given results to follow automatically from given material conditions: Nussbaum (1978), pp. 88ff.; Sorabji (1983), pp. 155–63; Charles (1988).

governed by intentional or purposive action.[19] However, few interpretations of Aristotelian teleology nowadays take it to depend on a
kind of agency or intentional action.

A quite different proposal is that the mechanistic is an ontological
commitment to avoid all reference to substances and substantial
natures. Waterlow characterizes the mechanistic by the rejection of
substantial forms.[20] Although this would certainly exclude Aristotelian
teleology, there are typically also a number of positive commitments
implicit in the claim that an account is mechanistic. Consider explanations of phenomena in domains where Aristotelians would not make
use of substantial form. Choosing among, for example, explanations of
magnetism or attraction or light or meteorological effects, modern
scholars characterize some as mechanistic, others not.

Waterlow, recognizing this, adds that it is the properties 'of bodies
as such ... mass, velocity, position, duration, etc.' that are invoked
by the mechanist.[21] Open-ended lists of the mechanists' explanatory
methods seem *ad hoc* unless they offer some justification why certain
properties are to be taken as explanatory at the expense of others, and
why certain properties are to be taken to be those of body, others
not.[22] Describing a causal explanation as 'mechanistic' is often taken
to mean that the only things that can function as *explanans* are
physical properties. However, it is not pre-theoretically evident
what properties belong to matter or body: witness the discussions
in antiquity whether matter or body can have weight, attraction,
tonos, active powers, vital heat, life, soul, *logos*. In the absence of an
agreed point of reference, there is no constraint on the properties that
can be stipulated to be material.

The problem is not merely that there is no agreement in antiquity as to what properties really pertain to body. They also lacked
any agreed *procedure* for deciding such questions. Later mechanical
philosophers shared a common point of reference, inasmuch as they
considered the properties of bodies to be those properties that would

---

[19] Dijksterhuis (1961), p. 498.   [20] Waterlow (1982), p. 35.
[21] Waterlow (1982), p. 35.
[22] The properties Waterlow lists reflect modern more than ancient discussions.

be employed *in the discipline of mechanics*. To describe ancient philosophers as 'mechanistic' before the fact risks obscuring important
features of their motivation. In the ancient context, the Stoics again
provide a test case for the adequacy of this definition, since they also
insist on action by contact, even while their whole system is deeply
teleological. Further constraints, concerning the kinds of interaction
and the kinds of entities involved in them, would need to be added to
limit the category to the kinds of interactions typically described as
'mechanistic'.[23]

The criteria others identify for a view to qualify as mechanistic
include – among other things – particular views about causal interaction. Balme, for example, focuses on the question whether the
atomists would have countenanced modern ideas about the laws of
motion. He argues that, far from implicitly accepting something like
Newtonian laws, the ancient atomists took motion to be generated or
renewed in collisions rather than subject to laws and equations.[24] He
is surely on common ground with other scholars in supposing that
the interactions of matter must be understood to work in the right
ways to count as mechanistic. Mechanism, these accounts suggest,
does not merely restrict itself to the use of material properties but
also uses them in a restricted range of ways.

Sometimes it is said that the definitive commitment of mechanists
is that they avoid the use of forces.[25] Immanuel Kant contrasts the
'dynamical' natural philosophy he advocates with a position he
thinks is shared by various figures from Democritus to Descartes.
He contrasts his own view with that of corpuscularians, who held
that atoms are absolutely impassive, 'mere instruments of external
moving forces', exerting no influence on one another by means of

---

[23] It is, incidentally, not clear that atoms are thought to be straightforwardly in
contact: Philoponus at least suggests that they could never be said to touch,
lest they fuse into a single whole, and he indicates that they must act on one
another by some kind of repulsion. See Kline and Matheson (1987); Godfrey
(1990).

[24] Balme (1941), pp. 24–5.

[25] On whether the matter theories of the early modern 'mechanical philosophers'
actually avoid ascribing forces, see J. Henry (1986).

their own forces of attraction and repulsion.[26] Some modern scholars echo this idea, for instance when they doubt that ancient atomists would qualify as mechanistic if they make claims about the attraction of like to like.[27] A version of this concern is expressed in terms of passivity: Pyle claims that a mechanistic account should avoid the spontaneous initiation of motion;[28] Dijksterhuis says that what is excluded by a mechanistic account is the notion that bodies have an internal source of motion.[29] It may be hard to use the presence or absence of forces to divide ancient natural philosophers into two camps, since it is not always clear what would count as a force, for example, or whether countenancing forces, powers or tendencies was always thought to be inimical to materialism. Passivity is hard to assess – witness the controversies over the atomist conception of weight – while the idea that passivity is definitive of materialism in the seventeenth century is also contested.[30]

Dijksterhuis moves away from the properties of matter altogether when he claims that the presence of a 'mechanics' can be taken as the defining feature of the mechanistic.[31] By this, he evidently means laws of motion of a particular kind. This characterization, however, merely defers the issue to one of deciding what qualifies a set of laws of motion as a mechanics. Not every attempt to characterize the principles governing motion would qualify as mechanistic: Aristotle's natural philosophy includes some generalizations about motion, but these are rarely characterized as a mechanics.[32] Some take the 'mechanical' to imply that the principles governing motion be mathematical.[33] But formal criteria such as mathematization of the laws of motion may not be necessary, and they are certainly

---

[26] Kant (2002), p. 242. I thank Monte Johnson for drawing my attention to this: see Johnson (2005), p. 32.

[27] E.g. Dijksterhuis (1961), p. 12; Hankinson (1998a), p. 208; Hirsch (1990).

[28] Pyle (1997), p. 142.   [29] Dijksterhuis (1961), pp. 177–8.

[30] See, e.g., J. Henry (1986).   [31] Dijksterhuis (1961), p. 498.

[32] Carteron (1975) denies that Aristotle's account of motion counts as a mechanics because its articulation of the principles of motion was not sufficiently thorough; cf. Balme (1941), 23–8. See Chapter 3 below.

[33] Balme (1941); Lonie (1981b), p. 116; Hirsch (1990), p. 225.

not sufficient: the Newtonian analysis of gravitational attraction, although thoroughly mathematical, did not seem to his critics – or to Newton himself – to be mechanistic.[34]

The above survey, which is far from exhaustive, shows that the criteria offered to define the 'mechanical' or 'mechanistic' are many and various: rejection of teleology, necessity, avoidance of substantial natures, use of only properties of matter, passivity of matter and absence of forces, appeal to laws of motion, mathematization. These ideas might seem to have displayed a certain affinity in a given context, but it cannot be assumed that this affinity should always have held. Some of the accounts discussed characterize the positive commitments of mechanistic thought by open-ended lists. Waterlow lists properties thought to belong to body;[35] Hesse likewise characterizes mechanistic thought as the reliance on certain properties of inanimate and passive matter: 'forces of expansion and contraction, suction, pressure, centrifugal force, and so on'.[36]

There is, I suggest, a good reason why the term both lends itself to so many distinct analyses and also gives rise to these open-ended lists. Thinkers inspired by a governing analogy to another field pick out different features of the point of reference: to describe a system of thought as 'psychologistic' or 'legalistic', for example, allows for a certain open-endedness and fluctuation in that characterization, as notions of psychology or law differ or evolve. It can thus be misleading to suppose that there is a single notion of the 'mechanical', and that this constitutes a unified and perspicuous conception.

In the appendix I show how recent scholarship on the seventeenth century has helped to disentangle several different strands interwoven in the complex cluster of meanings surrounding the terms 'mechanical' and 'mechanistic' as they are used today. Scholarship on

---

[34] Newton (1995), p. 442; cf. Dijksterhuis (1961), p. 497; Westfall (1971), pp. 143ff.; Nadler (1998), pp. 542ff.; Garber et al. (1998), pp. 606ff.; Dear (2001), pp. 160ff.

[35] Waterlow (1982), p. 35.

[36] Hesse (1962), p. 51. Salmon (1984), p. 241, notes that 'mechanism is often identified with the notion that explanations of physical phenomena are inadequate unless they are given in terms of levers, springs, pulleys, wheels, gears, deformable jelly, and so forth'.

the ancients – and on the concept of the mechanical – could benefit
from attention to this literature. It highlights the potential for confusion inherent in using a multifaceted term such as 'mechanistic' of
the ancients without due care as to exactly which sense is meant.[37]

The attempts to define the 'mechanical' discussed above assume
that the term is being used as a systematic description of the features
of a conception, not of the motivation of the conceiver. The focus of
this book is on the history of 'mechanical' or 'mechanistic' thought in
antiquity, using the term to refer to the history of the appeal to the
discipline of mechanics to understand the natural world. This will
include a study of the philosophical reception of mechanical theory
and its impact on theories of causation or of motion, as well as the
role that mechanical devices played in fostering a way of examining
the natural world, the functioning of organisms, or the nature of
causation in the cosmos.

The philosophical reception of mechanics in antiquity has not
been well studied. One reason is that conceptual confusion has
obscured the importance of this history. Secondly, a mistaken conception of the ancient view of mechanics has led some to think there
is no such history: that the ancients did not consider their mechanics
to be applicable to the natural world. A third reason is simply that
there is little and scattered evidence of the reception of mechanics in
antiquity, generally recorded in its detractors. The fact that a movement did not become dominant or succeed in its ambitions is no
reason to ignore it, however. Nor is the fact that its traces fared
badly in the process of transmission. There were those in late
antiquity who defended the need for ongoing intelligent direction
of the natural world, and they had good reason for rejecting this
optimistic programme. Still, its very formulation in antiquity is
significant. This work aims to trace a fragment of the history of
the role of the discipline of mechanics in *creating* a consensus about
the properties of matter and its motions.

---

[37] Gabbey (1993a), pp. 137–8, urges greater attention to 'disciplinary taxonomy', lest we
should miss the importance of problems that depend on such distinctions. See also
Clagett (1959), p. xx; Laird (1986); Gabbey (1992b), (1993b), (2001); Garber (2002).

CHAPTER 2

'Mechanistic' thought before mechanics?

In this chapter I consider issues that form an essential background to the question how the development of ancient mechanics might have impacted on ancient natural philosophy. Such an impact could take different forms, and it is important to be clear on what would count as a 'mechanical' or 'mechanistic' conception, using the term to describe a way of conceiving of the natural world by reference to mechanics. The question needs to be posed in a way that is neither too broad nor too narrow in scope, in order to appreciate what effects the discipline of mechanics might have had on natural philosophy.

At a time when mechanics was understood to work because of principles that could be identified and theorized, we might expect philosophers to consider the applicability of these principles to the study of other kinds of motion and its causes. But it is also possible for natural philosophers to take inspiration from mechanics independently of such a theoretical understanding. Experience with constructing devices might give rise to new ideas about the properties of matter, or the way it interacts. The presence of working artifacts that can approximate the functions taken to be definitive of animals might call into question the distinction in kind between organism and artifact, or suggest ways that animal functions might be realized by material means. Mechanics could serve as a heuristic, even without a precisely articulated understanding of the nature of mechanics or of the principles thought to be at work in the field.[1]

---

[1] For this role of mechanics, see Anstey (2000), p. 4; Des Chene (2001), p. 14.

This heuristic use of mechanics as a guiding analogy is not trivial. In the early modern period it is widely accepted that practical mechanics played a significant role as a point of reference in determining the properties that could properly be ascribed to matter, and the laws of motion and its causes. We could apply the same distinction to the ancient Greek world and ask both whether mechanical theory was applied to nature, and whether mechanical practice played a heuristic role in guiding investigation of the natural world.

Two conflicting answers to the latter question are suggested by the existing literature. On the one hand, some histories of technology suggest that there are 'mechanistic' conceptions of organisms in Greek literature at least as far back as Homer. On the other hand, it is more common, especially in histories of science or of philosophy, to assume that there is no story to tell about the philosophical reception of mechanics in antiquity, even after the Hellenistic period. Historians of science have offered elaborate explanations of why a discipline so important to early modern philosophy should have been excluded from philosophical consideration by the ancients.

In this chapter I shall argue against both of these suppositions. The first position, dating mechanistic conceptions back to Homer, implies that such ideas developed prior to the existence of mechanics as a discipline. This seems very unlikely, and for an interesting reason. I shall suggest that mechanics began from experience – that practical mechanics shows what results can be achieved by natural forces exactly by manipulating them – and that it would be too much of a coincidence to expect that imagination should settle on the laws of nature by happenstance.

This is meant as a non-trivial, substantive claim, and it is central to the idea that the emergence of mechanics played a role in forging a consensus as to what is possible in nature. The construction and use of mechanical devices offered a context in which it was feasible to manipulate and quantify a number of parameters involved in causing motion, including weight, distance from a fulcrum, time, and the elusive notion of force. By contrast, the parameters involved in free fall or projectile motion were very difficult to manipulate or to verify.[2] Although I do not think there is any way to show definitively that imagination unaided by experience *could* not have created such a consensus, it seems that, historically, experience with mechanical devices *did* lead to some convergence of views about the properties of matter, the principles of motion, and the nature of causation.

A corollary to this claim is that ideas based on speculation unconstrained by experience would not properly count as part of mechanics. To be sure, mechanical theorists – including Archimedes, Hero and Pappus – acknowledged a role for idealization in their theories and made claims based on extrapolation of their theories. Some of the constructions described by Hero seem to be theoretical combinations of well-known and tested techniques that can be made to work in isolation, but that in combination would be difficult to engineer sufficiently precisely with the kinds of materials and techniques that seem to have been available. However, what would not qualify as 'mechanical' is the imaginative 'construction' using materials or techniques whose properties are merely stipulation. Although ideas inspire practice, the field of mechanics is ultimately concerned with devices that work, not with fiction or imagination.[3]

In the first part of this chapter I shall consider the evidence for 'mechanistic' conceptions before the time of Plato and Aristotle. In the remainder of the chapter I shall examine the well-entrenched explanations in the literature of why the ancients would not have been interested in applying mechanics to natural philosophy. In contrast to those who see the influence of mechanics everywhere or nowhere in ancient Greek thought, I shall try to trace a more precise account of its reception and indicate how the development of Hellenistic mechanics affected ancient Greek natural philosophy. There is, I think, a story to be told.

---

[2] Witness, for example, the debates about projectile motion, or Strato of Lampsacus' valiant efforts to establish acceleration of falling bodies by pointing to the greater dent left by a body falling from a greater height: Simplicius, *in Ph.* 916.10.

[3] A significant application of this restriction is that I will claim that Aristotle's speculation about the properties of *pneuma* could not, by definition, count as 'mechanical'.

DIVINE VERSUS HUMAN TECHNOLOGY

It might seem that 'mechanical conceptions' of the natural world are found in ancient thought from the time of the earliest literary records. Some scholars – especially historians of technology – imply that anticipations of later 'mechanical beings' and automata can be found as far back as Homer. Hephaestus in the *Iliad* created golden handmaidens and self-moving tripods; Daedalus made statues that get up and run away. At first glance, these may seem like examples of automata: just as, for example, nineteenth-century literature is replete with fictional accounts of scientists and inventors building lifelike machines or artificial beings, so too the ancients might seem to have imagined this possibility. Histories of automata sometimes cite these stories as if they are anticipations or ancestors of the 'mechanical conceptions' of organisms found in later periods.[4]

References such as these illustrate the difficulty of assessing how ancient stories are conceived and understood. Descriptions in mythology and Homeric literature of devices that run 'by themselves' often involve the god Hephaestus. Since he is portrayed as a blacksmith, the stories about him seem to trade on ideas of both human and divine craft. In the *Iliad* Hephaestus is said to have bellows that work themselves, golden handmaidens obeying his will and tripods that enter the assembly by themselves.[5] In all three cases, these are technological devices that are described as though they were capable of self-moving but that at the same time seemed to be tools of their master's will.

The description of Hephaestus' workshop might seem to be one of productivity enhanced by clever technological aids, but it is not at all clear that the poet conceives of the god as using mechanical skill to

---

[4] E.g. Bruce (1913); Chapuis and Droz (1958); Price (1964); Maurice and Mayr (1980), p. 234; Mayr (1986). Espinas (1903), p. 705, treats the statues of Daedalus as machines. More recently, Humphrey, Oleson and Sherwood (1998), p. 61, list imaginary and real automata side by side in their sourcebook, as do Irby-Massie and Keyser (2002), p. 150. Krafft (1972), p. 364, treats myths as imaginary anticipations of mechanics; see also Lonie (1981b), p. 125.

[5] *Il.* 18. 414ff.

automate his tools. We are given no reason to suppose that the poet thinks of the god as building devices using material technology. Hephaestus is said to have few actual tools besides those of an ordinary blacksmith: hammer and anvil, tongs and bellows.[6] Hephaestus' tripods have wheels, but there is no evidence of other moving parts or starting devices, and nothing to explain how the tripods move by themselves. Nothing is said about internal mechanisms in the handmaidens or the bellows. Rather, they seem to be conscious and to respond directly to their master's will. The technology of the day, moreover, does not offer much to inspire the idea of building devices that work by themselves.[7]

The poem might merely be embellishing a kind of mystique surrounding craft ability. The actual available technology was understood to have divine origins, as the Prometheus legend illustrates. It is possible that the poem only exaggerates a kind of awe at those who make devices such as bellows, well-turned wheels and clever crutches.[8] It may be significant that the devices surrounding Hephaestus are not so much described as tools but presented as symbolic indications of his power.[9] His profession represents the height of the craftsman's art, as it was understood at the time.[10] While the bellows and handmaidens might have a practical use, equally important in the representation is that their master can enter the assembly of the gods with his own retinue of servants, created with just enough autonomy to obey their master's will. The account may simply be hyperbolic representation of the practical power and social status of craftsmen.

Another interpretation seems much more likely: that the devices are animated by divine power.[11] When Zeus wants a Pandora in Hesiod's *Works and Days*, he has Hephaestus make a female figure

---

[6] The crafts and tools mentioned in Homer are discussed in Seymour (1908).
[7] Prager (1974), p. 3, even suggests that parts of the story of Hephaestus' devices may have been interpolated into the Homeric text during the time of Philo of Byzantium.
[8] Seymour (1908), p. 295, notes that the handmaidens are crutches.
[9] On tripods as symbols of power, see Papalexandrou (1998), pp. 29–32.
[10] Harrison (1908–9); Delcourt (1982), pp. 156–70; Burford (1972), p. 122.
[11] Morris (1992), pp. 10–11; Burford (1972), p. 196.

out of clay and infuse it with human abilities.[12] While part of the process involves conventional craftsmanship – moulding clay – this is not presented as sufficient. The act of animation is a distinct process, adding divine art to the human. For a god to animate a statue by breathing on it is no technique of human craft. This story rather draws on the association of breath with life and on the view of the divine as life-giving. In the *Iliad* Hephaestus' tools not only move by themselves but seem to have minds: the handmaidens have rational attributes as well as human voice and strength.[13] The self-piloting ships in the *Odyssey* are likewise described as having minds rather than internal mechanisms that explain their abilities.[14] Just as Hephaestus or Pygmalion can breathe life into a statue, Hephaestus and the Phaeacians can create living, thinking things. These stories are not about the capacities of ordinary technological devices, but about the mysterious and unanalysable ability of the gods to convey life.

Mythology ascribes a number of clever inventions to Daedalus, who is the archetypal craftsman. Because Daedalus is human – albeit with divine connections – it is less obvious whether his creative powers are understood to involve animation.[15] Few of his artifacts have moving parts: the most plausible candidates for mechanical devices are the statues of Daedalus, which are said to need to be tied down lest they run away.[16] These could be fanciful stories about animate beings.[17] Although the comic dramatist Philippus suggests – apparently for comic effect – that the 'quickening' was achieved by pouring in quicksilver,[18] this seems to be a later gloss on the story, which does not contain much to suggest that it is plausible evidence of a mechanical invention. Even in the fourth century the story had

---

[12] *Op.* 60.   [13] *Il.* 18.419–20.
[14] *Od.* 8.555–62; I thank Douglas Frame for the reference.
[15] Some scholars take the magical creations of Hephaestus to encourage this view of craftsmanly production: Morris (1992), p. 11; Frontisi-Ducroux (1975), p. 101; cf. Brumbaugh (1966), p. 26.
[16] Plato, *Euthphr.* 11d; *Men.* 97d–e.   [17] Cf. Lucian, *Philops.* 19.
[18] Aristotle, *de An.* 1.3, 406b18. Mercury is often credited with magical powers because of its volatility, but the pun is English.

its sceptics. Palaephatus, who offers deflationary accounts of a number of myths, treats the story as an urban legend. He thinks it is based on the reputation of an innovative sculptor, whose lifelike figures startled onlookers accustomed to more stylized images. The poses were lifelike, suggesting motion, giving rise to a hyperbolic description that the statues of Daedalus could 'get up and run away.'[19]

These stories should not be read as evidence, then, that the creators of this early literature imagined the building of 'mechanical' automata. This is not only because there is positive evidence to suggest that divine animation is needed: it is *a priori* unreasonable to expect mechanical conceptions before the development of mechanics. In one sense, this statement verges on the tautological, but it could also be understood substantively. Trivially, mechanics needs to exist to inspire comparisons; but, more importantly, we should not expect people to be able to *imagine* what devices can actually achieve, without practical experience.

What would count as evidence that someone *imagined* some modern invention, unless they were informed by experience with technology? A vague reference to a 'box that thinks' should not be treated as a conception of a computer, absent some detailed evidence that the conceiver had ideas about how thinking might be brought about. While it may be tempting to read accounts of 'statues that move' as anticipating modern robots, this is not warranted, unless there is evidence of technology available that could give some content to such a conception. It would be risky to assume the conceivability of techniques that were only developed later, and to

---

[19] *Peri Apiston*, 21; Frontisi-Ducroux (1975), p. 100 n. 35. Palaephatus is generally taken to be fourth century, perhaps a contemporary of other debunkers of mythology such as Prodicus of Ceos. See Stern (1996), pp. 20–1, 52; R. M. Grant (1952), pp. 44ff. Diodorus Siculus, writing in the first century BCE, claims that Daedalus was a much better craftsman than others of his day and, because he made statues with open eyes and feet astride, created such wonder in his contemporaries that later generations said his statues were like living beings: Diodorus 4.76.1–6; Pollitt (1990), p. 13; Morris (1992), pp. 217–25. On the lack of evidence for such an artistic innovation, see Morris (1992), pp. 243–4; Pollitt (1974), pp. 154–8. I thank Gail Hoffman for references.

suppose that the ancient storyteller must be imagining something comparable. What seems possible to us may have seemed to an ancient to require intervention by divine or supernatural agency.

This point is easily missed by those who do not clearly distinguish different ways of using the terms 'mechanistic' or 'mechanical'. It should be at least puzzling that the ancients would have conceptions of the world that are systematically similar to modern notions based on mechanics, without having actual technology as a point of reference.[20] It may seem obvious to us how mechanical technology works: levers twice as long can lift twice as much; screws transmit circular motion in a continuous upward direction; springs or compressed air recoil forcefully once compression is released; steam or forced air in an enclosed space can be made to turn turbines, sound whistles, open valves; toothed wheels in series transmit motion in converse directions or even perpendicularly, according to the ratio of the teeth. But none of these beliefs about the operation of devices are *prima facie* evident; there was a time when they were first articulated. Experience with technology changed views about what results could be produced and under what conditions.

Ancient mechanics *surprised* its audience. We have become accustomed to the capacities of devices, and they are integrated into our views of the nature of matter and its motions. But this should not blind us to the role of experience with mechanics in shaping those expectations, and in *creating* a consensus about the properties of matter, of motion and its causes. The philosophical history of mechanics is the history of its role as a point of reference to determine what is possible, and its role in forging what we now regard as common sense about the capacities of matter and its motions.

In his study of mechanical comparisons in Descartes, Des Chene suggests that, for assessing Descartes' mechanical analogues for organisms, it is irrelevant whether the devices used as points of comparison were ever built or would in fact work.[21] But if, as Des

---

[20] I am grateful to Georges Rey for urging me to clarify this point.
[21] Des Chene (2001), p. 66.

Chene rightly proposes, the point of the analogy is to limit the explanatory options and to direct investigation towards the way things work in constructed devices,[22] there needs to be a real continuity with techniques that are available at the time. Once a consensus is reached as to the theoretical principles underlying mechanical devices, one may be able to detail a blueprint on the basis of that theory without actually building it. Some of the devices even in later ancient mechanics texts might have been theoretical extensions of well-known technology.[23] But this requires an experientially grounded theory about the functioning of the component parts and about the way these components interact.

WORKING ARTIFACTS BEFORE THE FOURTH CENTURY

Histories of technology, as mentioned earlier, have made implausible claims on the basis of literary references that seem to *imagine* automata. There are certainly reports from before the fourth century BCE describing impressive statues. Numismatical evidence supports a story in Pliny about a statue of Cephisodorus: the figure of a stag held in a god's hand was constructed to allow some sort of rocking motion.[24] However, Pliny's report leaves the details unclear, and there is no reason to suppose that its motion was caused by some mechanical device, rather than – like a modern rocking horse – simply continuing an oscillation initiated from outside.

Some stories mentioning animal-like artifacts are of the *homunculus* variety, only moving inasmuch as they contain living beings. The sixth-century Sicilian tyrant Phalaris is said to have built a bull-shaped torture device in which he roasted enemies alive: it had pipes crafted so that the screams of the victims came out as a bellowing sound.[25] Apparently self-moving devices that really depend on

[22] Des Chene (2001), pp. 14, 71ff.

[23] This point is made by, e.g., Tybjerg (2003), pp. 449ff.

[24] *HN* 34.19.75. Coins indicate that the moving part, the stag, was small and carried in the god's hand: Rackham (1968), p. 183 n.d.

[25] Lucian, *Phal.* 1.11. cf. Diodorus Siculus 9.18–19. I am grateful to Kai Trampedach, Elizabeth Kosmetatou, Myriam Hecquet and Manuel Baumbach for references.

hidden agents within, if anything, undercut the idea that we could construct self-movers by technological means. Rehm suggests that even in the early third century a reportedly self-moving snail used in the procession of Demetrius of Phaleron was most probably pedalled by people hidden inside turning a wheel.[26] Several centuries later, when Hero of Alexandria describes the construction of amazing devices that start moving by themselves, he cautions the builder to make them small enough so that no one will suspect that they are worked by someone hidden inside.[27]

Simple marionettes are another kind of simulacrum that should not be confused with automata. Herodotus describes images that were carried around in Egyptian Dionysian festivals and were worked by strings.[28] However, the idea that organisms *work like* marionettes would imply that there is an agent pulling the strings. Plato, for example, considers whether we might be puppets – *thaumata* – worked by the gods.[29] The marionette comparison merely relocates agency from the person to the implied divinity pulling the strings.[30]

Care is needed both in identifying apparent references to the existence of 'working artifacts', and in interpreting texts that seem to draw 'mechanical' analogies to such artifacts. Presocratic philosophy is sometimes said to contain 'mechanistic conceptions' of nature, because of the use of comparisons to artifacts. Ancient philosophers certainly appealed to technology in their accounts of the natural world; Presocratic thought is rife with artifact analogies. But it is not clear that every comparison of artifacts to the natural world is aptly called 'mechanical', even bracketing the question of

---

[26] Rehm (1937), pp. 317–30. The report in Polybius 12.13.9 is minimal: a snail moving by itself led his procession, emitting slime.

[27] Hero, *Aut.* 4.4.4.   [28] Herodotus 2.48.

[29] Plato, *Lg.* 644e: *golden* cords act differently, suggesting that the transmission of effect involves not merely physical pulling and pushing, but some kind of qualitative transmission also.

[30] Mere puppets are not presented by Plato as a particularly convincing point of analogy to human beings: elsewhere *thaumata* are deceptive imitations, only apparently self-moving, carried by people we cannot see: *R.* 514. Cf. also the deceptive wonders of the Sophist, called a *thaumatopoios*: *Sph.* 224a; 235b; 268d.

the existence of any such field so-called at the time. The interesting sense of an analogy to artifacts would have to be one that helped us understand the natural world and how it works: not just the appeal to artifacts that merely *look like* natural things, or are similar only in that both are made by divine design. The question is whether artifacts and natural things were thought to *work like* one another.[31] Not every artifact analogy would count as specifically 'mechanical'.

Some suggest that the Hippocratic texts show evidence of 'mechanistic' thought, and that the Hippocratic doctors looked to technology to explain the functioning of organisms.[32] However, the evidence for this is slight. The text *On the Nature of the Child*, perhaps dating from the end of the fifth century,[33] compares the sorting of materials within the body to the case of a bladder containing earth, sand and lead filings, filled with water. By blowing into the bladder through a pipe, it is claimed, different ingredients will sort by kind.[34] The function of the comparison is to suggest that sorting by kind can happen automatically as a by-product of the action of moving air: like Democritus' reference to a winnowing basket, it is only an illustration of the ways materials can be made to sort by kind. A passage in *Diseases 4* tries to explain the fluid distribution in the body by comparison to a series of cauldrons connected by pipes. The point is made that, just as water poured into one cauldron will flow through to the others until they are filled, so too the liquid will flow back if the first vessel is emptied before the others.[35] But however interesting they may be, these occasional uses of artifact analogies fall far short of a 'mechanistic' view of the organism. Lonie rightly rejects the idea that the Hippocratic corpus contains anything

---

[31] Mechanical devices are defined by functioning: see Chapter 3, below.

[32] Needham (1934); Brumbaugh (1964). Schiefsky (2007a) discusses the relationship of technical analogies to investigation of nature in the Hippocratics.

[33] Lonie (1981a), p. 71.

[34] *Nat. Puer.* 17. Keyser (1992), pp. 108–9, argues that this is the ancestor of a device found in later authors that uses pressure to precipitate the different substances by layers.

[35] The illustration does not particularly exploit the resources of technology, as the Hellenistic doctor Asclepiades saw: interconnected mud puddles would exhibit the same effect. See Cassius, *Problemata* 40, cited in Vallance (1990), p. 87.

comparable to the idea that 'a natural process is described in terms of the workings of a machine or an automaton', an idea for which he thinks that 'the materials, and to some extent the mood' are lacking until the Hellenistic period.[36]

Astronomy is another field where we might look for 'mechanical models' and 'mechanistic conceptions'. Physical models of the heavens are certainly ascribed even to the first philosophers. Cicero reports that Thales, whose astronomical interests are otherwise well attested, built a celestial globe.[37] There is no evidence that Thales' construction contained any moving parts, however: Cicero indeed contrasts it to later devices that do.[38] It seems to have been a kind of three-dimensional map of the 'fixed sphere' of the heavens. While such a device might be taken to suggest that the heavens have an invisible solid structure, as an artifact analogy it is no more complex than puppets that, without moving parts, do little to inspire mechanical conceptions of organisms.[39]

Another early Presocratic philosopher, Thales' pupil Anaximander, is sometimes said to have a 'mechanical model' of the cosmos.[40] He talks of there being great circles of fire in the cosmos, largely obscured by other bodies; the heavenly bodies are really points of fire seen obtruding through apertures. The sun and moon are said to fill the inside of great wheels, which allow the fire to be seen through vents; the stars seem to appear through holes in another such wheel.[41] There are many different attempts to reconstruct the reports into a systematic and coherent view. Some make the model of the heavens quite

---

[36] Lonie (1981b), p. 125.

[37] *Rep.* 1.14, 21. See White (2002), for discussion of the evidence regarding Thales' astronomical interests and his contribution to quantitative astronomy.

[38] Cicero, *Rep.* 1.14.22; Price (1975), p. 56; Savage-Smith (1985), pp. 3ff.; Evans (1998), pp. 78–95. See the next chapter for more on celestial globes and armillary spheres.

[39] For caution about the tendency to ascribe more sophistication to early astronomy than is warranted, see Dicks (1970); Goldstein and Bowen (1983). More on this in subsequent chapters.

[40] G. E. R. Lloyd (1966), p. 315; Brumbaugh (1964), p. 80.

[41] For the question whether the choice of 'wheels' here may be motivated by knowledge of the ecliptic, see Evans (1998), p. 56.

sophisticated, and imagine a technologically detailed model.[42] Others interpret the accounts in much simpler and more naturalistic terms, reading the 'wheels' as rings of mist.[43] Others again take the textual evidence to be too garbled to lend much certainty to any definitive interpretation.[44] Some reports indicate that Anaximander used organic as well as artifact models: the account in Clement describes its growth from seed like bark around a tree.[45] There is little reason to suppose that he is proposing a thoroughly 'mechanical' model of the heavens.

While turning wheels *could* be associated with machinery, an isolated comparison to a wheel need not be any more 'mechanical' than references to spinning bowls, caps, or other circular artifacts. Like Anaximenes' suggestion that the stars are fixed to the crystalline sphere 'like nails', Anaximander's view does suggest that a better account of the regular spacing of the stars is achieved by positing a continuous structure uniting the apparently separated stars. This is a significant idea, but it does little to support the possibility that the building of working heavenly models led to 'mechanical conceptions' of the heavens in this period.[46]

These early passages discussing artifact analogues either for animals or for the heavens lack the details concerning methods of functioning that would be needed to qualify as 'mechanical' or 'mechanistic'. It is, given the way I understand the notion of the 'mechanical', problematic to suggest that a 'mechanistic conception' could exist independently of mechanics. Not only does the discipline *called* 'mechanics' not seem to be evident before the fourth century, but also there is little to suggest that any substantial precursor existed in the form of 'mechanical conceptions' of organisms or of the heavenly bodies. Certainly there was interest in the explanatory or illustrative capacity of man-made devices, but it is dangerous to read too much into these early appeals to artifacts. There is little evidence from before the

---

[42] See Hahn (2001), pp. 177–218, for a survey of these attempts; also Couprie, Hahn and Naddaf (2003), pp. 175ff.

[43] Algra (1999), pp. 47–8. [44] Dicks (1970), pp. 45–6.

[45] *Strom.* 2, cited in Furley (1987), p. 26.

[46] For an interesting account of possible technological inspirations for Anaximander's philosophy, see Hahn (2001).

fourth century of devices sufficiently complex to suggest that the natural world might work 'just like that'. Moreover, the lack of evidence of such devices makes it difficult to ascribe mechanical analogies to early thinkers on the basis of the texts that survive.

ANCIENT ATOMISM AND THE MACHINE ANALOGY

There is, I suggested earlier, a marked tendency in twentieth-century scholarship on ancient Greek philosophy to refer to ancient atomism as the epitome of a 'mechanistic' account, or to regard the ancient Greek atomists as employing 'mechanical explanation'. This could be read as the claim that the ancient Greek atomists were drawing on ideas from the mechanics of their day to understand the motion of bodies. This is not often argued. More often, it seems, scholars intend rather to claim that ancient atomism conforms to some modern notion of the 'mechanistic', and that the conception of the properties and motion of atoms and its causes in Democritus, for example, is comparable to the conception of matter and motion found in seventeenth-century mechanical philosophers.

For the latter position, however, a real puzzle emerges. As Furley indeed noted, in Democritus' day there was little complex machinery – even less, mechanical theory – to serve as a point of reference.[47] If we accept this assessment, we need to ask *why* atomism's view of the properties and motion of matter and its causes should be so similar to those of Descartes and Boyle. These two were of course aware of ancient atomism, but they claim to have been motivated by ideas as to the nature of matter and causation illuminated by centuries of detailed work in the discipline of mechanics. It is thus worth pondering how Democritean ideas could anticipate the conception of matter and motion found in the later mechanical tradition, if they were not based on experience with mechanics.

This is a deep question. To be sure, atomist ideas seem to be based on everyday experience with moving bodies and thus ought to bear some continuity with the mechanical tradition. But that experience

[47] Furley (1987), p. 13.

would not be the same as ours, accustomed as we are to certain ways of looking at the world.[48] It is worth asking just how similar ancient atomism really is, especially on topics for which we simply lack evidence. David Balme importantly urged us not to assume that certain ideas, familiar since the seventeenth century, were *prima facie* obvious. This is a helpful reminder that some conceptions of motion and its causes were hard won. There was surely no consensus in antiquity, as there was among the seventeenth-century mechanical philosophers, as to the properties that could be ascribed to matter, precisely because there was no fixed point of reference – such as the discipline of mechanics – that could be appealed to to rule out the ascription of given properties to matter. As Edelstein warned, 'the fact that atomism has become the basis of progress in modern science should not make one forget the fundamental differences between the ancient and the modern atomic theory'.[49]

I shall argue here only for the less controversial claim that the ancient atomists were not motivated by the appeal to mechanics. Few scholars have overtly claimed that the atomists had, as Lindberg puts it, a 'vision of reality as a lifeless piece of machinery ...'[50] Hesse, for example, makes only a modest claim that the atomists drew on the model of a sieve to explain the automatic clustering and sorting of atoms to produce an apparently orderly cosmos.[51] This is an artifact or craft analogy but does not qualify as 'mechanical' in the sense that I am using the term. Brumbaugh is one of a few who try to make a more thoroughgoing case for the idea that the atomists are 'mechanists', in the sense that experience with actual technology fostered the atomist hypothesis.[52]

It is difficult – as subsequent chapters will show in more detail – to assess with confidence the technology available at a given time

---

[48] A point I owe to Max Weiss.
[49] Balme (1941); Edelstein (1967), p. 427. De Groot (2008), p. 44, notes that '[i]n antiquity, mechanics was not regarded as the natural ally of atomism'.
[50] Lindberg (1992), pp. 30–1; Steel (2007), p. 14. [51] Hesse (1962).
[52] Brumbaugh (1964). He notes that atomism was formulated in ancient Indian philosophy, and – in the absence of suitable technology – rejected as implausible: Brumbaugh (1964), p. 89.

merely from the surviving written records. Brumbaugh is more sanguine than Furley about the complexity of the technology available to Democritus: he makes much of an archaeological discovery of a *klērōtērion*, or voting device, in the Athenian Agora, dating from the fourth century.[53] While this is an interesting find, it is not very sophisticated, particularly when compared with the working artifacts of the Hellenistic period. It was used for 'blind' selection of citizens to various offices, dispensing a sequence of white or black balls to indicate whether participants were selected or not. The device seems not to have mixed the balls so much as merely dispensed them according to a pre-existing order by means of a simple crank.[54]

Brumbaugh does not offer much other positive evidence to show that an appeal to working artifacts was part of the atomists' motivation. He cites appeals to artifacts – a marionette and a lyre – directly operated by an agent, which at best offers evidence that the atomists were materialist, not that they appealed to the functioning of working artifacts.[55] Brumbaugh also cites artifact analogies found in early medical theories.[56] Still, as I argued earlier, Hippocratic use of artifact analogies is limited, and only in rare cases is it used to explain physiological functioning.[57] Even there, the commitment to materialist explanations is not thoroughgoing, since they are intertwined with animistic elements in some of the same texts.[58]

---

[53] He also notes that Anaximander had described the cosmos as a working device composed of two interacting wheels: I have discussed the evidence for this in the previous section.

[54] Diagrams can be seen in Thompson and Wycherley (1972), p. 54; Brumbaugh (1966), p. 66.

[55] Taking the view of the soul that Socrates rejects in the *Phaedo* as being that of the atomists, he thinks they are relying on puppet technology to 'reduce explanation of human behaviour to a "tense sinew" causing motion, or to "strings under tension" producing a harmony': Brumbaugh (1966), pp. 55–6.

[56] Ferrari (1984), p. 268, also thinks that Brumbaugh exaggerates the atomist interest in devices as a way to explain the motion of the soul as 'mechanical'.

[57] Lonie (1981b): he is responding to an eighteenth-century claim that 'Hippocrates' was an 'iatromechanist'.

[58] Lonie (1981b), p. 123.

Important to Brumbaugh's argument is a passage where Aristotle likens Democritus' materialist account of soul to the notion that pouring mercury into a statue would be an adequate account of animation:

Some go so far as to hold that the movements which the soul imparts to the body in which it is are the same in kind as those with which it itself is moved. An example of this is Democritus, who uses language like that of the comic dramatist Philippus, who accounts for the movements that Daedalus imparted to his wooden Aphrodite by saying that he poured quicksilver into it; similarly Democritus says that the spherical atoms owing to their own ceaseless movements draw the whole body after them and so produce its movements.[59]

Aristotle is not criticizing the atomists for appealing to mechanics, but rather the notion that animation can be explained by a technique as crude as pouring a special liquid into an inanimate object. Democritus' account of soul seems to rely on a particular kind of atom with an easily moveable shape to do the explanatory work. The account rejected is clearly materialist and involves contact action, but there is little to justify calling it specifically 'mechanistic'. The comparison to an artifact is *Aristotle*'s, and the specific artifact to which he appeals seems to require the power of a mythical craftsman to make it move. But his point is merely to ridicule the crudeness of the atomists' explanation, not to accuse them of using an artifact analogy.

Like other early natural philosophers, the first atomists certainly used analogies to simple artifacts such as a winnowing basket or a mirror. Artifacts, however, are not necessarily mechanical. Still – even given the problems with our incomplete evidence for the ideas of Leucippus and Democritus – we might rather be struck by how *little* use there seems to be in ancient Greek atomism of analogies to artifacts. Democritus might well have eschewed use of a machine analogy, even if machinery were available in his day, because it was taken to imply the existence of a designer.[60] In contrast to those who

---

[59] Aristotle, *de An.* 1.3, 406b16, trans. Smith.
[60] A point suggested to me by Tim O'Keefe.

did advocate machine analogies, atomism is most centrally concerned to deny the need for intelligent direction.

The work of later atomists supports the idea that they would be wary of machine analogies. Sedley has drawn attention to a debate between Epicurus and the mathematicians of Cyzicus on the usefulness of the analogy to cosmic simulacra of some sort in understanding the motions of the heavens: Epicurus is critical of the analogy.[61] Steel takes the passage in Cicero's *de Natura Deorum*, where an Epicurean critiques the Platonist for not explaining what tools the *dēmiourgos* uses in creating the world, as an endorsement by Epicureans of 'mechanical explanation' *grounded in mechanics*.[62] However, the point seems rather to ridicule the notion of a designer god acting on the universe by showing how absurd it is to try to think of mechanical techniques on a cosmic scale. Lucretius, who is writing at a time when there is much more evidence of complex working devices in public use, makes only very limited use of such analogies. He does refer to the principle of leverage in explaining how, in animal self-motion, a small motion at the origin can produce a large result: in this he seems to be following Aristotle.[63] Lucretius does offer – as one of several possible accounts of the regular and apparently coordinated motion of the heavenly spheres – the possibility that they are fixed to a solid wheel and turn like a water wheel. This would be a fairly recent invention at the time when he is writing.[64] However, this explanation is offered as one among several alternative explanations and is presented as no more convincing than the idea that the stars may be swimming in harmony of their own volition.[65]

Lucretius' use of the phrase *machina mundi* has been read as claiming that the cosmos is a machine.[66] But Lucretius talks of *moles et machina mundi* only to refer to the organization of the

---

[61] Sedley (1976). See below for more on the details of this debate.
[62] Steel (2007), pp. 13–14.
[63] Lucretius 4.901–6; Aristotle, *MA* 7, 701b25–32, to be discussed further below.
[64] See Oleson (1984).   [65] Edelstein (1967), p. 427.
[66] Mayr (1986), pp. 39, 206 n. 28.

world into earth, air and water.[67] The meaning of *machina* here could be little more than a vague sense of an arrangement or system, perhaps in contrast to mere undifferentiated mass; there is no suggestion of technology here. Although some have assumed that atomism is motivated by a machine analogy, there is little to support this, and some reason to suppose the atomists eschewed such a comparison even at a time when more sophisticated devices were available.

THE 'SHORTFALLS' OF ANCIENT TECHNOLOGY

So far I have been arguing that we should not expect to find, nor is there evidence for, mechanical conceptions of nature – in either sense of the term – before the fourth century, when we first have clear evidence of the development of Greek mechanics as a discipline. There are a number of accounts in the literature that suggest that we should not expect to find such conceptions in the ancient Greek world even *after* the development of mechanics. These are, I think, open to question.

The traditional complaint about the limitations of ancient Greek technology is sometimes expressed as a regret that the ancients, otherwise so impressive in their intellectual achievements, did not make comparable advances in technology, and sometimes as a grumble about the apparent lack of interest in the subject in ancient Greek intellectual circles. The first version laments the lack of economic application of ancient technology, or perhaps the absence of an industrial revolution in antiquity.[68] The frivolity of ancient inventions is sometimes disparaged: Dijksterhuis describes them as 'ingenious, trifling, trivial, and superfluous'.[69]

One explanation of the supposed poverty of Greek technology refers to the lack of physical resources: for instance, it is sometimes said that the lack of readily available cheap materials and fuel sources

---

[67] Lucretius 5.96. Cf. Lucan 1.80: I thank Maura Lafferty for the reference. For the view that *machina* is one of a number of terms that acquire a more restricted use in medieval Latin, see Elliott (1997), p. 6.

[68] See Cuomo (2007), p. 3, for a critique of this approach.

[69] Dijksterhuis (1961), p. 74.

made many of the kinds of techniques important to the modern
Industrial Revolution impractical. Greek technology had limited
impact, it is said, because the devices that were invented were not
economically viable as substitutes for human or animal labour.[70]
Others cite sociological factors that would not only affect the interest
in invention, but also the intellectual reception of ancient technology. These include the prevalence of slavery and the lowly status
accorded to craftsmen and engineers, or the relegation of the management of estates to functionaries.[71] Those with most experience of
technology were not those with an economic interest in exploiting its
possibilities; thus technology never flowered. In such an environment, it is reasoned, the most theoretically minded of Greek intellectuals would disdain to associate themselves with practical, lowly,
banausic manual labour.[72]

Still other scholars find these accounts insufficient and blame
conceptual or theoretical barriers to technological progress. Koyré
thinks that the conception of natural philosophy and the lack of
mathematization of nature are stumbling blocks to greater interest in
the implications of ancient technology by the natural philosophers
and scientists of the day.[73] In a similar vein, Vernant complains that
technology was not understood as 'applied science': the ancients did
not connect technology with experiment and observation and manipulation of the world, and thus they failed to develop a practice that
would 'through its own internal logic, be pledged to innovation and
progress'.[74]

---

[70] E.g. Landels (1978), p. 31; on the distinction between invention and widespread
deployment, also Finley (1965); G. E. R. Lloyd (1973), pp. 107–10; Green (1990),
pp. 467–9. On the secondary literature, see Oleson (1984), p. 402; Greene (2000),
(2004).

[71] E.g. Schuhl (1947); Forbes (1949), p. 928; Dijksterhuis (1961), p. 74; Farrington
(1961), pp. 303ff.; Hodges (1970); Vernant (1983), pp. 283–4; Green (1990),
pp. 467ff. For a critique of this claim, see Edelstein (1967), pp. 418ff.; Burford
(1972), pp. 119, 128–35; Pleket (1973), pp. 28–31; Oleson (1984), pp. 398–400.

[72] G. E. R. Lloyd (1973), pp. 111–12. See Culham (1992) for a contrast between
attitudes in Hellenistic and imperial times.

[73] Koyré (1961).

[74] Vernant (1983), p. 285; see Kuhn (1977), p. 143; on progress, see Edelstein (1967).

Others have challenged these negative assessments of the range of Greek technology, and indeed some of the assumptions underlying older work on the history of ancient technology.[75] The ancient Greeks did develop or borrow quite a number of technological devices, whether or not these found widespread application.[76] In developing devices for warfare and building and water distribution, the ancient Greek world was hardly stagnant, and there is ample evidence of astrolabes, spheres and calculators, measuring instruments, surgical machinery, hydraulic implements, time-measuring devices, musical instruments and theatrical shows. There has been an unfortunate tendency to underrate the significance of ancient technology by evaluating it purely on its practical benefits or range of application. Drachmann rightly decries the practice of underrating ancient technological invention because of a 'frivolous' interest in 'mere toys' rather than in 'serious' inventions with industrial or military applications.[77] Although the deployment and exploitation of technology might loom large in the eyes of economic historians, the *philosophical* reception of technological devices is a different matter.

It is difficult to form a reliable picture of the development or reception of ancient technology, since there are serious problems with the evidence. Not only are many works lost and the dates of the major figures in ancient mechanics often unknown, but the literary records are inadequately detailed in their descriptions. We often cannot tell if given devices worked, or were ever in fact constructed. Reports conflict; diagrams are poor and of later vintage; technical terms are sometimes obscure.[78] Literary reports – often all

---

[75] For the latter, see especially Greene (2004), who details recent historiographical shifts away from the 'triumphalism' of earlier writing about technology and towards a more contextual approach; and Cuomo (2007), who shows how a deeper understanding of technology requires a deeper knowledge of the social context in which it arose.

[76] E.g. Mumford (1934), p. 4; Finley (1965); Edelstein (1967), p. 409; G. E. R. Lloyd (1973), pp. 105ff.; Pleket (1973); Oleson (1984); Simms (1995); Greene (2000); de Gandt (2003), p. 337.

[77] Drachmann (1948), pp. 3, 45; also Greene (2004), p. 160; Tybjerg (2005).

[78] For discussion of the difficulties, see, e.g., Drachmann (1963a); Oleson (1984); Fleury (1993).

we have – do not give details of the workings of devices; even technical manuals are woefully thin on specifics. Physical evidence has shown how unreliable the written records are in tracking the availability of new technology. Archaeological findings demonstrate use of the crank and of the cart shaft long before they appear in the literary records;[79] interpretations of the Antikythera mechanism suggest that, in the Hellenistic period, the level of technological sophistication in gearing was far greater than that recorded in surviving texts.[80] The 'argument from silence' is thus problematic: not every device or technique available at a given period is mentioned in the surviving literary records; but nor should we rashly postulate the availability of mechanical techniques in a given period without sufficient reason. Nor should we assume that ancient technology followed a linear and cumulative development.[81]

Those who focus on the historical importance of technology often consider the intellectual reception of mechanics in the context of the social status of various fields of inquiry. A prejudice against the practical is said to be the motive for – as Plutarch famously portrays it – Archimedes' greater interest in abstract mathematical work, only undertaking practical problems in response to royal requests.[82] Yet Archimedes' own achievements seem to belie Plutarch's claim.[83] The question is a complex one. Evidence suggests that those who saw the benefits of technology were able to overcome prejudices against it. Diodorus Siculus attributes the inventiveness of Dionysius' engineers in 399 BCE to the personal attention they received: as well as offering high wages and prizes, Dionysius involved the most honoured citizens in supervising the workmen and took a personal interest, inviting the best to dinner.[84] In Ptolemaic Alexandria inventions were paraded in royal processions: the court seems to

---

[79] Hassell (1979); K. D. White (1984), p. 173.
[80] Price (1975); Simms (1995), pp. 84ff. More on this below.
[81] On this see Cuomo (2007).   [82] See Simms (1995), pp. 73ff.   [83] Simms (1995).
[84] Diodorus Siculus 14.41–2; see Oleson (1984), p. 392, on the role of Hellenistic monarchs as patrons of technology and sponsors of particular innovations; Dalley and Oleson (2003), p. 3: 'The high wages, performance bonuses, and focused work groups would not be out of place in a modern computer company.'

have patronized mechanics along with other arts and sciences. In the Greek and Roman world inventive theatrical pieces were commissioned by kings and emperors, displayed at dinner parties and exhibited at weddings.[85] Cuomo's careful work detailing the social status of specialists belies the claim that it was necessarily a mean one.[86] It is important not to overstate prejudice against the practical.

THE 'EXCLUSION' OF ANCIENT MECHANICS

One other preconception has affected existing accounts of the ancient reception of mechanics, and it needs to be addressed. Historians of science sometimes contrast the importance of mechanics to early modern natural philosophy with its reception in antiquity. Assuming that ancient natural philosophers took no heed of either the results or the investigative techniques of mechanics, a number of reasons are offered to account for the different reception of mechanics in the two periods: that mechanics works *against* nature; that natural and artificial things belong to isolated or incompatible fields of study; and that mechanical devices are marvellous or deceptive and thus not part of natural philosophy.[87]

Some of this stems from a misapplication of some remarks Galileo made in inaugurating his programme for integrating mechanics and natural philosophy. Galileo challenged aspects of a prevailing conception of mechanics, a conception that would have precluded the application of its ideas, methods and results to natural philosophy. This challenge is seen as a milestone, articulating a new approach to the study of motion, drawing on the discipline of mechanics to formulate new methods for the quantitative study of motion in other

---

[85] E.g. Polybius 12.13.9; Vitruvius, *de Arch.* 10.3; Athenaeus, *Deipn.* 5.198; Seneca, *Ep.* 88.22; Suetonius 5.21, 34.2; Philoponus, *in GA* 77.16.

[86] Cuomo (2000), (2007).

[87] Cf. Micheli (1995), p. 33. See also Schiefsky (2007a) for a challenge to Krafft's claim that a distinction between art and nature governed the understanding of mechanics in antiquity. This work came to my attention too late to take full account of it: I thank an anonymous reviewer for the reference, and the author for allowing me to see an advance copy.

contexts, inaugurating a new programme important to the mechanical philosophy. A problem arises, however, when it is assumed that the views of mechanics that Galileo rejects go back to the ancient Greeks. I argue in this section that this is not so.

'Against nature'

Apparently a number of engineers in Galileo's day regarded their art as operating by cheating or breaking nature's laws.[88] His *Le Mecaniche* begins with the expressed aim of showing that engineers were not, in fact, cheating nature when they used the power of the lever.[89] In thus naturalizing the operation of the lever, he showed that it is not 'getting something for nothing': the effort required to lift a given weight with a longer lever, while less in quantity at any given moment, needs to be applied over a proportionally greater time. The advantage gained by mechanical devices is merely to portion out the work required into quantities that a given person could apply conveniently.[90] The effect of this was to establish that the operation of mechanical devices depended on the principles of natural philosophy.

Because the view Galileo rejects is based on a distinction between art and nature, and between forced and natural motion, it would be easy to suppose that he is rejecting a view of mechanics that goes back to Aristotle. Despite the view of mechanics expressed in the *Posterior Analytics* – that it is a legitimate field, intermediary between natural philosophy and mathematics – scholars sometimes take as the view of antiquity in general, or the Aristotelian tradition in

---

[88] See Festa and Roux (2001), p. 252; Meli (2006), p. 19.

[89] 'Dei quali inganni parmi di avere compreso essere principalmente cagione la credenza, che i detti artefici hanno avuta ed hanno continuamente, di potere con poca forza muovere ed alzare grandissimi pesi, ingannando, in un certo modo, con le loro machine la natura ...' Galilei (1929–40), vol. II, p. 155. See also Galilei (1929–40), vol. VIII, p. 572: 'E perché io, gia gran tempo fa, mi era formato un concetto, e per molte e molte esperienze confermatolo, che la natura non potesse esser superata e defraudata dall'arte ...' I thank Michael Mahoney for the reference. Roux (1996), pp. 7–11; Crombie (1996), pp. 102–3.

[90] Galilei (1960), p. 149.

particular, that mechanics works 'against nature'.[91] Galileo's *Two New Sciences* challenges the common conception that effects produced by force are 'contrary to nature', claiming that only the impossible is contrary to nature.[92] This might seem to be a rejection of an Aristotelian view: the Aristotelian *Mechanica* describes mechanics as studying motions that are *para phusin*, that is, not according to nature, a category that includes all forced motions.[93] While motion *para phusin* is sometimes rendered 'contrary to nature' in modern translations of Aristotle or the Aristotelian *Mechanica*,[94] it is by no means clear that Aristotle's medieval and Renaissance interpreters took *contra naturam* to be the appropriate translation of Aristotle's Greek phrase *para phusin*, or that they understood forced motion to be 'against nature' in any strong sense.

In the Latin tradition Aristotle's categorization of forced or non-natural motion – the category into which motions caused by mechanical devices would fall – was not standardly translated *contra naturam*. Both the *translatio vetus* of the *Physics*, and Thomas Aquinas' exposition of the *Physics*, for example, render *para phusin* as *extra naturam*.[95] Wallace's work on the scholars of the Collegio Romano shows that there are explicit discussions amongst Renaissance Aristotelians concerning the correct translation of *para phusin*, and the classification of motions implied by the Latin prepositions. Vitelleschi, one of Galileo's sources, raises a question

[91] E.g. Hooykaas (1963); Krafft (1970a); (1970b); Pleket (1973), p. 20; Gabbey (1992b), p. 308; (1993a), pp. 142–3; Roux (1996), p. 7; Newman (2004), pp. 20–1, 299.

[92] Sagredo: 'Converrà dunque dire che, pur per violenza o contro a natura, il vacuo talor si conceda (benché l'opinion mia è che nissuna cosa sia contro a natura, salvo che l'impossibile, il quale poi non è mai)'. Galilei (1929–40), vol. VIII, p. 60.

[93] Ps.-Aristotle, *Mechanica* 847a18.

[94] Some prominent English examples include Ross (1936), p. 435; Hardie and Gaye's translation of *Physics* and E. S. Forster's translation of the *Mechanics* in Barnes (1984), vol. I, p. 365 and vol. II, p. 1299. See Chapters 3 and 4 below for discussions of authorship.

[95] From the *translatio vetus*: *violentus quidem enim extra naturam est* (*Physics* 4.8, 215a3); *violentia et extra naturam* (*Physics* 8.4, 254b14): Bossier and Brams (1990). From the exposition of Thomas Aquinas: *violentus enim est extra naturam* (*Physics* 4.8); *aut extra naturam et violentia* (*Physics* 8.4); Maggiòlo (1954), pp. 251, 539.

whether forced motion should be understood as *praeter naturam* or *supra naturam*, 'beyond' or 'above', rather than 'contrary to' nature. This is not a merely philological issue: Vitelleschi wants to make clear that the natural powers of bodies are not destroyed during forced motion.[96] Since bodies undergoing forced motion retain their weight – understood as a tendency to downward fall – forced motion is not best considered contrary to natural motion. In his 1627 commentary on the *Mechanica*, Guevara claims that mechanics studies the production of motions by smaller forces, 'whether such motions are in accord with nature, contrary to it, or beyond it'.[97]

These interpreters of the Aristotelian tradition did not take forced motion to be *prima facie* excluded from the science of nature.[98] There is no evidence of an *a priori* classification of mechanics here that forces an opposition of mechanical motion to natural. Although the classification of mechanics is still an open question, it would certainly be possible to look to mechanics for information on the natural world without thereby being forced into an anti-Aristotelian stance.

The *Mechanica* found in the Aristotelian corpus is a key text cited in discussions of the status of mechanics in antiquity. This text famously begins with a classification of the work of mechanics as *para phusin*, an idea that clearly echoes Aristotle's classification of forced motion more generally.[99] To those who read *para phusin* as meaning 'contrary to nature', this categorization seems to support the idea that the view of mechanics rejected by Galileo goes back to antiquity.[100] The Greek phrase can certainly be used in cases

---

[96] Wallace (1984), p. 163; cf. Weisheipl (1985), p. 64; Gabbey (1993a), p. 145. See Festa and Roux (2001), esp. p. 241 n. 13, where they take *praeter naturam* as the accepted translation of *para phusin* in the sixteenth century; Bottecchia Dehò (2000), p. 131, lists different translations.

[97] Wallace (1984), p. 210. See also Micheli (1995), p. 28.

[98] Wallace (1984), p. 202. Guevara describes mechanics as a science as well as an art: Wallace (1984), pp. 209–11.

[99] Although, as I shall argue later, the *Mechanica* departs significantly from the standard Aristotelian view in its account of the relationship between the two kinds of motion.

[100] Krafft (1970a), p. xv; (1970b), p. 191.

that involve transgression.[101] However, the phrase need not imply transgression against or opposition to, rather than merely going beyond, a given category. In the particular case of Aristotle's use of *para phusin*, there are reasons not to understand the Greek phrase to refer to phenomena opposed to or excluded from natural philosophy altogether.[102]

Aristotle does not think of the 'science of nature' as an attempt to give an account of everything that happens in the physical world, or even every occurrence in the lives of plants, animals and the four elements. The changes that happen *kata phusin*, 'according to nature', are those that happen 'always or for the most part', and for which the source of change and rest is internal to a substantial individual.[103] A large part of his study of the natural world focuses on the features of organisms that follow from their individual natures, but there is much else to say about regularities in the physical world that do not follow from the natures of substantial individuals. Although the matter of an organism is composed from kinds with their own essences, these in turn can only account for normal functioning, not for anomalies, coincidences, by-products or failures.[104]

Aristotle and his followers in fact recognize some awkwardness with this classification: some defects occur rather regularly. Theophrastus acknowledges that some causes of decay and death happen often and in a habitual way.[105] The Aristotelian commentator

---

[101] Plato, *Lg.* 636c6; 841d4; Dover (1978), pp. 167, 186. The transgression arises here because of a view about the moral implications of overstepping social boundaries, and not because the actions involved – homosexual acts – are thought to encounter some 'natural' obstacle or to lie outside the normal causal framework.

[102] This is argued in detail in Schiefsky (2007a).

[103] There is room for debate as to why Aristotle thinks these two categories are equivalent. It may be that, *because* of his observation of the regularities in nature and his belief that they cannot be accounted for by chaotic processes, he posits that these regularities must be the result of something internal guiding its development.

[104] Micheli (1995), p. 27, notes that spontaneous generation is *para phusin*: *Ph.* 2.6, 197b34–5.

[105] Theophrastus, *CP* 5.8.1. The idea that diseases have a nature is recognized in the Hippocratic text *Morb. Sacr.*: see G. E. R. Lloyd (1987), p. 117 n. 37.

Simplicius tries to accommodate the difficulty by emphasizing that the category of things that happen 'by nature', *phusei*, is larger than the category of things that happen 'according to nature', *kata phusin*.[106] Philoponus also tries to solve the problem by looking at the bigger picture within which things that are *para phusin* for the individual may be *kata phusin* for the whole.[107] The Aristotelian category of the *kata phusin* is too specific to encompass all that happens in the natural world.

The distinction between *kata phusin* and *para phusin* continued to be used in mechanical texts, including those of Hero and Pappus, where it does not seem to imply any deep allegiance to Aristotelian metaphysics.[108] It might have come to indicate little more than the results that occurred with or without intervention. The use of the terminology is no reason to assume mechanics was regarded as being opposed to natural philosophy. Certainly the *Mechanica*, supposedly the key exhibit for that assumed opposition, applies its results to cases in the natural world.

Art versus nature

Besides the relationship between forced motion and natural philosophy, a second aspect of Galileo's challenge to the status of mechanics concerns the relationship between art and science. Here again, it seems that Galileo is reacting to a tradition that had arisen in the intervening centuries, rather than to a view that goes back to antiquity. Medieval tradition followed a classification by Hugh of St Victor, which suggests that the 'mechanical' is imitative, with the clear implication of inferiority. An etymology, deriving the term for 'mechanics' from the term for 'adulterer', apparently gave rise to the view of mechanics as deceptive.[109]

---

[106] Simplicius, *in Ph.* 271.10ff.; Sambursky (1962), pp. 93–8; G. E. R. Lloyd (1987), p. 14 n. 43.
[107] Philoponus, *in Ph.* 201.10ff.; Macierowski and Hassing (1988), p. 86.
[108] On Aristotelian ideas as 'buzzwords', see Cuomo (2000), p. 104.
[109] J. Taylor (1961); Sternagel (1966). See the appendix for the story on this.

Aristotle, however, allowed that arts could be improving on nature rather than merely imitating it.[110] Given his classification of mechanics alongside optics, astronomy and harmonics, there is no reason to think that he saw mechanics as a purely productive rather than a theoretical pursuit.[111] Other ancient mechanics texts support this. The Aristotelian *Mechanica* describes its subject matter as common to mathematical and physical studies, *theōrēmata*;[112] Vitruvius cites a view that the architect – who is also the master mechanic – should be schooled in all arts and sciences;[113] Pappus introduces mechanics as a *theōria*, a theoretical study.[114] The best-known texts show that mechanics, in antiquity, had a theoretical aspect.

Galileo's project involved a reclassification of mechanics from an art to a part of natural philosophy.[115] However, there is no reason to think that the description of mechanics as a *technē* would be reason for excluding it from consideration in ancient Greek natural philosophy.[116] When Plato wants to classify arts as empty of theoretical principles, he calls them *tribai*, not *technai*;[117] medicine's classification as a *technē* was not thought to be in conflict with its considerable theoretical apparatus or the integration of its discoveries into natural philosophy. Aristotle characterizes *technē* by its ability to form universal principles from experience.[118] Indeed, *technē* is sometimes better translated 'science' than 'art'.[119] The idea that 'mechanical' applies to arts that are purely practical and lacking theory does not seem to stem from the ancient Greek tradition.[120]

---

[110] *Ph.* 2.8, 199a15–17. Plato indicates at *Lg.* 889b–d that the view that art is merely derivative is a partisan position advocated by challengers to teleology. On the idea that this view is pervasive in antiquity, see, e.g., Close (1969).

[111] Owens (1991). [112] *Mech.* 847a27.

[113] Vitruvius, *de Arch.* 1.1.11. [114] Pappus 8.1.

[115] Gabbey (1992b), (1993a). Bottecchia Dehò (2000), p. 136, discusses the controversy over the classification of the *Mechanica*.

[116] See Schiefsky (2007a) and Cuomo (2007) for some excellent recent work on the art–nature distinction in antiquity.

[117] E.g. *Grg.* 463b4. [118] *Metaph.* 1.1, 981a6–8.

[119] Cooper (2004), p. 6; see also Mourelatos (1991); Russo (2004), pp. 186–7.

[120] See Fleury (1993), p. 18, for doubts whether the theoretical–practical distinction within mechanics is really applicable in antiquity.

Wonder versus nature

There is a third possible obstacle to the understanding of mechanics as part of natural philosophy, which is also sometimes read back into antiquity. This is the idea that the ancients associated mechanics with wonder, magic and trickery, and thus did not take it seriously as part of natural philosophy. A common term for makers of theatrical devices in later centuries is *thaumatopoios*, 'wondermaker', or *thaumasiourgos*,[121] 'wonderworker', terms also used of jugglers and other performers more generally. Weightlifting technology is referred to by Pappus as the field of the *manganarioi*: this term has associations

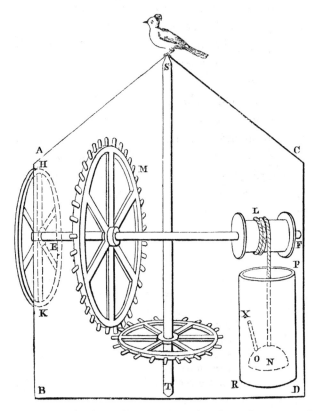

Figure 1 *Hagnistērion*, a device associated with purification rituals.

[121] Pappus 8.1.

with trickery.[122] Mechanical devices continued to be used in religious contexts, much like the statues with moving parts carried in Egyptian religious festivals.[123] The Aristotelian *Mechanica* talks of a series of wheels that turn one another in opposite directions, like those erected in temples:[124] Hero also describes a *hagnistērion*, a device based on the turning of a bronze wheel by passers-by at the entrance to a temple.[125]

Some scholars have made much of this association with wonder.[126] Vernant suggests that the opening of the Aristotelian text presents mechanics as a kind of trickery, since it talks of 'the lesser mastering the greater'.[127] This phrase recalls the sophistic knack for 'making the worse argument seem the better'; it ascribes the special power of mechanics to the wonderful properties of the circle.[128] Subsequent chapters will show that the association of mechanics with sophistry or trickery is not really representative of the Greek tradition.

While ancient mechanical texts certainly offer evidence that mechanics was associated with wonder or the marvellous *by its audience*, the mechanical theorists might have had reasons for maintaining this aura without being party to it. In war devices a factor of terror and surprise would be part of their function, as the reports of Archimedes' devices testify;[129] Philo of Byzantium rates his new invention not only on cheapness, range and ease of operation, but also on its imposing appearance, which is achieved by hiding the

[122] Liddell, Scott and Jones (1996), p. 1070; see Oleson (1984), p. 45. This is emphasized by Pleket (1973), p. 40, following Krafft; cf. *manganeuontes*, Francis (1995), p. 70.
[123] Herodotus 2.48.   [124] *Mech.* 848a25.
[125] *Spir.* 2.32, cited in Drachmann (1963a), p. 13. Faraone (1992), p. 5 discusses the belief that smooth stones had fallen from the sky and thus had special powers: these were placed at doorways for protective purposes and could be the origin of this practice.
[126] Vernant (1983); also Close (1969); Pérez-Ramos (1996a), pp. 112–13; Newman (2004), p. 22. On wonder in later natural philosophy, see Daston and Park (1998).
[127] Vernant (1983); cf. Crombie (1994), p. 179.
[128] Ps.-Aristotle, *Mech.* 847a20ff.; 847b16ff.; Vernant (1983), pp. 286–7.
[129] Plutarch, *Marc.* 14ff.: see Dijksterhuis (1956), p. 27.

moving parts from the front view.[130] With show pieces this feature is even more essential. Popular reactions, then, are unlikely to reflect the understanding of the discipline by its theorists. Lloyd notes that other sciences were sometimes likened by detractors to 'mumbo-jumbo or wonder-work'.[131] We do not take the presentation of scientists by Aristophanes as representative of the views of their practitioners.

A number of passages show that this association with wonder is maintained for the sake of the watching public and is not part of the engineer's own understanding of the craft. The Aristotelian *Mechanica* indicates that craftsmen maintain wonder by hiding the source of motion, so that only wonder is evident and the cause is unseen.[132] Several ancient writers echo Aristotle's claim that, to the more experienced – for those who perceive the cause – wonder vanishes.[133] Wonder is thus presented as a prelude or spur to inquiry, rather than as a category important to inquiry itself. Hero recognizes the value of surprise and novelty in his art: he instructs us to keep the mechanisms hidden from view to maintain the surprise.[134]

Tybjerg, who recognizes the distinction between the perspective of the audience and that of the mechanical theorist in the ancient texts, nonetheless tries to show that wonder plays an important intellectual role in Hero of Alexandria's work. She argues that the category of wonder found in mechanics is used as justification for regarding mechanics as more than merely useful: it parallels the role of wonder in philosophy and adds an element of 'divine cunning' to the claims of mechanics.[135] While mechanics never abandoned its aura, I suggest that this is a feature of the *display* value of mechanics,

---

[130] Philo, *Bel.* 56.23–4; 62.11–12: see Cuomo (2000), p. 100.

[131] G. E. R. Lloyd (1987), p. 333.

[132] *Mech.* 1, 848a34. See Micheli (1995), pp. 140ff., for the idea that wonder was a factor of human ignorance only, not an ontological category. Bottecchia Dehò (2000), p. 19 n. 9, discusses some translations of the terminology of 'wonder' in the *Mechanica*.

[133] Aristotle, *Metaph.* 1.2, 983a12; Seneca, *Ep.* 88.23; cf. Michael, *in MA* 117.20ff.; Asclepius, *in Metaph.* 22.12; Philo, *Bel.* 77.26; pseudo-Alexander, *Pr.* 1.33.

[134] *Aut.* 17.1; 26.1–2; 30.6.   [135] Tybjerg (2003), p. 443.

not of its theory. Hero's or Pappus' claims for the intellectual status of mechanics depend more on its connection to the mathematical tradition; Vitruvius' situation of mechanics within the body of architecture, validated by its place within the sober tradition of the arts and sciences, also forfeits the mystique. Cuomo notes that the association with wonder-working was downplayed by Pappus: not only is he concerned to stress the theoretical aspect of mechanics, but he was also writing in a time when wonder-working had gone out of favour.[136]

Although recent historians have been concerned to stress the real presence of the magical, occult and mysterious in even the canonical texts of the history of science, it is important not to let this interest support the thesis of the 'exclusion' of ancient mechanics from natural philosophy. Maintaining an air of illusion might have been part of the trade of the mechanic, but this should not lead us to think that the mechanics took their devices to be insulated from theories in other disciplines, or that philosophers regarded this association with illusion as central to the intellectual status of the field.

The notion that mechanics works against nature, the rigid distinction between mechanics as an art and a science, and the notion of mechanics as a deceptive or magical trickery, all take the form that Galileo is rejecting from medieval rather than ancient discussions. All three notions *could* be read back into ancient texts, but none really represent the way mechanics is treated there by those most closely associated with the field.[137] If we set aside these preconceptions, then, it seems that there are reasons to look for evidence of the philosophical reception of ancient mechanics in antiquity. References to mechanics appear in the fourth century. It is to the evidence for the early history of the discipline that I now turn.

[136] Cuomo (2000), pp. 106, 124. Pappus uses the term *thaumasiourgoi* to refer to the practitioners of one of the branches of mechanics: for the use of this term to refer to various kinds of sorcerers and wonderworkers, see Francis (1995).

[137] This point is made against Krafft by Micheli (1995), pp. 34–5.

CHAPTER 3

Mechanics in the fourth century

The origins of mechanics – both the practical development of devices and the creation of a body of theory about their operation – are obscure. Doubtless elements of the discipline, such as the use of lever and balance, axle-and-wheel, clepsydra and siphon, predated the fourth century BCE. However, the creation of a discipline requires more than the use of certain kinds of technology: there needs to be some kind of unifying idea, some perception of commonality. Looking at the disparate elements that came to be included in the Greek discipline of mechanics, it is difficult to identify exactly what that perceived commonality was. It may be that the reason why mechanics came to be recognized as a discipline – a field of knowledge – was no more than a recognition that certain devices make possible results that would not have occurred without them, and that some of them worked in similar ways. The contribution of mechanics to the history of philosophy arose from its ensuing theories, as well as a more general commitment to the idea that the principles at work in mechanics can also be found in the natural world.

This chapter will examine the evidence concerning the creation of a discipline *called* 'mechanics' during the fourth century. Such a reconstructive project requires great caution against reading back assumptions about what 'mechanics' means, or about what is self-evident. In the end, I find the evidence from the fourth century to be inconclusive. Some may find this reading of the fourth-century evidence overly cautious: others have reconstructed more positive accounts of the founding of mechanics in the fourth century. But such speculation leaves much unexplained.

Aristotle is, of course, the key figure here, since he is the first to mention a discipline of mechanics, and it is to his corpus that the first surviving work of mechanics is attributed. If we took the Aristotelian *Mechanica* to be Aristotle's work, we would have a good deal of information about the development of mechanics in the fourth century, but with it a puzzle as to why Aristotle elsewhere makes so little use of such a powerful theory. Some have thought it was because of a distinction in kind between art and nature that Aristotle does not see the relevance of mechanics to understanding natural philosophy. I have already suggested, however, that this supposition is unsupported. Other scholars attribute the *Mechanica* to the early third century, especially since an ancient tradition ascribes the work to Strato of Lampsacus, third scholarch of the Peripatos. But if this is so, we have rather little information about the history of mechanics in the fourth century. While I favour the latter interpretation, it should be acknowledged that the evidence is less than conclusive.

THE SCOPE OF ANCIENT GREEK MECHANICS

A history of the concept of mechanics should begin with the evolution of the term 'mechanical,' or rather, its Greek equivalents.[1] The noun *mēchanē*, from which *mēchanik-* is derived, is so broad in range as to mean nothing more precise than 'device' or stratagem.[2] The privative term, *amēchania*, is used in early Greek poetry as a term for human helplessness before the gods, in contrast to Odysseus' resourcefulness or *polumēchania*.[3] Klytemnestra's robe is described

---

[1] These are the neuter plural noun *ta mēchanika* or the feminine adjective *mēchanikē*. The first expression is generally thought to refer by implication to the neuter plural *problēmata*, i.e. 'mechanical problems': *tōn problēmatōn mēchanika*, ps.-Aristotle, *Mech.* 847a25; Aristotle, *APo.* 1.13, 78b37; Diogenes Laertius 8.83. The feminine adjective typically implies the noun *technē*, i.e. 'the mechanical art': Aristotle, *Metaph.* 13.3, 1078a16; Plutarch, *Marc.* 14. Aristotle also refers to 'mechanical demonstration,' *apodeixis*: *APo.* 1.9, 76a24; Pappus to 'the mechanical study', *theōria*: 8.1.

[2] See Micheli (1995), pp. 9–11: he notes Plato's etymology at *Cra.* 415a. Fleury (1993), pp. 20–2, claims that, etymologically, *mēchanē* derives from a root sense of 'power'.

[3] Fränkel (1960), p. 29; Snell (1953), pp. 52–62. I thank Kai Trampedach for the references.

by Aeschylus as a *mēchanēma*, a device for implementing a purpose.[4] Aristotle accuses Anaxagoras of introducing *nous* or mind into his system as a *mēchanē* to fix all insoluble problems: *nous* is surely the antithesis of a machine. This breadth of meaning is also true of the earlier meaning of the Latin *machina*, and, for that matter, of early English usage: the *Oxford English Dictionary* lists, as representative of seventeenth- and eighteenth-century English usage, application of the term to things as simple as a hat-box or as abstract as society or language.[5]

While scholars often note this very general range of the term *mēchanē*, it is important to recognize that the use of the term *mēchanikē* is much more specific and it is the relevant term to focus on when it comes to the understanding of the discipline. There are occasionally cases where derivatives of *mēchanik-* have a non-technical sense: Aesop describes an elderly lion who is too weak to feed himself and attempts to live *mēchanikōs*, that is, by clever tricks.[6] But *mēchanikē* came to be used principally as a technical term, naming one of a number of branches of a particular discipline.[7] The term *mēchanēma* was also used more specifically of manufactured artifacts such as war engines.[8] Terminology was not used rigidly: terms with other derivations such as *kataskeuē*, 'construction', were also commonly used of the devices produced by mechanics.

The perceived character of the field of mechanics seems to be, I suggest, that its subject matter *does* something. It was not used so much as a catch-all term for technology or for tools generally, but for a new category of what I shall call 'working artifacts'. Its primary subject matter includes devices for lifting weights or moving fluids; ballistic devices for throwing projectiles; devices imitating living beings; devices that show the relative motions of the heavenly bodies. It is hard to divine the perceived unifying element too precisely, but the discipline of mechanics seems to focus on function,

---

[4] *A.* 1126; *Ch.* 975; noted by Morris (1992), p. 61.
[5] Simpson and Weiner (1989), vol. IX, pp. 156–9.   [6] Aesop, *Prov.* 37.
[7] On the practice of designating *technai* with the *-ik-* suffix, see Zhmud (2006), p. 61.
[8] E.g. Plutarch, *Marc.* 14.4; cf. Aeschylus, *Pr.* 469, cited by Micheli (1995), pp. 122–3 n. 3.

not on mere form. A stick is not a lever, although they may be morphologically identical: a lever is a functional kind, and mechanical devices seem to be such when they are considered in their functional roles.

The taxonomic classification of the field in the surviving literature appears to be somewhat fluid. Mechanics is often classified as a branch of architecture, a classification that seems to go back in the Greek tradition to at least the sixth century BCE and is echoed centuries later by Vitruvius, Galen and Procopius.[9] This is because the master-builder or *architektōn* was responsible for weight-moving technology on the site of public buildings such as temples, which required hauling huge stone blocks. Sculptors were credited with inventing some early mechanisms, such as starting gates for races.[10] Plutarch complains that mechanics became part of the art of war; and it is certainly true that the term *mēchanopoios* is commonly applied to a maker of large war implements. Neither category, however, indicates the full extent of the field, which includes display pieces for temples and public ceremonies, household serving implements, theatrical displays, cosmic models, water organs, fountains, timekeeping devices, and so forth.

'Mechanics' seems only to have come into use as a category in the mid fourth century. There is no mention of *mēchanikē technē* or the practitioner *mēchanikos* in Plato's work, despite Plato's abundant use of analogies to the arts and crafts of his day. Plato once uses *mēchanopoios* of a maker of military devices,[11] but mechanics is not among the mathematical disciplines mentioned in the *Republic*. There are later references to the development of a field called 'mechanics' by Archytas, a Pythagorean and associate of Plato's. He is credited with having systematized 'mechanics' – *ta mēchanika* – using mathematical principles. In Aristotle's *Posterior Analytics*, mechanics is listed alongside optics, harmonics and astronomy as

---

[9] Coulton (1977); Vitruvius, *de Arch.*; Galen, *Pecc. Dig.* 5.68–9; 99–100; *Libr. Propr.* 19.40; Procopius, *Aed.* 1.1.24; Simplicius, *in Cael.* 563.6–8.

[10] Coulton (1977), pp. 16ff.; Burford (1972), p. 102.   [11] Plato, *Grg.* 512b5.

one of the sciences subordinate to mathematical principles;[12] it is also mentioned with optics and harmonics in the *Metaphysics*.[13] Unfortunately, however, there is little to tell us what the term *mēchanikē* refers to in these texts. Aristotle gives us little to go on, and the sources concerning Archytas – Plutarch (first century CE) and Diogenes Laertius (third century CE) – are late and notoriously difficult as sources.

The earliest surviving treatise, the Aristotelian *Mechanica*, is primarily concerned with a group of devices centred around the balance and the lever, including pulley, wheel, wedge, rudder, forceps, mast and oar – though not the screw – and with the mathematical principles thought to underlie them. Particularly since this branch of mechanics has come to be one of the principal associations of the term in contemporary English, it is easy to assume that this is also what the fourth-century texts refer to. Mach, for example, confidently asserts that Archytas 'founded the theory of pulleys'.[14] However, it is important not to presuppose that we know what 'mechanics' refers to in the fourth century BCE.

There are several branches of the discipline of mechanics, as it later came to be understood. One of the more comprehensive accounts of the scope of the discipline, that by Pappus of Alexandria (fourth century CE), names practitioners of several branches, which he ascribes to 'the ancients'. The *manganarioi* are those who use devices to lift great weights with a lesser force; the *organopoioi* make catapults to hurl stone and iron armaments; the *mēchanopoioi* build irrigation instruments for raising water more easily from a depth; the *thaumasiourgoi* imitate living beings by pneumatic devices, or by cords and ropes, or by floating bodies, or by timepieces worked by water; the experts in *sphairopoiia* – literally, 'sphere-making' – make images of the heavens.

Unfortunately, we cannot take these classifications as definitive or the terminology as fixed. Generic terms such as *mēchanopoioi* could as easily refer to other branches of the field; elsewhere, similar terms

---

[12] *APo.* 1.13, 78b37; cf. 1.9, 76a24.   [13] *Metaph.* 13.3, 1078a16.
[14] Mach (1907), p. 510. For the view that Aristotle is referring to Archytas' achievement, see, e.g., Micheli (1995), p. 22.

are applied to the builders of war machinery.[15] Pappus' text seems to be including the study of floating bodies and the making of water clocks within the work of *thaumasiourgoi*, the 'wonder-workers'. The notion of 'wonder' is most often associated with display pieces and theatrical shows, and not with Archimedes' geometrical work on floating bodies.[16] Pappus' list seems to conflate the classification of 'pneumatic' devices according to one main use of the field – to create display pieces that seem to be animate – with a more analytic classification of the field in terms of the underlying dynamics of water pressure and equilibrium that explains the effects. A further puzzle is the suggestion that 'sphere-making' employed circulating water to make images of the heavens. While there are reports of water-driven timepieces that show the rotation of the heavens, the water is not circulated;[17] it is not clear how other kinds of celestial spheres might be water-driven.

It seems that this list of categories comes from an original list that underwent revision by various hands. Pappus makes clear that he is reporting what others say, and from some time ago.[18] Proclus (fifth century CE) gives what is on some points a strikingly similar list with some parallels in phrasing and structure; he seems to be citing a classification by Geminus.[19] The two surviving lists differ in some of the categories used: Proclus does not specifically mention weightlifting devices, water-lifting, floating bodies or water clocks. He seems more interested in situating mechanics within a broader picture of natural philosophy: he includes a general category of equilibrium and 'centres of weight',[20] and he includes a final, general category of the entire art of moving matter. Despite these differences, the two lists present the categories they share in common in the same order,

---

[15] Procopius in the sixth century CE uses it to refer to builders: *Aed.* 1.1.24.

[16] G. E. R. Lloyd (1973), p. 92 n. 1, notes the oddity of including Archimedes' abstract work on hydrostatics in this capacious category.

[17] Vitruvius, *de Arch.* 9.8–14; Manilius 4.267–8; see Chapter 4, below.

[18] κατὰ τοὺς ἀρχαίους λεγομένων; καλοῦσι δὲ μηχανικοὺς οἱ παλαιοί, Pappus 8.1024.14, 1024.24–5 (Hultsch).

[19] See Evans (1998), p. 83.   [20] Cf. Simplicius, *in Cael.* 543.30.

and they use similar wording.[21] This suggests that Pappus is also drawing on a doxographical tradition.

The categories mentioned by Pappus roughly correspond to the contours of the discipline indicated by the work of other Hellenistic authors. Archimedes (d. 212 BCE), who was regarded in antiquity as a practitioner of mechanics as well as mathematics, certainly worked with weightlifting technology, ballistic devices, irrigation instruments, floating bodies and sphere-making. The surviving parts of the nine-book *Mechanikē Syntaxis* of Philo of Byzantium (late third or second century BCE) are devoted to artillery and to pneumatics; there is a reference to a lost book on the lever.[22] However, there are still other possible categories. Philo, whose emphasis seems to be on civil engineering, included books on harbour-making and siege defence; Vitruvius (first century BCE), in a Latin collection of building techniques, includes musical instruments and a hodometer. Devices that 'imitate living beings' appear in both Hero's 'pneumatics' and his 'automatic theatre' collections.

Philoponus (sixth century CE) comes closest to suggesting a general characterization of mechanics as a discipline, when he describes it as focusing on two questions: how to lift a given weight or raise water.[23] While the notion of 'lifting' is simplistic, two of the principal techniques exploited by mechanical devices – the 'power of the lever' and the 'power of the void' – are nicely captured by Philoponus' classification. Still, it may be significant that there does not seem to be an agreed characterization of the subject matter of mechanics. The classificatory fluidity seems to be endemic to a field that began with the success of its devices and only later evolved theories to explain them, or even to determine which devices belong within the field.

---

[21] τὰ δὲ διὰ νεύρων καὶ σπάρτων ἐμψύχους ὁλκὰς καὶ κινήσεις ἀπομιμουμένων, Proclus, *in Euc.* 41 (Friedlein); οἱ δὲ διὰ νευρίων καὶ σπάρτων ἐμψύχων κινήσεις δοκοῦσι μιμεῖσθαι, Pappus 8.1024.26–7 (Hultsch).

[22] Philo, *Bel.* 59.12.

[23] ἴδοις δ' ἂν τοῦτο μάλιστα ἐπὶ τῶν κατὰ μηχανικὴν εὑρημάτων, οἷον πῶς ἄν τις βάρη κινήσειεν ἢ μετεωρίσειεν ὕδωρ ἤ τι τοιοῦτον, Philoponus, *in Cat.* 119.6–7 (Busse).

Although the catalogues recorded by Pappus and Proclus are from late antiquity and do not exactly correspond, they do provide some sort of template for inquiring what the term *mēchanikē* might refer to in the fourth century. I shall provisionally adapt these lists for use as a rough forensic template, in order to consider the state of the art of the various branches of mechanics as it came to be understood in late antiquity. That is, I shall consider the evidence for fourth-century discussions of balancing and equilibrium, lifting weights, hurling armaments, imitating living beings, lifting water, timepieces, and making models of the heavens. I shall then use this survey as a background to consideration of the evidence concerning Archytas and Aristotle. This is not a perfect solution to the problem of using ancient rather than modern categories, but it at least avoids assuming that we know what 'mechanics' ought to mean.

Balancing and equilibrium

The balance was known to the Greeks from early days.[24] A mathematical account of a principle underlying the operation of the balance is discussed at some length by Plato, who makes clear that the 'weighing art' considers not only the fact that different sized weights can be compared with each other on a balance, but also that their distance from the fulcrum affects the relative power of a given weight to displace the balance.[25] Plato's dialogue focuses on our ability to judge the value of various pains and pleasures but nonetheless envisions the possibility of a systematic study of measurement problems and distortions. Since we need to choose those things that are genuinely greater, the measuring art, *hē metrētikē technē*, helps us to adhere to the truth.

Weiss suggests that, while Socrates is not necessarily endorsing the hedonism implicit in the idea of a calculus of pleasures and pains, he is offering Protagoras a legitimate role in assisting hedonists to make better choices.[26] Plato takes the measuring art seriously elsewhere, since it fosters the idea of an impartial standard and

---

[24] Furley (1989), p. 91. [25] Plato, *Prt.* 356b. [26] Weiss (1990).

perhaps of a currency of exchange: measurement establishes a standard rather than merely comparing relative quantities.[27] He uses the idea of a calculating art to counterbalance the illusions of the artist.[28] Instruments make the measuring arts more respectable and reliable. Although Plato is sometimes portrayed as hostile to technology, he does not necessarily associate it with trickery or illusion.

In Plato's discussions the art of weighing is presented as standing in close parallel to optics. The latter, because it studies the systematic principles of perspective and the creation of visual illusion, enables us to anticipate or even correct for distortions.[29] Once it is understood that things closer appear larger than those further away, this opens the possibility that an art of measurement would enable us to correct for misleading appearances. Proclus, who regards himself as Plato's follower, lauds the value of optics in *understanding* illusion and thus enabling us to correct for as well as produce illusions.[30] There are certainly arts exploiting illusion: *skēnographia*, or scene painting, uses general rules of perspective to produce a given impression. Knowing that more distant objects appear smaller and darker, a painter might darken the edges of a painted image to make it appear rounder or use foreshortening to represent depth on a two-dimensional painting.[31] Architects in this period standardly corrected for illusions such as the apparent sag of a long building by manipulating the dimensions so as to produce the

---

[27] *Plt.* 283c–285c.

[28] *Phlb.* 55e–57d; *Plt.* 260a–b; 283dff. Crombie (1994). The art of weighing also appears in the Platonic dialogue *de Justo*, generally considered spurious, to aid in comparing just and unjust things.

[29] Plato, *Prt.* 356c. Cf. *Phlb.* 55e, *Chrm.* 166b: see Krafft (1970a), p. 143. G. E. R. Lloyd (1987), pp. 241–2 n. 100, 271–84, challenges the practice of blaming Platonism for a supposed resistance to quantification in Greek science.

[30] *in Euc.* 40. Proclus includes optics with mechanics as one of the arts that are for human benefit: *in Euc.* 63.

[31] Burford (1972), pp. 133–4; Coulton (1977), pp. 68–9; cf. Plato, *R.* 602c–e. Russo (2004), p. 58, claims that the earliest documented paintings using scenographic techniques date from Alexander's reign, although Vitruvius ascribes the theory to Anaxagoras and Democritus.

desired appearance.[32] Knowledge of these effects can also help us judge truly.

The *Protagoras* shows that Plato's audience would be expected to recognize the mathematical relationships ascribed to the balance. Awareness of the relationship of distance from the fulcrum to balance was presumably developed in the context of trade.[33] It seems to be only later that this notion was connected to the mathematical problem of finding centres of weight. There is discussion in Presocratic and fourth-century philosophy of *isorrhopia*, the notion of equal force. This takes different forms and is not necessarily connected to the idea of a balance. One of the areas in which this discussion occurs is that of the stability of the earth. The account of the stability of the earth in Anaximander is formulated in terms of the equality of reasons to move in every possible direction.[34] The presentation of an object with equal tendencies to go in any direction is not connected to the balance.

Plato is certainly taken by other ancient Greek philosophers to have asserted that inequality is the cause of motion, based on a remark in the *Timaeus*.[35] There, Plato asserts that for motion to be instigated requires both a mover and a moved; he attributes rest to uniformity and motion to anomaly, *anōmalotēs*, the cause of which is inequality.[36] This seems to be in accord with the general recognition that a change requires a specific cause to make it happen at one time rather than another, in one direction rather than another. While it does not provide specific evidence of the impact of the balance model on ideas about the causes of motion, the reference to inequality is suggestive. Simplicius, in discussing this passage, credits Plato's associate Archytas with the idea that inequality is the cause

[32] Coulton (1977).
[33] The ancient Greeks credited the Phoenicians with developing arithmetic because of their commercial needs, just as the Egyptians developed geometry for purposes of land measurement: Proclus, *in Euc.* 65.
[34] Kahn (1960), pp. 76–81; Makin (1993), pp. 101–5; Hankinson (1998a).
[35] Simplicius, *in Ph.* 431.4 and Proclus, *in Euc.* 41: see Bodnár (2004), p. 144.
[36] *Ti.* 57e7–58a1.

of motion. This needs to be considered in the light of Archytas' said connections with the founding of mechanics.[37]

Plato also mentions an idea that became important in the *explanation* of the action of a balance in later discussions. Plato's *Laws* discusses the motion of a circle spinning around a fixed centre, remarking on the 'wonders' produced by the fact that the outer circle moves faster than the inner.[38] The fixed proportion between the movements is emphasized.[39] The differences in the distance travelled between two unequal circles on the same centre is the principle used in the *Mechanica* to account for the 'wonderful' results obtained in mechanics: the shared terminology is marked. Here, inequality refers to differences of dimension, in a context where the circling bodies may be thought of as moved by the same force: the point is that the larger circle moves through a greater distance in the course of a single revolution. This was later connected to the idea that points on the same moving radius move different distances in a context where – if the radius is conceived as a rigid body – the radius as a whole is moved by a single force.

It is a further question whether and how the idea of the balance came to be connected to the idea of a lever. Heidel suggests that unequal arm balances might have provided the connecting link.[40] Although it is certainly true that an unequal arm balance helps to establish that the ratio between weights in balance varies inversely with their distance from the fulcrum, it is nevertheless a further problem how to link the question of the amount of weight required to balance a given weight to the question of the amount of effort required to lift it. Although the Aristotelian *Mechanica* claims that the lever works on the same principle as the balance,[41] it does not say

---

[37] I thank an anonymous reviewer for urging me to reconsider this further, and for supplying additional references.

[38] *Lg.* 893cff. See Mourelatos (1981); Micheli (1995), p. 50; Krafft (1970a), pp. 143ff.

[39] Mourelatos reads this passage as separating the mathematical description of heavenly motions from a complete mathematical science of the visible world: Mourelatos (1981), p. 7.

[40] Heidel (1933), p. 62; De Groot (2008).   [41] *Mech.* 848a14.

how the two are connected.[42] The mathematics of leverage might have developed independently from that of balancing, and a method for connecting the two might have needed to be worked out.

Lifting the greater weight with the lesser force

The prehistory of the theory of the lever seems to lie in building technology. It is easy to imagine how the association of weight-moving devices with quantification could have occurred in the context of devices used in building, especially in large public works such as the building of great temples. The weights involved would be roughly proportional to size; a foreman would know the size of block he could expect a single individual to lift, and there would have been many of them. Thus construction sites would provide a context where rough numerical assessments came naturally, in order to complete a given job in a limited time. Because of the need to move large quantities of stone by means of human labour and various expedients – ropes, ramps, rollers, levers – it is plausible that master-builders would want to compare the relative effectiveness of different devices for lifting weights.[43]

After studying the size of stone blocks used in temple building at different dates, Coulton argues that a sudden increase in the size of stone used in the seventh century indicates the introduction of new techniques for lifting them.[44] Monumental temple designs required production of standard-size blocks in distant quarries, with increased concern for careful measurement and new techniques for transportation.[45] Coulton argues that, by the end of the sixth century, the blocks must have been set in place by cranes with compound pulleys and winches.[46] The technology available for lifting weights was the

[42] For the suggestion that the Greek term for lever might be connected to an Egyptian term for balance, see Bernal (2001), p. 262.
[43] At least in Vitruvius' day architects knew by what proportion the weight of limestone diminished during firing: *de Arch.* 2.5.3.
[44] Coulton (1974). On the importation of weightlifting techniques from Egypt, see Couprie, Hahn and Naddaf (2003), pp. 75ff.
[45] Coulton (1977), pp. 39ff.   [46] Coulton (1977), p. 48.

limiting factor in building techniques: design was constrained by the size of block that could be lifted to span between columns.[47] Thus the whole building operation was organized around the weight of stone block that could be moved by the methods available.

Moreover, the supply of labour available was finite, and the use of subcontractors in large public works projects would have placed a premium on the estimation of the time and labour required to accomplish a given task. Subcontractors were fined for not completing a task on time.[48] It was the business of the architect or master-builder to supervise the weight-moving processes;[49] technical treatises on architecture, which started to appear in the sixth and fifth centuries BCE, apparently discussed these problems.[50] There would be good reason, then, to pay attention to the quantities of weight moveable by given methods and to recognize the proportionality between the dimensions of weightlifting devices and their efficacy.[51]

Another context where lever technology was used for increasing human power is medicine. The Hippocratic text *On Fractures* discusses the use of free-standing frame devices for stretching dislocated joints. The advantage of such devices is not only that of increasing the power that a doctor can exert, but presumably also that the frames help to stabilize the limbs and apply the power at a specific point. Ankle joints are stretched by inserting a lever into the hub of a wheel to pull leather thongs tied to the foot; another technique uses the end of a board on which the patient lies as a pivot, with windlasses underneath stretching the thongs.[52] The frames not only apply force

[47] Coulton (1977), p. 144.
[48] Coulton (1977), pp. 21–2; 144. On the continuing value of fines for architectural overruns, see Vitruvius, *de Arch.* 10.1.1.
[49] Burford (1972), pp. 93–4, 192.   [50] Coulton (1977), pp. 21–5.
[51] Cuomo (2001), p. 9, notes the use of proportional ratios in temple building as early as 540 BCE; G. E. R. Lloyd (1987), pp. 244, 295, argues that the technique of studying qualitative phenomena quantitatively and of varying conditions to isolate causally relevant factors was used in early research on harmonics.
[52] Landels (1978), p. 10.

but apply it in a controlled and localized manner suited to the joint in question.[53]

These techniques are described in the text as devices by which human power can be increased. The text claims that, of all the tools devised by men, axle-and-wheel (i.e. windlass), lever and wedge are the most powerful: without them, men would be unable to complete the tasks needing the greatest force.[54] In this context, however, there would be no particular need to focus on *quantifying* force. Significantly, three devices are classified together, inasmuch as they all enable one to extend human power beyond what is possible. Still, there is no mention of a theory of their operation, nor any suggestion of a mathematical proportionality between dimension, weight, time or force.

Although the Hippocratic text does not draw out the analogy between the use of devices and the functioning of joints in organisms, this analogy is seen by Aristotle. Aristotle describes the rudder as a device whereby a small change at one end can produce a considerable displacement at the other; in *On the Motion of Animals*, he explicitly compares this to the operation of limbs.[55] The rudder is one of the examples used in the Aristotelian text of a device operating by the power of the lever. Aristotle's discussion of the motion of animals draws parallels to leverage, focusing particularly on the need for an unmoving point against which the mover presses.[56] Aristotle's interest is in the contrast between the moved mover and the unmoved mover, taking the role of the fulcrum as unmoved to offer support for the idea that all sequences of motion begin from an unmoved first principle.[57] This needs interpretation: the fulcrum, after all, hardly

[53] There seem to have been specialists: a big-city doctor is advised to provide himself with a frame comprising all the necessary techniques for stretching various dislocated joints: *Fract.* 13. Aristotle refers to some perhaps less cumbersome devices at *Pol.* 7.17, 1336a11.

[54] *Fract.* 31.

[55] Aristotle does not say what is moving: he seems to mean that the expansion of a particular material, *pneuma*, at one end of the limb is pushing aside a rigid body at one end, resulting in a considerable motion of the other end of the limb: *MA* 7, 701b25; 10, 703a9–28. See Berryman (2002a).

[56] *MA* 1, 698a17ff.   [57] *MA* 3.

provides the *origin* of motion, merely playing a necessary role in the operation of leverage.[58] The analogy to the 'unmoved mover' may be better understood as an attempt to understand the transfer of force: the downward thrust of the body weight, meeting an unyielding surface, is transferred into an upward and forward thrust. Aristotle's discussion is not very clear.

In a distinct explanation of the ability of the agent to originate motion, limbs are said to work like a lever and rudder, wherein a rigid body resting against a fixed pivot is able to move a greater distance at one end by means of a lesser motion at the shorter end. The small internal movements at our core, caused by desire, can produce substantial movement of arms and legs.[59] In the case of organisms, however, Aristotle introduces a theoretical substance, *pneuma*, to explain how this is possible, apparently because other materials would not be able to expand without becoming rarer and hence losing their power to press other bodies aside.[60] He does not think the analogy to mechanical devices offers sufficient explanatory power to account for the situation in organisms, since in the latter case the pressure has to be produced by the expansion of a bodily fluid by heating. The problem is that ordinary fluids such as air and water become rarer on expansion, thus losing their ability to exert pressure.

Aristotle's concern is that 'the natural bodies master one another according to their excess: the light is overpowered downward by the heavier, the heavy is forced up by the lighter'.[61] His point seems to be that any of the four elements would need to exceed the others in total mass in order to succeed in pushing something aside. Excessively heavy bodies push down smaller light ones, while light

[58] In the case of a limb getting its leverage by pressing against a firm base, the earth, it might seem that the fixed point is an 'origin' in the sense of being at an extreme. The 'unmoved mover' comparison seems unhelpful here.

[59] *MA* 7, 701b24–7.

[60] *MA* 10, 703a18ff.; see Berryman (2002a), where I discuss other interpretations, and D. Henry (2005).

[61] *MA* 10, 703a25–6. Cf. Nussbaum (1978), 155–8: she takes the account of *pneuma* to be unclear.

ones can buoy up smaller heavy bodies. The implied contrast is that *pneuma* can act on bodies without being in quantitative excess. A new substance seems to be introduced here precisely because it is not subject to the kinds of quantitative regularities characteristic of the rest of the natural world, and it therefore helps to account for the fact that organisms have capacities that are not found in the inorganic world. This would not count as 'mechanistic' thought, in my sense, since it does not depend on practical experience to establish what results can be achieved but rather introduces a theoretical material with stipulated powers. Aristotle seems to be agreeing that there are fixed proportionalities required to produce motion in the case of mechanical devices and the materials they work with, while denying that these can be what produces the comparable effect in organisms.

Hurling armaments

Some texts indicate that the work of a *mēchanikos* was to make military devices, especially those which increased the range of fire beyond that of a person throwing projectiles or stretching a bow by hand. Some devices without moving parts are also included in this category, such as the large shields carried overhead by several men, or large scaling ladders. Vitruvius' description indicates that devices that merely coordinate the action of several persons are classified as 'mechanical', alongside those that increase the power of one person.[62] This would certainly provide a context for the inclusion of the building of large war implements without moving parts within the field of 'mechanics'. However, the field primarily concerns devices that work to some degree independently.

In the fourth century the making of ballistic devices and other war implements became an important speciality.[63] Changes in military technology were evidently affecting daily life: while Plato claims that city walls produce cowards, Aristotle derides this view as out of

---

[62] Vitruvius, *de Arch.* 10.1.3. [63] Plato, *Grg.* 512b5.

date, endorsing the need for walls in the light of recent inventions.[64] Times were changing.

Diodorus Siculus writes of the invention of the *katapeltikon* in 399 BCE, in the arsenals of Dionysius of Syracuse, who paid a handsome price to attract engineers from Italy, Greece and Carthage.[65] Marsden argues that the device referred to in this report is a *gastraphetēs*, a form of crossbow, and that catapults were only in use by the middle of the century.[66] Cuomo, who raises doubts about Diodorus' story about invention, thinks they could be torsion devices and might have already been in use in Carthage.[67] The first torsion catapults worked from the tension placed on twisted skeins of sinew or hair held vertically in a large, freestanding wooden frame. The handle end of a paddle was inserted between the strands of one of these twisted skeins, and the other end was pulled back in a circular pathway, further tensioning the skein. A stone held against the paddle would then be propelled forward when the tension was released.[68]

At some point during the fourth or early third centuries, catapult makers devised a method for developing new variants based on the idea that the range of a ballistic device and the weights it could most effectively throw depended on the relative size of its parts. In other words, the most efficient proportions were decided by trial on a small prototype, and those proportions then used to build larger devices with a greater firing range. Rather than needing elaborate and expensive trials to find the ideal proportions of a larger device, the accepted procedure to increase range was to replicate the relative proportions of a successful prototype on a larger scale.

---

[64] Plato, *Lg.* 778d; Aristotle, *Pol.* 7.11, 1330b32. See McNicoll (1997), p. 1; Keyser (1994).

[65] Diodorus Siculus 14.41–2.

[66] Marsden (1969); Krafft (1970a), p. 152; Keyser (1994), p. 31; Huffman (2005); Cuomo (2007) discusses the evidence against Marsden's account.

[67] Cuomo (2007), pp. 41–6.

[68] Marsden (1969), pp. 16–24, p. 60: he argues that these torsion devices were first deployed during the campaigns of 353–341 BCE, but see Cuomo (2007).

Torsion catapults in particular required a complex formula to increase their size proportionally, because the weight of the stone that could be most effectively thrown was found to stand in a given relationship to the diameter of the twisted skein of hair or sinew used as a spring. A formula that has been preserved in the work of Philo of Byzantium is that the diameter of the springs in *dactyls* should be 1.1 times the cube root of the weight, given in *minae* multiplied by 1000.[69] It is not clear exactly when mechanics began to use this relationship in building larger torsion catapults. Philo ascribes this formula to Alexandrian craftsmen, presumed to be those employed by the Ptolemies at the end of the fourth and beginning of the third centuries.[70] Still, the formula for calibrating the size of catapult required to throw a given weight would have required considerable experience to refine it to so precise a ratio and might have been recognized during the fourth century.

This recognition that mechanical devices could be built according to a given formula seems to have given rise to the sense that ballistics was based on mathematical principles, although the creation of the prototype was not driven by a mathematical theory of the physics. This will prove important in considering what the term 'mechanics' referred to, in Aristotle's text. The connection of methods for finding cube roots to the 'systematization' of mechanics is also important in considering the evidence linking Archytas to mechanics. These issues will be discussed further below.

Imitating living beings

Devices imitating animals, humans and mythological beings can be found in the Hellenistic treatises on pneumatics and theatre-making. Although stage scenery may have moving parts representing thunder and lightning, for example, the focus of theatre-making is on a narrative involving the motion of agents, whether human, animal or god. In Hellenistic pneumatic technology many devices

---

[69] Marsden (1969), p. 62.   [70] Marsden (1969), p. 62.

involved figures representing traditional mythological narratives; others simply produced sounds or opened temple doors.

Given that both fields are somewhat broader in scope, the apparent classification of pneumatics and theatre-making as 'imitating living beings' *may* indicate that the ability of certain devices to initiate movement – to function – was enough to classify them broadly as 'like' living things, even if they were not overtly tricked out in animal guise.[71] Self-motion was, for Aristotle, one of the definitive features of living things, characteristic of animal life in particular. Many Hellenistic showpieces were designed to work without a human agent directly moving them: to use the flow of water, the unwinding of ropes, the pressure of steam, to create special effects of a sort that watchers would think require a living agent to produce. Unlike projectiles or weightlifting devices, they did not merely extend an agent's power but operated independently, producing complex results as if 'at will'.

There might have been some such devices even in the fourth century. Although I suggested that there is limited use of mechanics in Hippocratic texts, Aristotle gives some credence to the possibility that an artifact might 'imitate' the functioning of living things. In two passages, one discussed already, he seems to be referring to a genuine automaton, a kind of puppet with the ability to move 'by itself,' that is, to continue moving in the absence of an agent in contact with it, and moreover to respond to inputs in ways that are determined by the construction of the device.[72]

In *Generation of Animals* he uses the analogy to convey the idea that causation is transitive: A moves B, B moves C, just as happens in automata.[73] The point at issue is that the father is responsible, by means of his seed, for starting the motions that produce an embryo, even though the parent is no longer in direct contact. The form of the father produced the seed, and the seed imparts the form-producing motion to the maternal blood. The analogue seems to be a wind-up

---

[71] On the idea of devices as self-movers, see Des Chene (2001).

[72] See most recently D. Henry (2005); De Groot (2008).

[73] ἐν τοῖς αὐτομάτοις, *GA* 2.1, 734b12; cf. 2.5, 741b8.

toy that keeps going once the puppet master lets go. Such a device need not be very sophisticated to illustrate the point that the causal agent is no longer in direct contact as the changes instigated affect a further part. The reference in *Motion of Animals* fits this under-standing. There the intention is to compare a case where one kind of cause produces different kinds of effect: the device is such as to transform the impetus into a different sort of result.[74]

Although there are different attempts at reconstructing the device he describes, I suggest that a good candidate can be found in an ancient source, albeit from a later period. A device Hero ascribes to Philo seems to meet Aristotle's description and does not require any technology incongruous to the fourth century.[75] It is a standing display, used as part of a dramatic narrative: a figure of Hephaestus painted on a background has an arm that moves up and down, as if hammering. It is worked by a trip-hammer device behind the scene, worked by a falling weight. The device runs by itself once the starting mechanism is disengaged.

David Charles suggests that Aristotle's comparison to automatic puppets is intended to allow that, by analogy, a complete *physical* account is possible in the case of organisms.[76] This may be right; however, the fact that one of the necessary physical components is a theoretical substance with stipulated powers disqualifies the approach from being *mechanistic*. This is because mechanics as a

---

[74] The careful analysis in D. Henry (2005) shows that the two uses of the 'mechanical' analogy cannot be quite the same, as I had previously thought. However, in *GA* 2.1 and 2.5, Aristotle still regards the subsequent processes in the organism as forming a sequence of sorts, although all parts of the sequence have the form of the organism as final and formal cause, and the efficient causal sequence instigating them is insufficient alone. I disagree with Henry's suggestion that the mechanical device used as analogue in *GA* is necessarily different; rather, the use of the analogy in the latter case is limited.

[75] Hero, *Aut.* 24. D. Henry (2005), p. 5, suggests that 'wooden pegs' refers to the teeth of toothed axles. This seems unlikely: it is not obvious that the motion is 'generated *internally*', rather than that it is generated by the agent winding up the device, stored and then released. As he recognizes p. 6, it is an external stimulus that causes the motion in the analogous case of the organism.

[76] Charles (1988), p. 26.

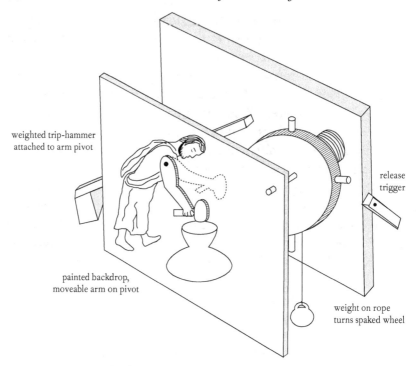

weighted trip-hammer
attached to arm pivot

release
trigger

painted backdrop,
moveable arm on pivot

weight on rope
turns spaked wheel

Figure 2 Sketch of a working model, built by the author, of a standing
theatre-piece ascribed to Philo of Byzantium; based on descriptions by
Hero of Alexandria and drawings by Schmidt.

field works by determining what results can be achieved with the
materials available, and not by speculating about imaginary
substances.

Other passages show Aristotle's lack of confidence in the capabilities of devices. When he wants to say in *Motion of Animals* 10 that
bodily actions are in some sense automatic or self-governing, he does
not use a mechanical analogy to make the point. Instead, he says the
body works like a well-run city. This simile suggests that when the
city is functioning smoothly there is no need for a ruler to preside
over each part or offer ongoing direction and intervention.[77] A city is

---

[77] *Pol.* 1.3, 1253b33. Irwin (1988), p. 620 n. 21, recognizes that this is only a
mythological possibility. I see no evidence that this passage visualizes the possibility
of automata and attendant social problems, *pace* Hammerstein (1986), pp. 15–16.

the best analogue Aristotle has for a complex system working by series of action and reaction, or, as we might say, working according to laws.[78] Aristotle does consider the idea that tools could run by themselves in his defense of slavery: if shuttles could weave and the plectrum play the lyre, there would be no need of human instruments to execute one's will.[79] He talks of instruments that can obey or anticipate the will of others, such as the statues of Daedalus or the tripods of Hephaestus that enter the assembly of their own accord. By referring to mythology, Aristotle is not suggesting that this is a conceivable development or arguing that technological progress will make slavery obsolete, but rather ridiculing those who wish to dispense with slaves. The idea that devices might be sufficient to model the complex functions of an organism is dismissed as a fairy tale. Living beings, to him, are simply different in kind.

Lifting water

I know of no evidence before the Hellenistic period that the development of devices for moving fluids in particular ways came to be considered as a distinct field. However, the field that later came to be called 'pneumatics' seems to have developed a number of its central ideas in the fourth century: devices such as siphons, cupping-glasses and clepsydras were thought to effect the motion of fluids in unusual ways, drawing fluid from wounds or pulling water uphill.[80] In contrast to the 'power of the lever', the central principle at work is pithily referred to as the 'power of the void'.[81]

There are many different attempts to articulate and classify the phenomena in question. In antiquity, the effect – sometimes described as a form of attraction – was credited in some way to the void. The problems raised by the 'power of the void' had received considerable philosophical attention by Aristotle's day. The traditional approach

---

[78] On the prevalence of the political metaphor for natural order, see G. E. R. Lloyd (1966).

[79] *Pol.* 1.3, 1253b33.   [80] Prager (1974) surveys early devices.

[81] Philoponus, *in Ph.* 569.18; 570.17. There are a variety of phrases used to describe this effect: see below and Chapter 5.

was to think that if one region empties, it has a tendency to refill. This effect was characterized differently by those who accept, and by those who reject, the existence of void. This difference is evident in Aristotle's report of two closely parallel Presocratic explanations of fishes' ability to extract air from water. Diogenes of Apollonia claims that air is moved *by the void*; Anaxagoras says air is moved *because there is no void*.[82]

Some phenomena ascribed to the 'power of the void' are found in nature: the operation of lungs or the movement of clouds and wind; others involve movement artificially induced by bellows, siphons, clepsydras and cupping-glasses. The bellows had been known in Homer's time; the clepsydra, a narrow-necked vessel with a strainer at the base, used for lifting and serving liquids, was known from Minoan and Mycenean times.[83] When the neck is stoppered, liquid is trapped in the container, to be released through the holes when the finger is removed. Cupping-glasses work by the cooling of enclosed air that has previously been heated: they are placed on the skin to draw pus from a wound as the heated air within them cools and contracts. Often the effect is described as 'attraction', a *helxis* or *holkē* holding or drawing material against its natural direction.[84] Fluid flows upward in a siphon; it is held suspended in a stoppered clepsydra despite the holes in the bottom; it is extracted from flesh when a warmed cupping glass cools.

I have argued elsewhere that there are at least four different approaches to the explanation of this effect, all in evidence by the fourth century.[85] Some of the Hippocratics seem to take the attraction of bodies to one another to be explanatorily basic. The treatise *On Ancient Medicine* takes the constitution of the tissue or the power and strength of humours of the body to be responsible for the attraction.[86] The idea that qualitatively different powers attract

[82] *Resp.* 8(2), 470b35–471a6.   [83] See Prager (1974), pp. 4–5.
[84] The category of 'attraction' was broader and included magnetism and the attraction of amber to chaff.
[85] Berryman (1997); (2002b); (2002c). For a critique of my approach, see Lehoux (1999).
[86] *VM* 24; cf. Hesse (1962), pp. 54–6.

from a distance encountered opposition from those who deny that bodies can act on one another without contact. Plato explicitly denies the existence of attraction, as do members of Aristotle's school.[87]

The atomists, who think all change occurs by physical contact, also reject attraction.[88] The atomists seem to have the most ingenious reductive account of apparent cases of attraction: that atoms gravitate towards a void under pressure of continual collisions with bodies in all other directions. The atoms will tend to drift in the direction in which they encounter fewest collisions, an effect that – at the macroscopic level – might look as though the void is positively attracting them. Evidence for a 'drift' account of attraction is uncontroversially evident in Lucretius, and I have argued that reports of Democritus' and Epicurus' accounts of magnetism implicitly rely on the tendency towards a void.[89] A passage in Aristotle suggests that Democritus recognized this 'drift' and offered an account of it in terms of the movement of atoms bombarding one another.[90]

Continuum theorists, who deny that void exists and take matter to be a cohesive mass, not an aggregate of smallest parts in constant motion, could not make use of drift as an explanation of the tendency of bodies to move into emptier spaces. The discussion in Plato's *Timaeus* denies that bodies attract one another, arguing that apparent cases of attraction really involve pushing from behind.[91] This idea of *antiperistasis*, circular mutual replacement, is used to explain breathing, magnetic attraction and related phenomena. Still, the range of phenomena to which *antiperistasis* could apply is limited, and his explanation would seem too weak or slow for some phenomena. There are problems such as the retention of water in a clepsydra for

---

[87] Plato, *Ti.* 80c2; Theophrastus, *Vent.* 5.33–5; Simplicius, *in Ph.* 663.2; [Aristotle] *Pr.* 16.8–9, 915a17.

[88] For discussion of the supposed 'attraction' of like to like, see Furley (1989), p. 79; Berryman (1997), (2002c).

[89] Berryman (1997). Vallance takes them to be different accounts: (1990), p. 92.

[90] Berryman (2002c). [91] Plato *Ti.* 79e–80c2.

which *antiperistasis* could not be the explanation, as no circular replacement can occur when the top of the clepsydra is stoppered.

Aristotelians seem to have evolved a distinct, fourth explanation of the creation of movement to avert a void, wherein the notion of matter's *continuity* seems to be pressed into service.[92] While Aristotle's theoretical discussions of *sunecheia* or continuity focus on the problem of infinite divisibility of extended bodies, in practice he discusses the continuity of matter in a quite different sense of 'holding together'.[93] In a number of passages he takes the continuity of matter to be explanatory of the movement of masses. This usage is even more marked in a passage in the Aristotelian *Problemata*, where the *sunecheia* of matter is given as the explanation of the retention of water in a clepsydra.[94]

These four alternative explanations of what I call 'rarefaction effects' are all available in the fourth century, although there is little to suggest that what came to be called 'pneumatics' was demarcated as a distinct field of inquiry. This designation is attributed to the Hellenistic inventor Ctesibius, whom I shall discuss below. Nor is there much evidence of development of pneumatic devices more complex than the traditional siphon, cupping-glass and clepsydra, and some water-driven timepieces, to be discussed below. Reports of Plato's 'alarm clock' and Archytas' 'dove' have occasioned speculation: I offer a more reserved reading of these reports below. The emergence of pneumatics as a distinct field, marked by technical manuals and a building programme, may not pre-date the early third century BCE.

Timepieces

It is not clear whether the earliest timepieces were considered to be part of mechanics, or whether it is only the later addition of

---

[92] Hesse (1962), pp. 54–6, suggests that Plato's explanation by *antiperistasis* is widely accepted among continuum theorists, but there is little evidence of this.

[93] Aristotle, *Mete.* 1.3, 341a2–4; 1.7, 344a12; 3.1, 370b29–371a2; *Cael.* 2.9, 291a17, 4.6, 313b17–22; cf. Theophrastus, *Sud.* 25. See Berryman (1997), (2002b).

[94] [Aristotle] *Pr.* 16.8–9, 915a17–20.

mechanical refinements to traditional pieces that led to their inclusion in the art. As Pappus indicates, the making of sundials was a distinct art, namely 'gnomics'; its problems would be mathematical and astronomical, not mechanical, and it does not seem to be classified as mechanics.[95] Sundials depend on shadows cast by a moving body: they track motion, rather than being designed to move themselves. Although in a sense they represent the motion of the heavens, they do so in a way that depends on the causal processes of the heavens themselves, and that does not suggest a causal hypothesis for how that motion might be produced.

Another kind of device is based on dripping water. Recent archaeological work on the fourth-century Agora in Athens has unearthed some such public time-keeping devices.[96] These are quite simple: a timer for courtroom speeches involves a pot with a hole in the bottom, which would drain into a lower basin in about six minutes. It was reset by hand.[97] A larger version of this had a water container built into a wall and drained in the course of a day; it seems to have had a float device attached to a pointer, so that it could be read easily.

Plato is credited with using a timepiece in the Academy that signalled members to wake up. Athenaeus mentions it in the course of describing Ctesibius' water organ: while Athenaeus' second-century source makes clear that the water organ was unknown to the musical theorist Aristoxenus, a member of Aristotle's circle, he does have Aristoxenus reporting that Plato built an 'alarm clock'.[98] Diels attempts a reconstruction of this alarm clock, rejecting a proposal that gradually rising water would reach a certain height

---

[95] Pappus 8.1026.1.

[96] See especially Thompson and Wycherley (1972); Boegehold (1995).

[97] See the texts mentioned in the previous note, and also American School of Classical Studies at Athens (1976), pp. 248–9.

[98] Ἀριστόξενος μὲν οὖν τοῦτο οὐκ οἶδε. λέγεται δὲ Πλάτωνα μικράν τινα ἔννοιαν δοῦναι τοῦ κατασκευάσματος νυκτερινὸν ποιήσαντα ὡρολόγιον ἐοικὸς τῷ ὑδραυλικῷ οἷον κλεψύδραν μεγάλην λίαν. καὶ τὸ ὑδραυλικὸν δὲ ὄργανον δοκεῖ κλεψύδρα εἶναι, Athenaeus, *Deipn.* 4.174c (Kaibel).

and knock a lead pebble off a dish so that it fell with a clang. Diels argues that this would not be sufficiently noisy to rouse an Academy of sleeping students, and also that such a device would hardly inspire a water organ.[99]

Diels speculates instead that the device uses what later came to be called a *diabētēs*, a self-starting siphon that activates only when the water reaches a certain level, then empties in a rush. In effect, there would be three vessels: an upper storage tank letting water out gradually through the night into a middle vessel. The middle vessel would empty via the self-starting siphon when the run-off reached a certain level, rushing down forcefully into a lower vessel. The lower vessel would be sealed, with the only egress for escaping air through a whistle device, which would sound off suddenly. Diels' reconstruction belies Vitruvius' claim that Ctesibius found out how to use forced air through tubes to make sound, and requires supposing that the *diabētēs*, described in the work of Philo of Byzantium from about 200 BCE, was available in the fourth century.[100] It is risky to read so much from a scant report.

Even simple timekeepers might have had a social impact. Much has been made of the impact of clockwork in late medieval and Renaissance Europe as devices of automation and regulation of public life.[101] Plato complains that courtroom timing devices warp people's sense of importance by forcing them to conform to an external measure.[102] There is evidence of other devices to ensure public impartiality, such as the voting *klērōtērion* that dispensed coloured balls. Although not immune from rigging, such a device – if used with appropriate safeguards – could make voting procedure blind and reduce the potential for public friction.[103] Nonetheless, the degree of automation of public life in fourth-century Athens does not seem to have been very extensive.

---

[99] Diels (1915).

[100] Vitruvius, *de Arch.* 9.8.3; Philo, *De Ing. Spir.* 10. Drachmann (1948) is more receptive.

[101] E.g. Mayr (1986).   [102] Plato, *Tht.* 172d–e.

[103] Brumbaugh (1966), p. 61, talks of allotment devices used in classical Athens for the 'automation of honesty'. It is not clear how to prevent them being rigged. Plato, after all, advocated rigging a marriage lottery: *R.* 460a.

Sphere-making and models of the heavens

The making of *sphairai* came to be classified as part of mechanics in the summary lists from late antiquity. Much debate surrounds the kinds of 'spheres' – various kinds of models of the heavens – that could have been constructed at various periods.[104] From the scant evidence available, it is hard to determine either what kinds of heavenly models were built in the fourth century BCE, or whether the building of these was considered a branch of mechanics. Nonetheless, the work of Eudoxus and Plato has given rise to much scholarly speculation on this score.

There are at least six kinds of cosmic devices that might be described as 'imitating the revolutions of the heavens' and that are potentially in question in ancient reports.[105] Autolycus of Pitane, probably writing about 300 BCE, describes a sphere turning on an axle that is oblique to the horizon. This could be a refinement of Thales' star map, since it would show the rotation of the sphere of the fixed stars about its axle. Simple as this may sound, such a device would be a great aid in visualization and in determining the changes in the visible stars at different latitudes.[106] This geometrical knowledge would assist an observer in sorting out which stars should be considered 'fixed,' or which stars should be visible at a particular time and latitude.

More complex is an armillary sphere. It is described in detail by Geminus in the first century BCE, although it was probably available much earlier.[107] This device uses welded circular bands to represent the shape of the celestial sphere. Different bands represent the celestial equator and tropics; a band representing the plane of the ecliptic would be marked with the signs of the zodiac. The sphere

---

[104] On the meaning of *sphairion*, see Keyser (1998); more on the kinds of devices built during the Hellenistic period and late antiquity in Chapters 4 and 6 below.

[105] I suggested above that the traces produced by sundials are not what is usually meant by imitation.

[106] Autolycus' treatise is concerned with the mathematics in question: Aujac (1979); Evans (1998), pp. 87–8.

[107] See, e.g., Evans (1998); Savage-Smith (1985); Maurice and Mayr (1980).

rotates about its central pivot, with a central ball representing the earth. The angle of obliquity of the sphere could also be set with respect to a stand representing the horizon, depending on the latitude of the observer on earth: the device would thus show what portions of the celestial sphere would be visible at different times with respect to the earth's horizon.

Of the fixed stars, only the constellations of the zodiac would be shown, but the bands would enable an observer to estimate longitudes and latitudes of other stars. The circle of the ecliptic represents roughly the plane on which the sun, moon and planets are found, but not their positions.[108] Bands representing the celestial equator and tropics would mark the extreme northerly and southerly rotations of the sun throughout the year at equinoxes and solstices and would aid in calculating the exact position of the sun.

A similar device, projected onto a two-dimensional surface, is the planispheric astrolabe. This is a calculating device used to find the time of day or time of year from the stars visible – or vice versa – by adjusting a dial projecting the celestial coordinates for a particular latitude onto a plane surface, against a rotating dial with a map of the visible stars.[109] Construction requires mathematical techniques for projecting spherical maps onto a plane surface: these were developed by Hipparchus (second century BCE). A report by Pliny seems to suggest that Hipparchus built an astrolabe, although astrolabes are only definitely attested some centuries later.[110]

A fourth device, also exploiting the potential of this planispheric projection, is the anaphoric clock. Vitruvius describes a kind of clock that works by running water and uses a rising float to run a drum that

---

[108] For modern armillary spheres representing the motions of the sun by a separate mechanism, see Maurice and Mayr (1980), pp. 294, 302. I will use the English 'planets' to refer to Mercury, Venus, Mars, Jupiter and Saturn; the Greek category *planētes asteres* or 'wandering stars' includes sun and moon. For accessible introductions to ancient Greek astronomy, see, e.g., Kuhn (1957); G. E. R. Lloyd (1973), pp. 53–74; or, in more detail, Evans (1998).

[109] See Evans (1998) for a helpful introduction to the astrolabe, as well as plans for constructing a working model.

[110] Pliny ascribes a calculating tool to him at *HN.* 2.24. See Neugebauer (1975), vol. II, pp. 868–79.

shows the position of the constellations even during the day, when they would not be visible.[111] Although this kind of device might seem to belong to the field of timekeeping rather than sphere-making, it does include a circular disk that might be said to 'imitate' the rotation of the sphere of the fixed stars with the passage of time.[112]

Different again – perhaps used in conjunction with an astrolabe – are calculators, which mark features such as calendar date, phase of the moon, and position of sun and moon in the zodiac. They work by means of gear trains turning wheels through an appropriate number of revolutions relative to one another, and displaying current information on the calendar. Two examples of this have survived: the Antikythera mechanism recovered from a first- or second-century BCE shipwreck, and a fifth-century CE Byzantine example.[113] Reconstruction of the former is problematic, since the surviving remains are considerably damaged: there is some uncertainty as to exactly which celestial features are being calculated by the interlocking toothed wheels. Reconstruction indicates that the technology available was more sophisticated than is known from surviving literary records. On the calculator, information is read from dials: calculators do not purport to represent the *topography* of the heavens.

An orrery is a sixth kind of device that some speculate might have been available in antiquity. The term is modern, named after the Earl of Orrery: it is a model that aims to be isomorphic to a heliocentric solar system, and it shows the relative positions of earth, moon, sun and planets. Complex gearing coordinates the rotations of celestial

---

[111] Vitruvius, *de Arch.* 9.8: see Drachmann (1948); Chapter 4 below.

[112] If this type of device were included within the category of 'sphere-making', it *might* help make some sense of the puzzling claim in Pappus' catalogue that sphere-making involves water-driven devices: μηχανικοὺς δὲ καλοῦσιν καὶ τοὺς τὰς σφαιροποιΐας [ποιεῖν] ἐπισταμένους, ὑφ' ὧν εἰκὼν τοῦ οὐρανοῦ κατασκευάζεται δι' ὁμαλῆς καὶ ἐγκυκλίου κινήσεως ὕδατος, 8.1026.2 (Hultsch). I thank Alexei Kojevnikov for noting that the water in the clepsydra is not circulating, however.

[113] Field and Wright (1985); Price (1975); Freeth, Bitsakis, Moussas *et al.* (2006).

bodies so as to show their mutual locations after a given time lapse.
The alignment of earth, moon and sun relative to one another would
thus allow for prediction of eclipses and other phenomena by showing relative positions of various bodies. Modern heliocentric orreries
show the mutual rotations of the planets and their moons relative to
one another from the turning of a single central drive mechanism,
whether automated or turned by hand. The technical problems of
construction would be greater for a geocentric model.[114]

Because of the vagueness of Greek terms such as 'sphere-making,'
there is uncertainty about the kinds of devices that are referred to
in different reports.[115] Moreover, much controversy surrounds the
early history of Greek astronomy, and speculation about constructed
models intersects with speculation about the astronomical theory
used.

Concerning the fourth century in particular, a debate has arisen
whether Eudoxus, a mathematical astronomer contemporary with
Plato, constructed physical models of the heavens. Eudoxus' work
has not survived; reconstructions are based on a report by Aristotle
and a more extensive commentary by Simplicius.[116] According
to the classic reconstruction proposed by Schiaparelli in 1875,
Eudoxus attempted to model the motions of the 'wandering stars'
by a series of nested, homocentric spheres turning on axes tilted
with respect to one another, some of them in opposite directions of
rotation.

Simplicius subsumes this model to the famous project of 'saving
the phenomena', which Plato is said to have instigated: Eudoxus
is said to have used his geometrical model to try to show how
the observed phenomena could be produced by regular geometric
motions. The hippopede, a figure-eight path, results from the motion
of a point around a sphere that is both rotating with the same period

---

[114] I thank Jim Evans for discussing the technical problems and some possible
solutions.

[115] The terms for armillary sphere, *krikōtos sphaira*, and astrolabe, seem to have been
used interchangeably in some cases.

[116] Aristotle, *Metaph.* 12.8; Simplicius, *in Cael.* 488.18–24; 493.4–506.18. See Heath
(1913), pp. 193ff., for an overview.

on its own axis and also simultaneously carried by an outer sphere rotating in the opposite direction on an axis tilted from that of the first.[117] This figure was taken to approximate the observed motions of the planets. Precise reconstruction is difficult, as we do not know what angles Eudoxus gave to the respective poles, and there is much uncertainty about the planetary data available at the time.

Plato's account of the heavens in the *Timaeus* is sometimes thought to be inspired by Eudoxus' work; Aristotle is said to have interpreted this model more literally, with some modifications, positing a cosmos that consists of spherical shells imparting motion to one another by physical contact.[118] But there are problems with reconstructing both Eudoxus' theory and the celestial models Plato and Aristotle reportedly developed on the basis of his theories. Heath argues that Schiaparelli's reconstruction of Eudoxus' theory has major differences from the principal phenomena concerning Venus and Mars: given the values that Simplicius reports, they would not show retrogradations at all.[119] Recent scholars have questioned how Eudoxus' model could be made to work physically, given that the poles for the inner spheres move with the 'carrying' spheres, and the spheres producing the motions of different planets would need to be superimposed to model the motions of more than one 'wanderer' at a time.[120] It seems more likely that Eudoxus was concerned to defend the possibility that the motions of 'the wanderers' could be given a mathematical basis than that he took a physical model to offer insight into the causal processes involved in coordinating the motions of the heavenly bodies.

There are questions about the accuracy of Simplicius' history of astronomy, in which Simplicius claims that its early history was driven by Plato's requirement to 'save the phenomena' by reducing

---

[117] Heath (1913); Neugebauer (1975), vol. ii, pp. 677–83; Evans (1998), pp. 305–10; Zhmud (2006), pp. 273ff. Schiaparelli's work is collected in Schiaparelli (1997).

[118] More on Plato below; on Aristotle, see Heath (1913), pp. 197, 217; Hussey (1991); Mendell (2000), pp. 81–3.

[119] Heath (1913), pp. 210–11; Bowen (2002b), p. 159.

[120] Brumbaugh (1961), p. 523; Dicks (1970), pp. 120, 237 n. 164; Keyser (1998).

apparently irregular motions to regular, homocentric spheres.[121] Goldstein suggests that Eudoxus' model was purely qualitative and was not seriously applied to individual planetary motions.[122] Bowen has raised the most sweeping criticisms of the interpretations based on Simplicius' reports, noting a lack of evidence that the Greeks knew of planetary stations and retrogradations before the second century BCE.[123] He proposes a 'minimalist' interpretation of Aristotle's testimony, which does not attribute a hippopede or planetary stations and retrogradations to Eudoxus. Rather, Bowen suggests, the planets were thought to speed up and slow down with respect to one another rather than with respect to the fixed stars:[124] on this interpretation, the phenomena Eudoxus was concerned with involve only the observed risings and settings of planets at the horizon.[125]

Speculation about Eudoxus' building of devices was fuelled by some remarks in Plato's *Timaeus*, which seem to suggest that Plato is describing physical models of the heavens. Some take the description of the Demiurge building the world from circular strips turning about an axis, with the circle of the Different turning in a reverse direction to the circle of the Same, to be suggestive of an armillary sphere.[126] Further speculation has been occasioned by a remark of Plato's that it would be futile to describe the 'dance of the planets' without a visible imitation.[127] Cornford, for example, suggested that Plato is referring to a 'sphere or orrery'.[128] There is reason to be cautious about reading too much into Plato's remark, however.[129]

---

[121] Knorr (1990); Goldstein (1997); Mendell (2000); Bowen (2001), (2002b). See Zhmud (2006), pp. 86–7, for discussion of the late dating of the report that Plato set astronomers the problem of 'saving the phenomena'.

[122] Goldstein (1980), p. 135.   [123] Bowen (2002b).

[124] See also Knorr (1990), p. 317.   [125] Bowen (2002b), pp. 163–6; (2001).

[126] See Guerra and Torraca (1996); Evans (1998), p. 81. Dicks (1970), p. 119, doubts that it is anything but a celestial globe; Knorr (1990) endorses the idea that Plato's discussions are based on some kind of physical model.

[127] *Ti.* 40d.

[128] Cornford (1937), p. 135. The frontispiece for the volume shows an armillary sphere.

[129] On the existence of the two-sphere model in Plato's day, see Goldstein and Bowen (1983), p. 335; Berggren (1991), (unpublished). The slightly different

Although *Republic* 10 and the *Statesman* are thought by some to be describing actual physical models,[130] and Theon of Smyrna says he made a model after Plato's description in the *Republic*,[131] the account does not suggest anything mechanical. Several nested whorls turn about a spindle, with the inner whorls turning in the opposite direction to the whole. Although there are references to Necessity turning the spindle, this is an anthropomorphic figure, whose daughters are turning the outer and inner whorls by hand.[132]

It seems unlikely that it was possible at this date to build a device that could be taken to be structurally isomorphic to many of the heavenly bodies, imitating the motions of the 'wanderers' with any degree of fidelity to the observed phenomena. An armillary sphere – the closest physical analogue to the cosmos described by Plato – is, from a mechanical point of view, simply a number of bands welded around a globe that could be spun on its axis. If this is all that lies behind the remarks, there is less reason to suppose that 'sphere-making,' even if it was considered a discipline in the fourth century, would have been connected to the construction of 'working artifacts'.

ARCHYTAS AND THE FOUNDATION OF MECHANICS

Aristotle lists *ta mēchanika* – along with optics, harmonics and astronomy – as one of the fields subordinate to mathematics. Reports by two later authors claim that Plato's associate and older contemporary, Archytas of Tarentum, first 'systematized' the study of *ta mēchanika* to mathematical principles. Although it is generally assumed that both Aristotle and the reports concerning Archytas are referring to the branch of mechanics centred on the lever, in neither case is it obvious what *ta mēchanika* refers to. I will examine the

use of 'two-sphere model' in Mendell (2000), pp. 62–3, presupposes that Plato envisaged a spherical earth in the middle of the sphere of the fixed stars (the Same) and added a third sphere (the Different) inside that of the fixed stars.

[130] Heath (1913), p. 155, mentions interpretations in his own time suggesting this; Brumbaugh (1961) discusses those from the mid twentieth century.

[131] Theon 146.4; Heath (1913), p. 155.   [132] *R.* 616cff.

evidence in the light of the foregoing survey of the state of the art of mechanics in the fourth century.

In his biographical entry on Archytas, Diogenes Laertius reports:

He first systematized mechanics using mathematical principles and first introduced the motion of instruments to geometrical diagram, seeking in the duplication of the cube to grasp two mean proportionals through section of the half-cylinder.[133]

The background to this passage includes the ancient Greek practice of identifying 'first discoverers';[134] this trope can overemphasize the role of the founder of a field at the expense of its subsequent development. Plutarch may be the source of this association of the use of tools in geometry with the 'mechanical'; he even seems to imply that the sense in which Archytas was concerned with 'mechanical' depends on his use of devices to solve the problem of duplicating the cube. Plutarch claims, in his *Life of Marcellus*, that the latter was condemned by Plato as a violation of geometry's abstraction from the sensible world:

Eudoxus and Archytas and their followers began to set in motion this prized and famous science of mechanics, by embellishing geometry with its subtlety, and, in the case of problems which did not admit of logical and geometrical demonstration, by using sensible tools and patterns as supports. Thus, they both used constructed tools for the problem of the two mean proportionals, which is a necessary element in many geometrical figures, adapting to their purposes certain mean lines from bent lines and sections. But, when Plato was upset and maintained against them that they were destroying and ruining the value of geometry, since it had fled from the incorporeal and intelligible to the sensible, using again physical objects which required much common handicraft, the science of mechanics was driven out and separated from geometry,

---

[133] οὗτος πρῶτος τὰ μηχανικὰ ταῖς μαθηματικαῖς προσχρησάμενος ἀρχαῖς μεθώδευσε καὶ πρῶτος κίνησιν ὀργανικὴν διαγράμματι γεωμετρικῷ προσήγαγε, διὰ τῆς τομῆς τοῦ ἡμικυλίνδρου δύο μέσας ἀνὰ λόγον λαβεῖν ζητῶν εἰς τὸν τοῦ κύβου διπλασιασμόν, Diogenes Laertius 8.83. I thank an anonymous reviewer for noting that the reference to mathematics is a conjecture, though widely accepted: Marcovich (1999), p. 625.

[134] Cambiano (1998), p. 311; Zhmud (2006), p. 176. Zhmud's first chapter gives a thorough history of the 'first discoverer' trope.

and being disregarded for a long time by philosophy, became one of the military arts.[135]

If Plato had merely been objecting to the use of tools in geometry, this passage might have little to do with the discipline of mechanics. There was a long-standing debate about the extent to which it is acceptable to use tools in geometry, since proofs and problems are thought to be about exact ratios that hold amongst the properties of abstract objects, not approximations read off constructions produced by non-geometrical means. Archytas' solution involved rotating a physical object to trace a semicylinder perpendicular to the plane of a two-dimensional diagram in order to find the point of intersection.[136] While Diogenes' and Plutarch's description of this action as involving tools might thus be appropriate, Plutarch's suggestion that this procedure introduced the *mechanical* into geometry could be misleading.[137] No branch of the ancient classification of mechanics concerns the use of objects or devices to construct mathematical figures. Bowen suggests that Archytas' constructions might have come to be labelled 'mechanical' on account of an issue about the

---

[135] τὴν γὰρ ἀγαπωμένην ταύτην καὶ περιβόητον ὀργανικὴν ἤρξαντο μὲν κινεῖν οἱ περὶ Εὔδοξον καὶ Ἀρχύταν, ποικίλλοντες τῷ γλαφυρῷ γεωμετρίαν, καὶ λογικῆς καὶ γραμμικῆς ἀποδείξεως οὐκ εὐποροῦντα προβλήματα δι' αἰσθητῶν καὶ ὀργανικῶν παραδειγμάτων ὑπερείδοντες, ὡς τὸ περὶ δύο μέσας ἀνὰ λόγον πρόβλημα καὶ στοιχεῖον ἐπὶ πολλὰ τῶν γραφομένων ἀναγκαῖον εἰς ὀργανικὰς ἐξῆγον ἀμφότεροι κατασκευάς. μεσογράφους τινὰς ἀπὸ καμπύλων γραμμ[ατ]ῶν καὶ τμημάτων μεθαρμόζοντες· ἐπεὶ δὲ Πλάτων ἠγανάκτησε καὶ διετείνατο πρὸς αὐτούς, ὡς ἀπολλύντας καὶ διαφθείροντας τὸ γεωμετρίας ἀγαθόν, ἀπὸ τῶν ἀσωμάτων καὶ νοητῶν ἀποδιδρασκούσης ἐπὶ τὰ αἰσθητά, καὶ προσχρωμένης αὖθις αὖ σώμασι πολλῆς καὶ φορτικῆς βαναυσουργίας δεομένοις, οὕτω διεκρίθη γεωμετρίας ἐκπεσοῦσα μηχανική, καὶ περιορωμένη πολὺν χρόνον ὑπὸ φιλοσοφίας, μία τῶν στρατιωτίδων τεχνῶν ἐγεγόνει, Plutarch, *Marc.* 14.5–6 (Ziegler). Translation by Huffman (2005), p. 366, slightly modified: I have preferred 'sensible tools and patterns' for δι' αἰσθητῶν καὶ ὀργανικῶν παραδειγμάτων, in place of Huffman's 'sensible and mechanical models', to avoid rendering ὀργανικῶν as 'mechanical'. See Patterson (1985) on *paradeigmata*.

[136] Huffman (2003), p. 14, offers a diagram and a discussion of the mathematics.

[137] Cf. ὀργανικὰς καὶ μηχανικὰς κατασκευάς, Plutarch, *Quaest. conv.* 8.2, 718e.

relationship of theorems and problems in mathematics: that Plutarch is incorrectly attributing to Archytas a view that all mathematical demonstrations are really problems, in that they involve constructing objects.[138] Although the term 'construction', *kataskeuē*, does apply to both geometrical constructions and mechanical devices, it would be odd for Plutarch to take this ambiguity alone as grounds for claiming that Archytas founded the discipline of mechanics.

The following three claims need to be distinguished:

A. The theory of mechanical devices can be explained in geometrical terms.
B. The construction of mechanical devices uses geometrical solutions.
C. Geometrical constructions require instruments.

Aristotle's classification of mechanics in *Posterior Analytics* would require that claim A be true. There is some reason – to be discussed presently – to think that the association of Archytas with mechanics may concern claim B, since Archytas' solution to the duplication of the cube was important in the construction of mechanical devices. The introduction of claim C in the same reports may be a red herring.

Although the passage from the *Life of Marcellus* is well known and might thus have affected subsequent perceptions of Plato's attitude to technology, it better reflects Plutarch's concerns than those of Plato. The story of Plato's anger about the tainting of mathematics with mechanical devices is suspect: Heath noted the oddity of supposing that Plato would distinguish categorically between the use of ruler and compass and other manual aids, since any physical diagram would be suspected by a Platonist.[139] The story of the criticism of Archytas' solution is also unconvincing: Archytas'

---

[138] Bowen (1983), pp. 16, 23.

[139] Heath (1921), vol. 1, p. 288. Pappus uses the term *organikōs* in the context of constructions using a ruler and compass: 8.1082.2; Ver Eecke (1933), p. 851 n. 5.

solution, scholars have argued, is remarkably abstract and would not even be practicable using physical bodies.[140] Plutarch belabours the trope of the high-minded mathematician only turning to design war implements under royal suasion, in contrast to the active Marcellus.[141] The association between keeping mathematics pure and leaving mechanics – namely war machinery – to vulgar labourers seems to arise from the same philosophical agenda that drives Plutarch to draw such a sharp contrast between Archimedes and Marcellus. Plutarch's representation is ideologically laden and may not tell us much about the historical Archytas or about the conception of mechanics in the fourth century.[142]

There are different possible lines of interpretation of the story that Archytas was the first to 'systematize' mechanics to mathematical principles. One account, argued by Krafft and more recently by Zhmud, takes the key idea of 'mechanics' to concern the motion of concentric circles of different sizes. Tracing this principle to Archytas – based on some remarks in Plato's *Laws* and a report on Archytas' views – they suppose that Archytas is being credited with originating the geometrical analysis of the different speeds of concentric circles moving at equal angular speed.[143]

They are surely right to connect the discussion of the peculiarities of concentric circles at the beginning of the *Mechanica* to the passage in Plato's *Laws*. There is evidently a recognition in the fourth century that the ability of a smaller movement to produce a greater is somehow connected to the geometry of concentric circles, and that this is somehow involved in the explanation of the power of the lever. However, there is a further question of what implications to read from this for the history of mechanics. In Plato this fact is

---

[140] Huffman (2005), esp. 386–99. See Cuomo (2001), p. 58; Zhmud (2006), p. 85.

[141] Culham (1992), p. 189; I thank Hans Beck for discussion of Plutarch's use of characters to illustrate positions or ideas.

[142] Culham (1992) discusses some inaccuracies in Plutarch's report that stem from his lack of interest in technology. Tybjerg (2004), p. 46, suggests that Plutarch is in fact reacting to the work of Hero of Alexandria, whose terminology shows some striking parallels to Plutarch's terms of abuse here.

[143] Krafft (1970a), pp. 143ff.; Zhmud (2006), p. 97.

expressed in terms of *motion* alone.[144] While a report by Eudemus credits Archytas with correcting Plato's view that motion *is* the great and small, to the view that these are *the causes* of motion, the context is quite general and not specific to mechanics.[145] It could equally refer to a situation such as Plato discusses in his account of breathing, in which an unequal pressure from one direction sets up a circular current.[146] Further, the Aristotelian *Problemata* connects Archytas with the idea that motions occur proportionally and that circularity is somehow important in motion.[147] However, these suggestive remarks do not add up to the developed and quite detailed account of the operation of mechanical devices given in *Mechanica*.

Krafft treats this account of the origin of the mathematics of the *Mechanica* as part of an argument that the *Mechanica* is a genuine text by Aristotle. In his account Aristotle merely added the 'dynamische' explanation of the motion of concentric circles, already understood geometrically by Plato. Zhmud, whose focus is on the history of mathematics, despairs of finding another competent mathematician amongst the early Peripatetics who could have formulated the mathematical theory of the *Mechanica*, and he concludes that – since Aristotle mentions mechanics as a theoretical subject – Archytas must be its founder.[148]

This is too quick. If we keep in mind that we do not know which branch of mechanics *Posterior Analytics* refers to, there is little reason to ascribe the full-fledged theory of the Aristotelian *Mechanica* back to Aristotle's time. All we know is that Archytas is credited with formulating the mathematics for *some* field; the nature and extent of that discipline is yet unclear. The discussion of the peculiarities of mechanical motion in the beginning of *Mechanica* does not rely on notions of 'anomaly' or 'inequality', central to the Platonic and Archytan passages. Moreover, the connecting idea of the vector addition of motion would need to be articulated. Finding the author of the mathematical analysis of concentric circles is not enough to

---

[144] *Lg.* 893d. [145] Simplicius, *in Ph.* 431.4ff.; Huffman (2005), pp. 508ff.
[146] *Ti.* 79b–c. [147] *Pr.* 17.9, 915a29; cited by Zhmud (2006).
[148] Zhmud (2006), pp. 97–8 n. 83.

account for the discipline of mechanics: the central idea of the treatise is not the mathematical analysis of the reasons why a smaller motion is able to produce a greater in a context of concentric circles, but the unification of a wide range of cases, both natural and artificial, which are understood as problems of leverage.

A problem with the ascription of the Aristotelian text to Aristotle is that he elsewhere makes little use of such a powerful and far-reaching theoretical unification of so many physical problems to a single principle. Krafft's solution – that the distinction between natural and artificial is the reason why Aristotle otherwise ignores mechanics in his natural philosophy – is unconvincing. Although there is clearly a recognition of the power of circular motion in the fourth century, and some interest in the properties of the balance and lever, it is far from clear that the full-fledged theory of *Mechanica* was available to Aristotle.

Krafft's conjecture, treating the *Mechanica* as Aristotle's early work, might lead one to expect some mention of mechanics as a discipline in Plato's writings. In this connection, Zhmud draws attention to a recently interpreted text of Philodemus, which mentions mechanics and optics in connection with the Academy.[149] However, the text is very fragmented at the relevant place.[150] Plato consistently mentions only harmonics and astronomy in his 'quadrivium';[151] mechanics, like optics, seems to have been in its early stages in Plato's day.

A weaker version of this reconstruction, connecting Aristotle's mention of mechanics and the story that Archytas founded it to the analysis of the geometry of concentric circles, is that 'mechanics' in this fourth-century context refers only to the 'art of weighing'. This is surely the interpretation best supported by the evidence from Plato; the mathematics of the concentric circles was indeed formulated in the context of the balance. Although the Aristotelian *Mechanica* refers the lever to the balance, this connection is not evident in the Platonic material. This weaker reading of the idea

---

[149] Zhmud (2006), p. 88.
[150] See Gaiser (1988), p. 152; Dorandi (1991), pp. 127, 209, for reconstructions of the text.
[151] Zhmud (2006), p. 63.

that there is a mathematical discipline connected to concentric circles would lend less credence to the ascription of the full theory of the Aristotelian *Mechanica* to Aristotle.

On the other hand, there is another possible explanation of the story that Archytas 'systematized' mechanics. Huffman lays out a detailed argument suggesting that Plato, as reported by Plutarch, is really taking issue with the practice of *solid geometry* in his own day. The criticism about the crude physicality of Archytas' work was really directed, Huffman suggests, at the fact that practitioners tended to focus on solving problems with practical import, such as the duplication of the cube, without making the field into a systematic discipline. This focus is 'mechanical' only to the extent that it is in the field of mechanics that the solution is needed. His plausible suggestion is that Archytas might be said to have 'systematized' mechanics only to the extent that his construction came to be used in making certain devices.[152]

It may be significant that the stories of Archytas' mechanical endeavours are reported alongside his solution to the duplication of a cube, a long-standing problem in Greek mathematics. In other works Plutarch reports that the Delians were told by an oracle to produce an altar double the size of the original, whereupon Plato interpreted the god as enjoining them to study geometry.[153] Although the chronology suggests that elements of this story are apocryphal, duplicating the cube is certainly a problem that the Platonists took seriously, and it became one of the three classic problems of mechanics.[154]

In the fifth century Hippocrates of Chios had discovered that the solution was equivalent to finding two continuous mean proportionals, such that

$$a : x = x : y = y : 2a$$

---

[152] Huffman (2005), p. 384.

[153] *De E apud Delphos* 386e; *de Genio Socratis* 579c. Theon of Smyrna quotes a version of the story by Eratosthenes, who adds that the oracle was consulted during a plague. Although Heath (1921), vol. 1, pp. 245–6, credits Eratosthenes' version, others have disputed the chronology: Van Der Waerden (1961), p. 161; Cuomo (2001), p. 53; Zhmud (2006), p. 84.

[154] Pappus 8.1028,18–21; Huffman (2003), p. 25.

If the terms are found that stand in this proportion, the first mean proportional x – the required length of the side of the duplicated cube – will provide the solution.[155] A number of attempts at a solution are reported by Eutocius in his commentary on Archimedes' *On the Sphere and the Cylinder*. Many of those proposing solutions are the figures most centrally associated with the history of Greek mechanics: besides Archytas, Philo of Byzantium, Hero of Alexandria, Diocles and Pappus all offered solutions.[156]

Cube roots, as mentioned above, are needed to solve a formula that was used to correlate the diameter of the springs of torsion catapults to the weight of a projectile. Archytas is credited with being the first to systematize mechanics: the verb translated 'systematize' here – *methodeuō* – means subjecting something to a rule. This statement would certainly be apt if his achievement was fundamental to a mathematical formula that enabled the field to take a systematic approach to the development of devices. Archytas was a general and an ally of Dionysius I – the great promoter of military technology – and could have been involved in the research and development of catapults.[157]

There is little direct evidence to show whether Archytas was interested in the technical applications of his mathematics. Diogenes Laertius tells us that some report the existence of another person called Archytas, an architect, who wrote a book *Peri Mēchanēs*, *On Devices*: this figure, whom Diogenes resists identifying with Archytas of Tarentum, credits his knowledge to an otherwise unknown figure, Teucer of Carthage.[158] However, Vitruvius implies that Archytas of Tarentum wrote on devices,[159] and Athenaeus mentions his treatise

[155] Heath (1921) vol. I, pp. 244–70; Van Der Waerden (1961), pp. 136ff.
[156] Knorr notes that the style of geometrical argument in Philo's text has more in common with the fourth century and Aristotelian tradition than with the Euclidean style: Knorr (1989), p. 43. Knorr also indicates that the Heronian solution might be Archimedes' p. 54.
[157] See Keyser (1994), pp. 27–59, p. 31.
[158] I thank Paul Keyser for noting that Dionysius I recruited Carthaginians for his arsenal.
[159] Vitruvius, *de Arch.* 1.1.17. Aristotle also attributes a child's toy to Archytas: *Pol.* 5.6, 1340b26, cited by Van Der Waerden (1961), p. 149.

in a book on ballistic devices.[160] This is of course only circumstantial evidence towards the claim that Archytas was involved with ballistics.[161]

The other report attesting to Archytas' 'mechanical' interests is the story that he made 'a wooden dove that flew'. The one surviving report is found in Aulus Gellius (second century CE), who quotes an earlier Greek source. All he says about its construction is that it includes weights and a current of air. He does give a direct Greek quotation from his source, Favorinus, but this unfortunately breaks off after telling us that Archytas was a *mēchanikos*, and that the dove did not rise up again once it had landed.[162]

Attempts to reconstruct the device assume that it is a model of a flying bird and employ the kinds of techniques available in later pneumatic technology.[163] However, what we have preserved of Gellius' rendering of his Greek source into Latin does not inspire confidence: Gellius tells us that it is a *simulacrum* of a dove, whereas the Greek source he paraphrases uses the word 'dove' as a *name* for the device. The difference is not trivial, as it was common to call complex constructions, especially war engines and their parts, by the names of animals – crane, ram, tortoise, crow, scorpion, raven, dolphin – without implying that the devices were simulacra.[164] If the story is about a device called a 'dove', rather than a model of a dove, it could refer to a catapult, or more likely the projectile it launched. But none of this is more than speculation.

If Archytas might be credited only with a solution to the duplication of the cube, or even with merely the mathematics used in the

---

[160] Athenaeus, *Peri Mēchanēmatōn* 5.1. There are other figures listed, however, who have no known interest in ballistics, including Aristotle and Strato. For evidence supporting Archytas' involvement with ballistics, see Keyser (1994), p. 31.

[161] Huffman (2005), pp. 15–17, 82, is more sceptical about the evidence of Archytas' involvement in developing ballistic devices. Russo (2004), p. 191, notes that Archytas' classification of the branches of mathematics does not include mechanics.

[162] *Noctes Atticae* 10.10.8–10.   [163] See Huffman (2005), pp. 571–9.

[164] See von Staden (1998); Fleury (1993), p. 193. Whitehead and Blyth (2004), pp. 83, 88, discuss stories of the rationale for naming the tortoise and raven; Schiefsky (2005), p. 260, notes Hero's explanation of the naming based on similarity of shape.

analysis of the balance, Plutarch's report would give us little reason to date the theory of the *Mechanica* to the fourth century. The question becomes one of the extent to which Aristotle recognized the kinds of principles articulated in the Aristotelian *Mechanica*. It is to this that I now turn.

ARISTOTLE'S 'MECHANICS' OF MOTION

In *Posterior Analytics* Aristotle classifies *ta mēchanika* with astronomy, optics and harmonics, sciences understood to be systematically subordinate to mathematics.[165] Unfortunately, the text is equivocal even here regarding which branch of mathematics is at issue. 'Mechanics' is described once as an application of geometry,[166] another time as based on stereometry.[167] If Aristotle understood by 'mechanics' the ideas expressed in the Aristotelian *Mechanica*, it would be reasonable that he took the field to be subordinate to geometry: the 'lifting of greater weights with a lesser power' is explained in terms of the theory of the balance, and the balance in turn by reference to the geometry of the circle. If, on the other hand, Aristotle is referring to the field of ballistics,[168] it would be equally reasonable for him to take mechanics to be subordinate to stereometry. Stereometry is characterized by the Platonic *Epinomis* as the discipline concerned with mean proportionals such as that used in the duplication of the cube.[169]

There has been much disagreement on whether Aristotle should be said to have a 'mechanics', using the term to refer to a systematic body of laws of motion. Carteron, for example, doubts that Aristotle should be said to have a 'mechanics', because his statements on the mathematics of the causes of motion are insufficiently systematic and sometimes inaccurate.[170] Drabkin considers as evidence not only

---

[165] *APo.* 1.13, 79a1.   [166] *APo.* 1.9, 76a24.

[167] *APo.* 1.13; 79a1. Philoponus notes the difference, but contributes nothing towards understanding what Aristotle has in mind: *in APo.* 179,14–16.

[168] Micheli (1995), p. 22.

[169] *Epin.* 990e–991b; Van Der Waerden (1961), p. 138.

[170] Carteron (1975): Carteron does consider the *Mechanica* to be Aristotelian.

those generalizations that are specific to local motion, but also those that apply to change generally, including qualitative alteration.[171] He offers an optimistic assessment of Aristotle's tendencies to 'mechanism', but one that is based on some extrapolation from Aristotle's explicit statements. Owen takes a more critical look at the 'laws of motion' Drabkin finds in Aristotle, and doubts the generality of the claims made. He more cautiously notes that, while Aristotle certainly makes some general claims about the proportionalities involved in non-natural motion, he offers few quantitative statements about *natural* motion.[172] De Gandt, who stresses the scope of the proportionalities offered by Aristotle, regrets that Aristotle fails to offer any justification for them.[173]

Because of a tendency to take for granted that the mathematization of natural philosophy is appropriately described as 'mechanics', scholars do not always consider whether these mathematical principles found in Aristotle might have been based on investigation of the properties of devices. Bodnár argues that the discussion of leverage in two of Aristotle's works shows some structural similarities to the accounts of the Aristotelian *Mechanica*, but even so, suggests that the authentically Aristotelian texts do not seem to recognize quantitative proportionalities in discussions of leverage.[174] Hussey has reconstructed an account wherein Aristotle's theory of motion is presented as a thoroughly mathematical treatment, and moreover one that is based on empirical evidence from the sciences of the fourth century, including mechanics.[175] De Groot also argues for Aristotle's use of mechanical theory, although he thinks that the particular analysis central to the Aristotelian *Mechanica* is not found in Aristotle.[176]

Hussey takes Eudoxus' mathematical treatment of astronomy as Aristotle's main inspiration. Nonetheless, he further argues that some puzzling claims about the nature of motion can be shown to be part of a coherent account if we assume that Aristotle must be

---

[171] Drabkin (1938). Cohen and Drabkin (1958), p. 182, write of Aristotle's failure to integrate different branches of physics because of lack of success in formulating laws.

[172] Owen (1986).   [173] De Gandt (1982), pp. 108–9.

[174] Bodnár (2004).   [175] Hussey (1991).   [176] De Groot (2008).

working from experience, and particularly experience with devices. On Hussey's reconstruction, Aristotle supposes that the 'power' or *dunamis* exerted by an agent stands in proportion to the time of change, the quantity of change and the quantity of the changed thing.[177] He also suggests that Aristotle thinks of power as a quantity of the agent's action, not as a quantity necessarily measurable by the perceivable effect. This is needed to make sense of the idea that there are minimal thresholds for motion, and that a compound motion can be analysed into components.[178]

Hussey argues that some remarks about the faster motion of heavier bodies make most sense if Aristotle is thinking of comparing weights on a balance, and taking the heavier weight to be moving one arm downward because it has the stronger power.[179] On a balance, the heavier weight has an overpowering effect on the lighter. Hussey thinks this makes best sense of a claim that otherwise contradicts ordinary observation of falling bodies. Besides the balance, Hussey also suggests that pulley technology might be part of the inspiration for Aristotle's belief in the co-variation of different quantities involved in motion, since it allows someone to lift twice the load at half the rate.[180]

Hussey points to the importance, for Aristotle, of establishing proportional relationships between various quantities, in order to avert the possibility of infinites. The claim that he derives these proportions from devices is plausible. However, the evidence that Aristotle accepted the mathematical composition of motion of the kind found in *Mechanica* seems less than conclusive.[181] Hussey's prime example for demonstrating that Aristotle recognized the

---

[177] Hussey (1991), p. 216, suggests that this could be either the weight or the volume, depending on the kind of change involved. 'Power' means rate of input by the agent, not total input.

[178] Hussey (1991), pp. 219, 222.

[179] Hussey (1991), p. 224. He notes that the verb *rhepein*, from which Aristotle's *rhopē* or downward tendency is derived, has its core meaning in the idea of a scale tipping: p. 229.

[180] Hussey (1991), p. 219.

[181] De Gandt (1982), p. 126, denies that there is precedent for the composition of motion in Aristotle's work.

so-called 'parallelogram of velocities' is a passage in *Meteorology* concerning the production of meteorological effects by the motions of exhalations.[182] Throughout this text, Aristotle certainly accounts for a number of effects by the causal action of masses pushing one another aside. However, the passage does not seem clear enough to determine whether 'the parallelogram rule is used explicitly', as Hussey claims.[183]

Aristotle is arguing that the direction of the subsequent motion – up, down or sideways – depends on the disposition of the exhalation. He adds that most move sideways as a result of two other motions, an upward natural motion and a forced downward motion. He follows this with a general statement that, in such cases, the motion that occurs will be diagonal. Although this is only offered casually, in explanation of the fact that shooting stars tend to travel sideways, it does seem to be a general assertion that two motions in different directions produce a third 'along the diagonal'.

However, it requires some interpretation to read this as asserting explicitly the use of a parallelogram to diagram the resulting motion produced by two forces. One reason is that the two components lead in opposite directions. Hussey argues that, while the natural motion is exactly upward, the downward motion is only approximately downward.[184] Still, all that could safely be extrapolated from this reference is that the *direction* of motion is sideways between the two component forces. Nothing suggests that the length of the diagonal is used to determine the extent or speed of the motion: indeed, the context suggests otherwise, as the diagonal of two motions virtually opposed to one another would be very short, whereas Aristotle is trying to explain the motion of shooting stars.[185] He could be saying little more than that opposed forces make things shoot out sideways.

As Sambursky rightly notes, Aristotle elsewhere makes only a very general reference, in *Physics* 8, to the idea that an oblique

---

[182] *Mete.* 1.4, 342a16–27; Hussey (1991), p. 221, also noted by Micheli (1995), p. 60.
[183] Hussey (1991), p. 221.   [184] *Mete.* 1.4, 342a21ff., Hussey (1991), p. 221.
[185] The point here is not of course whether Aristotle is *right*, but whether his physics shows that he knew of the discussions in the *Mechanica*.

motion is not contrary, and so – by implication – does not simply cancel an upward motion, as its opposite would.[186] While one could certainly elaborate this thought into an endorsement of the idea of a parallelogram, as Philoponus does in his commentary on this passage centuries later, Aristotle's text does not draw that figure.

Hussey cites other contexts where the phrase *kata diametron* is used and refers to the tendency of a four-footed animal to move diametrically opposite feet simultaneously: these seem like red herrings. By contrast, the *Mechanica* clearly notes that the *length* of the lines involved represents the distance, and that the diagonal between two components in a fixed proportion represents the *extent* and not just the *direction* of motion.[187] This presentation also recognizes that circular movement must be produced by motions that are not in fixed proportion. The idea that the resulting displacement is a mathematical sum is clear here, as it is not in the *Meteorology* passage.

In order to make a case that there is a systematic attempt at quantitative summation of powers, Hussey depends on a particular reading of Aristotle's notion that a stronger motion 'overcomes', 'stops' or 'dislodges' a weaker. There are two interpretative possibilities: one is that Aristotle thinks that a significantly smaller action ceases to operate in the case where a much stronger one prevails; the other is that the effects of the weaker are still present and contributing to the result. Hussey argues that Aristotle is embracing the latter alternative. This seems to be important to his case that Aristotle's analysis of motion is quantitative and not qualitative.[188] However, it is also possible that Aristotle is thinking in terms of minimal thresholds: that the effect of weaker motion is not just indistinguishable by an observer, but becomes inoperative.

There are certainly cases where Aristotle notes that a forced motion added to a natural motion makes for a faster motion overall.[189] But this may not be quite so clear in cases where forces act in opposite directions. Hussey assumes that Aristotle does think this,

[186] *Ph.* 8.8, 262a11; Sambursky (1962), p. 88; see Chapter 6, below.
[187] *Mech.* 1, 848b10–35.   [188] Hussey (1991), pp. 221–2.
[189] *Ph.* 4.8, 215a15–17; 7.2, 243a20–b2.

but the evidence could be read either way. In *Meteorology*, discussing
contrary winds, Aristotle contrasts the case of winds that are directly
opposed and those that are at an angle to one another. When winds
are directly opposed, the weaker is said to be overpowered by the
other and to cease; those at an angle, conversely, can both blow
simultaneously, as evidenced by the fact that sailors making for the
same point from different directions can use them.[190] The implication here is not that a new compound of the two is produced, but that
each operates independently. Sailors can tack, because the two winds
are independent, and it is possible to exploit one against the other.
On the other hand, sailors cannot sail upwind: when there are two
opposed winds, the weaker is completely cancelled. While the notion
that forces produce a composite motion may seem obvious to us, we
shall see that even some mechanics thought there was more evidence
that the stronger power prevailed over the lesser.

The idea of analysing motion into components certainly has
precedent. Mourelatos argues that the roots of the idea of such an
analysis can be found in Plato's work, and that Plato's account of
heavenly motion allows for the possibility of a 'general and pure
kinematics'. Still, he does not suppose that Plato was familiar with
the analysis of motion found in the *Mechanica*.[191] The case for a
mathematical composition of the causes of motion was by no means
obvious: we shall see figures disputing or arguing for it some
centuries later. There is room to recognize that some of the ideas
found in the *Mechanica* had a fourth-century precedent without
thinking that all aspects of the theory are accepted by Aristotle.

Hussey draws an interesting parallel to the case of the 'powers' of
different ingredients in a mixture, another case where Aristotle needs
to show that different powers can act together without the contribution of either being distinguishable. It would certainly be suggestive
if it could be shown that Aristotle posits a linear relationship between
properties of the parts and properties of the whole in non-mechanical
contexts. Cooper has argued, conversely, that Aristotle's claim

---

[190] *Mete.* 2.6, 364a26. Hussey takes this passage as evidence for his reading.
[191] Mourelatos (1981), pp. 9–10.

that ingredients in a mixture do not need to be distributed evenly throughout suggests that the form of the mixture is a separate entity rather than a product of the powers of the ingredients.[192]

Hussey may be right in suggesting that the investigation of devices might have fostered a quantificational approach to the notion of power or force in some contexts. Many ideas that became important in mechanics can be found in some form in fourth-century texts. Nonetheless, Aristotle does not seem to pursue consistently a quantificational approach to the causes of motion, or to recognize principles of mechanics with the systematicity of the programme expressed in the Aristotelian *Mechanica*.

The evidence for the meaning of 'mechanics' in Aristotle's text remains slight. Although there is enough unclarity in the evidence to allow for competing interpretations, the situation may be comparable to that in optics. While passages in Aristotle's *Meteorology* presage the kind of theory developed in the Euclidean *Optics*, the account does not show all features present in the third-century account.[193] The situation with mechanics may be similar.

My reasons here for scepticism that the discipline of mechanics Aristotle refers to in *Posterior Analytics* is the full-blown theory found in the Aristotelian *Mechanica* are based on the paucity of evidence elsewhere in Aristotle's work that he knew of this discipline, rather than on any positive reason why he would not have accepted ideas from mechanics in other contexts. I do not think we should suppose that he knew of the *Mechanica* and explain Aristotle's disinterest in the topic as a consequence of a distinction between art and nature, as some have asserted. My suggestion is that Aristotle's somewhat scattered and piecemeal use of ideas that came to be characteristic of the mechanics tradition is best explained by the embryonic nature of the discipline in the fourth century.[194] But the overall picture of the state of mechanics in the fourth century is less than clear.

---

[192] Cooper (2004).
[193] I argue this in Berryman (1998), (forthcoming 2).   [194] Owen (1986).

CONCLUSION

This chapter began from a suggestion that we should not assume that we know what 'mechanics' refers to in a fourth-century context. Taking the best-preserved lists of the branches of the discipline in late antiquity as the best-available *ancient Greek* template, however imperfect, I considered the fourth-century state of the art of several possible fields of mechanics: balancing, leverage, ballistics, water-lifting, imitating living beings, timepieces and sphere-making. There are some reports concerning all these fields from the fourth century, but only the first three are plausibly fields 'systematized' to mathematical principles. I concluded that we do not know precisely what 'mechanics' in *Posterior Analytics* – or in the reports concerning Archytas – refers to. While it is commonly thought to refer to the art of leverage – the discipline expanded in the Aristotelian *Mechanica* – it could equally refer to the use of mathematical formulae for determining proportions in ballistics.

I have argued that, despite his interest in quantitative proportions holding between some parameters involved in non-natural motion, the evidence does not show clearly whether Aristotle knew of or accepted the analysis of compound motions found in the *Mechanica*. There is some suggestive evidence of the use of proportional co-variations associated with the balance and the lever, and that these had some impact on theories of motion and its causes. But unless we take the *Mechanica* text in the Aristotelian corpus to be Aristotle's own work, or that of the first generation of his school, the evidence concerning the theoretical understanding of the discipline of 'mechanics' in the fourth century remains disappointingly inconclusive.

While the beginnings of a theoretical discipline of mechanics are evident in the fourth century, it is clear that it had not yet acquired the authority it came to hold in the Hellenistic and imperial periods and in late antiquity. By the time of Philo of Byzantium, a new discipline had consolidated with various branches and a number of theories to account for its effects. It is to this fascinating period that I turn next.

CHAPTER 4

The theory and practice of ancient Greek mechanics

It is a commonplace that the Hellenistic period was a time of great productivity in the sciences. The patronage of the court of the Ptolemies made Alexandria in particular a centre for work in many fields, including medicine, mathematics, mechanics and astronomy. Many scientific and philosophical texts from the period are lost or survive only in part; the dates of many key figures are unknown. Nonetheless, there is evidence of much work in mechanics – theory and practice – in the post-Aristotelian period. Some texts have survived that attempt to unify, analyse and explain the techniques of mechanics. There are reports of devices involving valves, pistons and pumps, water-lifting screws, water organs, catapults, steam devices, pneumatic toys and display pieces, theatrical automata and planetary models. Archaeological finds have also yielded some physical evidence of the technology available and indicate that the sophistication of the technology exceeds that described in the surviving literary evidence. Despite much uncertainty and questionable evidence, it is clear that engineering advanced considerably, particularly during the Hellenistic period; there were also attempts to develop theories to explain the operation of mechanical devices.[1]

There is some uncertainty about the extent to which scientific ideas filtered through to the Athenian philosophical schools during the

---

[1] There is some debate about the degree of continuity in natural philosophy between the classical and Hellenistic periods, particularly on the most general issues of the development of deductive methods and 'scientific' methodology. Russo (2004), e.g., stresses discontinuity while, e.g., Van Der Waerden (1961) and Giannantoni (1984) place more weight on continuities with the classical period.

Hellenistic period.[2] Athens continued to be the philosophical centre for more than two centuries following Aristotle's death, spatially separated from the major hub of the natural sciences in Egypt. Philosophers during this period seem to have increasingly turned away from natural philosophy to other topics.[3] However, we should not overestimate the degree of separation. Although there was an increasing tendency for fields such as astronomy or mechanics to become the province of specialists and to be less thoroughly integrated into the systems of the philosophical schools, the specialization was never complete. Practitioners of technical fields engaged with questions of natural philosophy; some philosophers of the Hellenistic period and later acknowledged new work in medicine, optics or astronomy. It cannot be assumed that Hellenistic mechanics was isolated from natural philosophy.

THE ARISTOTELIAN *MECHANICA*

As mentioned in Chapter 2, above, the earliest surviving text on mechanics is the *Mechanica* found in the Aristotelian corpus. The *Mechanica* presents its subject matter as the moving of heavy bodies by art, for human benefit. It focuses on what is presented as an instance of the augmentation of human abilities by the use of devices, that is, cases where 'the lesser masters the greater, and things having a small downward force move great weights'.[4] The treatise centres around devices said to work by the same principles as the balance and lever. It also includes some theoretical material of a broader scope, including discussion of projectile motion[5] and analyses of composite motions.[6] It considers some cases occurring in nature that seem to work by similar means: the rounding of pebbles by the tide,[7] the

---

[2] Giannantoni (1984), p. 45.
[3] For a detailed examination of the evidence supporting this view, see G. E. R. Lloyd (1991). Zhmud (2006), pp. 285ff., surveys evidence for the interest in the exact sciences in the Hellenistic philosophical schools.
[4] *Mech.* 847a22: *rhopē* is explicitly used for downward tendency at 32, 858a15.
[5] *Mech.* 31–4; 858a2–b4.   [6] *Mech.* 23, 854b16.   [7] *Mech.* 15, 852b29.

movement of objects in a whirlpool,[8] and the angle of the limbs required to stand up from a sitting position.[9]

The introductory discussion notes that using a lever enables one to do what was not possible without it. Although this might seem outlandish, *atopos*, it is really not so, inasmuch as this marvellous feat is accomplished by something more marvellous – the circle – which contains opposites within itself. Although this passage is sometimes thought to present mechanics as magical or sophistical, it is more so in style than content.[10] The circle's 'opposites' are features such as the tracing of concave and convex surfaces by a single line, or the fact that some points on a circle are moving forward relative to a fixed point while others are moving backward. This explains how two circles in contact move each other in opposite directions. Different points on a rotating radius also move more quickly or more slowly: this feature is the one used to account for most of the phenomena in question.

Although the text was once considered Aristotle's own, nowadays it is often ascribed to his early school.[11] Heath noted that the terminology shares more in common with that of Euclid, who was working about 300 BCE, than does Aristotle's own.[12] Since a treatise by that title appears on the book lists of both Aristotle and Strato,[13] a long-standing suggestion is that it is by Strato of Lampsacus, scholarch from 288/7 to 269/8 BCE.[14] The treatise is unlikely to have been

---

[8] *Mech.* 35, 858b4.   [9] *Mech.* 30, 857b21.

[10] See Chapter 2, above. Micheli (1995), pp. 44–50, downplays the significance of the emphasis on contraries, pointing to precedents in Aristotle and Plato.

[11] For an extensive survey of scholarly opinions on its authorship and more detail on the ancient attributions, see Bottecchia Dehò (2000), pp. 28–51.

[12] Heath (1921), vol. I, p. 344.

[13] The manuscripts differ on whether to read *mēchanikon* or *mēchanikōn*: Marcovich (1999), p. 351. A proposed emendation, followed for example in the Loeb edition, appends this title to the previous one to read *Peri tōn metallikōn mēchanēmatōn*, i.e. 'On Mining Machinery': Hicks (1972), pp. 512–13.

[14] E.g. Moody and Clagett (1952), p. 11; Clagett (1957), p. 68; Drachmann (1963a), p. 10; Forbes and Dijksterhuis (1963), p. 56; De Camp (1963), pp. 119ff.; Fleury (1993), p. 17; less conclusively Knorr (1982), p. 100. For challenges to this orthodoxy, cf. Krafft (1970a), (1970b); Ferrari (1984), p. 252. Krafft (1970a), p. 18, gives further sources from the German tradition ascribing the work to Strato.

written after Archimedes' time, as it does not mention the screw among the list of simple devices. Moreover, as Drachmann notes, the Aristotelian text makes no use of anything comparable to the Archimedean notion of centres of gravity, even in the context of problems where such a concept would seem appropriate.[15] The text has something of the style of the Peripatetic *Problemata* collection.[16] The treatise mentions a device based on turning wheels, said to be used in temples: it resembles a device in the work of Hero of Alexandria, who talks of passers-by touching a wheel as they enter a temple (see figure 1). Elaborate devices were apparently built exploiting this rotation to make a bird turn on a different plane by a hidden mechanism. There was certainly a practice of touching temple stones in Egypt, and not in Greece;[17] some of the first two generations of Aristotle's students, especially Strato, worked in Alexandria as royal tutors.[18]

We have only circumstantial evidence. Although no works by Strato have survived, he was known for his empirical approach and interest in natural philosophy, for his interest in quantifying motion[19] and for a willingness to revise Aristotelian ideas.[20] Zhmud concludes that the author of the treatise must be a 'gifted mathematician',[21] which does not fit with what we know of Strato. However, the author of the treatise need not be the originator of the analysis of motions of concentric circles. The distinctive feature of the branch of mechanics that centres on the law of the lever is its attempt to reduce a wide and diverse range of practical problems to a simple model that can then be given a mathematical treatment. The latter could have developed separately.

[15] Drachmann (1963b), p. 95.
[16] Asper, in an unpublished manuscript, notes that there are texts of this form from before and after Aristotle's time.
[17] De Camp (1963), p. 121; Oleson (1984), pp. 44–5, 90.
[18] Diogenes Laertius 5.58   [19] Simplicius, *in Ph.* 710.33; 916.10.
[20] E.g. Stobaeus, *Ecl.* 1.14.1; Simplicius, *in Cael.* 267.19ff.; Cicero, *Acad.* 1.9.34; 2.28.121; Plutarch, *Adv. Col.* 14.1115b. See Wehrli (1951); a new edition of the fragments of Strato is in preparation by R. W. Sharples, to appear in the series *Rutgers Studies in the Classical Humanities.*
[21] Zhmud (2006), p. 97 n. 83.

Nothing definitively precludes Aristotle's authorship. However, the theory of the *Mechanica* has few echoes in the parts of the Aristotelian corpus now considered genuine; there are only passing references to a discipline of mechanics in *Posterior Analytics* and *Metaphysics* 13.3. The *Mechanica* moreover posits a distinction between natural and non-natural motion that is different from Aristotle's and hard to reconcile with it. The *Mechanica* accounts for the greater effect of a weight on a larger balance by considering the two arms of a balance or lever as if they were different points on the same radius tracing concentric circles simultaneously. The motion of each circle is divided into a horizontal and a vertical displacement; the treatise takes the difference between the vertical displacements of the larger and smaller circles to account for the greater displacement of a weight on a larger balance.

The natural motion is said to be along the tangent, the forced motion towards the centre. The division into natural and non-natural is thus unrelated to the Aristotelian notion that downward motion is natural to heavy bodies. It might have depended on the observation of a stone whirled in a sling: at the moment of release, the stone would continue unconstrained along the tangent, seeming to indicate that it was held in a circular orbit by force. The author of the treatise might have known of the Aristotelian treatment of projectile motion, since it later claims that a projectile continues a motion 'not its own'.[22]

Motion along the circumference of the circle is described as a compound of two different motions, much as motion along a diagonal is said to resolve into motions along two sides of a parallelogram.[23] However, in the case of circular motion, the two components are in no fixed proportion. The analysis is introduced to show why a point further out on a radius moves more quickly than one closer to the centre. The point closer to the centre – the extremity of the

---

[22] *Mech.* 33, 858a17ff.
[23] A later passage discusses the fact that the resolution of two motions at oblique angles to one another may be shorter than either of the components (*Mech.* 23, 854b17).

shorter radius – is more impeded in its travel than the point further out.[24] The idea of 'impeding' seems to be that an object is held in orbit by constraint, and that this constraint is greater in smaller circles, slowing down its rotation. A geometrical demonstration argues that, for a given displacement along the tangent, the greater circle undergoes less displacement towards the centre. The argument tries to give a causal account for the fact that, in order for the two points to remain on the same radius, the point further from the centre needs to undergo a greater total displacement in the same time, and this makes the degree of change more manifest.

The idea that circular motion is really complex has precedent in Aristotle's work, although not in the form in which it appears in the *Mechanica*. Although the argument of *On the Heavens* 1.2 supposes that circular motion is simple, Aristotle states that forcible circular motion is produced by a combination of pushing and pulling.[25] Wardy plausibly suggests that Aristotle uses a distinctive term *dinēsis* here because he means to refer to the act of *giving* circular motion to a body, which involves simultaneously pushing and pulling on different sides of, for example, a spindle. Both components occur around a circle, not in a straight line; and – in contrast to the *Mechanica* – Aristotle would not classify either component as 'natural'. The *Mechanica* analysis of forced motion seems to be incompatible with central Aristotelian doctrine.

Whoever its author, the most striking feature of the treatise lies not so much with the particular geometrical analysis offered of the peculiarities of circular motion, but rather – as Duhem noted – with its attempt to unify the action of a number of different devices under

---

[24] *Mech.* 1, 848b36ff. I thank an anonymous reviewer for noting a difficulty in the crucial passage over the placing of a comma, such that *Mech.* 1, 849a13 could be claiming either that the lesser radius is pulled more towards the middle and therefore moves more slowly, or that the lesser radius is pulled more and therefore moves more slowly *towards the middle*. Here I accept the reading of Forster (1913) in favour of the latter: the point of the chapter is to explain the quicker motion of the outer circle in the same time – its overall displacement – not just its greater centrifocal displacement. Cf. Bottecchia Dehò (2000), pp. 66–7.

[25] *Ph.* 7.2, 244a1–3. Wardy (1990), p. 135.

a single analysis, and to offer a mathematical account of their action.[26] The treatise claims that the peculiar features of the balance can be reduced to those of the circle, and the lever in turn to the balance. This approach to explanation presupposes the desirability of reduction to simple principles.

The explanation of the balance arises in the context of the problem of why a larger balance is more accurate than a smaller. This is referred to the fact that a point on a radius further from the centre is moved faster or further than one closer to the centre, although the radius as a whole is moved with the same force.[27] Factors such as the weight and thickness of the balance arm are not ignored by the treatise but treated as irrelevant except where they become important.[28] The discussion of the ability of the lever to move a greater weight begins by comparing the lever to a balance: it considers the force moving the lever as equivalent to a weight. This provides a way to quantify effort or force. The treatise asserts a proportionality: the weight moved has the inverse ratio to the 'weight' moving it that the length of the arm moved has to the length of the arm on which the force is exerted.[29]

A discussion of the wheel and its ease of motion also draws on the idea of balancing weight. A wheel moves easily both because it minimizes the area in contact with the ground, and because it can be regarded as balanced on a diameter drawn through its point of balance. A moving circle slightly inclines forward, so that there is more weight in the direction of movement.[30] This analysis links the idea of momentum to weight and treats friction as a factor to be minimized by minimizing surfaces in contact. Both of these ideas are further utilized in later Greek mechanics.

The analysis of the 'power of the lever' in terms of a relationship of the motion of a larger and smaller circle rotating together is not the only respect in which the *Mechanica* presents a mathematical basis for analysing motion. The text contains problems wherein a

---

[26] Duhem (1991), p. 13.   [27] *Mech.* 1, 848b1–9.
[28] *Mech.* 847b15; 1, 849b35ff.; 2, 850a1–29; 3, 850a32.
[29] *Mech.* 3, 850a35–b2.   [30] *Mech.* 8.

single complex motion is analysed into two different components, treating the resulting motion as a sum of two component motions.[31] Such analysis is important to the idea that we should think of motions as results of their causes, sometimes diverging causes whose effects may only be inferred from the result. Methods for adding together causes, and for separating a single motion into components, are thus essential to the analysis of the causes of motion as distinct forces, sometimes acting obliquely to the resulting motion. Thus the use of this kind of analysis is significant for the history of a mathematical analysis of motion, and of its causes.

Besides the analysis of circular motion, two other cases of composite motions involve parallelograms. The better-known and more commonly occurring of the two, the famous parallelogram of motion or velocity, suggests that the motion resulting when a body is moved in two different directions can be found by imagining a parallelogram formed by tracing two additional sides parallel to, and in the same ratio as, the component forces. The resultant motion will be along the diagonal beginning from the starting point of the two component motions.[32] The idea that a single motion could be caused by two forces acting obliquely does not, of course, provide a unique analysis of any given motion. However, it would allow us to infer the second cause if one component and the resultant sum are known.

The other, more complex, case concerns the result produced when two bodies move at the same speed towards one another along a trajectory that is itself moving. Although both bodies move at the same speed, the trajectories they trace will be quite different in length. This analysis attempts to consider the motion of something moving while itself being carried on a moving body. The context for this problem is not clear. Mourelatos suggests that understanding the kinematics of this kind of 'carrying' was important to early astronomy.[33] The idea that motions could be added together to produce a subsequent motion continued to be a subject of interest and

---

[31] Mourelatos (1981).   [32] *Mech.* 1, 848b23ff.
[33] Mourelatos (1981). See also Cleomedes 1.2.12, Bowen and Todd (2004), p. 39.

controversy; geometers sometimes considered complex lines as products of different motions.[34] The question whether the *causes* of motion, represented as line segments, could similarly be added together, or whether a greater force cancelled and prevailed over a lesser, continued to be a topic of debate.

The idea that successive circles in contact transmit opposite motions to one another is presented as a surprising result that would not be familiar to non-experts. The text claims that craftsmen build constructions to exhibit this marvel, keeping the cause hidden. This may be similar to a device Hero describes, wherein enmeshed wheels connecting to one another are hidden in a cabinet. The watcher who turns the first wheel sees only a bird above the cabinet revolving in a different plane to the first wheel as she turns it.[35]

Although the text does not make this clear, it seems likely that the transmission of motions – especially between circles perpendicular to one another – depends on interlocking teeth on the bronze wheels. Drachmann is sceptical of the suggestion that toothed wheels are needed here, and he suggests that a series of wheels in contact could turn one another by friction alone.[36] He notes that toothed wheels seem not to be used in Hero's theatre works or the medical joint-stretching devices and takes this as evidence that they are not available until the first century CE.[37] Archaeological evidence, however, shows that the silence of literary sources is problematic: toothed wheels are used extensively in the Antikythera mechanism dating from no later than the first century BCE. Price's reconstruction of this excavation from a shipwreck suggests that not only sophisticated systems of interlocking toothed wheels but possibly even differential gearing were available.[38] Oleson notes that, closer to the likely date of the *Mechanica*, a rack-and-pinion device was used by Ctesibius during the early third century, and that Archimedes, working at the end of the third century BCE, meshed a gear with an

[34] See, e.g., Proclus, *in Euc.* 105ff.
[35] Hero, *Spir.* 32; cf. Drachmann (1963a), p. 13.
[36] Drachmann (1963a), pp. 13–14; *Mech.* 848a33.   [37] Drachmann (1963a), p. 32.
[38] Price (1975). Freeth, Bitsakis, Moussas *et al.* (2006) suggest an earlier date than does Price.

endless screw and probably used toothed wheels in his planetarium.[39] However, toothed wheels were laborious to make. A Byzantine calculator surviving from the late fifth century CE indicates that toothed metal wheels were still ground by hand, not cast to shape.[40]

A problem that came to be called 'Aristotle's Wheel' concerns the case of two wheels of different sizes turning about the same centre. The question is how the two radii can trace out a path of the same length as the wheel rotates once, given that the points on the radius would describe circles of different sizes. The paradoxical appearance is that one cause moving both circles produces a faster and a slower movement in the different circles. The author might have been thinking about two wheels of different sizes fixed to an axle, as Hero's discussion seems to suggest.[41] There the problem is that the horizontal displacement along the ground is the same for the outer circumference of a wheel, and for any other point along the radius, including the axle, yet a point close to the axle traces a smaller circle for each rotation, even while it travels the same horizontal distance as the rest of the wheel.

The treatise does not introduce new or extraordinary devices and is not a technical how-to manual. Rather, it seems to be an attempt to make philosophical sense of the 'law of the lever' and its operation in various situations. Moreover, while it focuses on artificial devices, it allows that the same analysis can be applied to cases of motion involving concentric circles or other compound motions in nature. The discussion of whirlpool effects and the angles of knees of a person standing up, for example, apply the analysis beyond artificial cases. While probably not by Aristotle himself, it shows that the Aristotelian school had no antipathy either to the mechanical, or to the analysis of motion that is not 'according to nature'. The fact that the analysis is applied to some cases in nature belies any claims about a systematic separation of the mechanical from natural philosophy.

---

[39] Oleson (1984), p. 371.   [40] Field and Wright (1985), p.125.
[41] See Drachman (1963a), p. 32; Drabkin (1950).

CTESIBIUS

Ctesibius, an important if not very well-known inventor, lived during the first decades of the third century BCE in Alexandria.[42] His work is known only through second-hand reports.[43] He wrote treatises that were available to Philo of Byzantium and Vitruvius but that have been lost.[44] His most famous inventions depended on compressed air. The story goes that Ctesibius, the son of a barber, began experimenting with devices to take the weight of heavy mirrors as they were raised or lowered.[45] He discovered that air driven down a closed tube by a falling weight is forced out and produces a sound; artificially compressed air will return forcibly to its previous volume. This technique is used to make various devices including a force pump, worked by pistons pushing water out of cylinders through valves.[46] Fleury notes that this is the only water-lifting device listed by Vitruvius that is made with bronze cylinders: metal parts were used sparingly, suggesting that the device would be a rarity.[47]

Ctesibius tried to adapt the power of pistons to a catapult device, although Philo, who reports on this, was sceptical as to its practicality.[48] Ctesibius' basic technique was to force in a piston by hammering in wedges as far as possible; the piston leapt out when the wedges were removed. We are told about this device in a collection on catapults simply for the sake of thoroughness, since Philo had little faith in its practical usefulness for ballistics.[49] The sheer quality of engineering

---

[42] Dalley and Oleson (2003), p. 2, characterize him as a 'young Thomas Edison'.

[43] Drachmann (1951) argued against the evidence for a second Ctesibius. There are different views on the degree of Ctesibius' theoretical interests; Russo (2004), p. 52, compares him to Archimedes, while others regard his interests as primarily practical.

[44] Philo, *Bel.* 77.12; Vitruvius, *de Arch.* 1.1.7; 7.pr.14; Oleson (1984), p. 301.

[45] Vitruvius, *de Arch.* 9.8.2–3; Athenaeus, *Deipn.* 4.174; Drachmann (1948).

[46] Vitruvius, *de Arch.* 10.7; Oleson (1984), pp. 301–25; Landels (1978), pp. 76ff.; Fleury (1993), pp. 165–9.

[47] Fleury (1993), p. 146.   [48] Philo, *Bel.* 78.8ff.

[49] Philo, *Bel.* 78.8ff.; Marsden (1971), p. 184.

required might have been why it was not suitable for widespread application.

Philo sees a connection between Ctesibius' piston-driven catapult and his water organ, since the latter also worked by the force of compressed air. The crucial point, in the case of the piston at least, is that the air contained is compressed into a smaller space than it would normally occupy and returns violently to its original shape. This compression-and-recoil was apparently Ctesibius' discovery, and it was also used in pneumatic devices worked by what I shall call 'compression effects'. These will be discussed further in the next chapter.

There are enough detailed reports surrounding Ctesibius' work to lend credence to other stories of devices in public use about this time. Fraser suggests that Ctesibius might have been the builder of a huge statue used in a procession by Ptolemy Philadelphus.[50] The statue is described as standing up mechanically, *mēchanikōs*, with no one touching it, and, after pouring a libation from a bowl, sitting down again.[51] Although it is clear in the account that the statue was drawn along on a cart by human beings, the standing of the statue seems to have been achieved by a mechanism. Rice's suggestion is that the rolling of the cart was used to push the device up and down by means of a cam, namely a piece fixed to an axle that, by means of its own irregular shape, produced an up and down motion at different stages of each rotation of the axle.[52]

This is not the only report of an apparently 'self-moving' device from the royal processions of the early third century. There is also a report of a snail 'moving by itself' in the procession of Demetrius of Phaleron in 309/8 BCE.[53] The report tells us little else, except that it left a trail of slime. Rehm suggests that this could have been a kind of pedal-cart operated by someone hidden inside pedalling a large

[50] Fraser (1972), p. 426.   [51] Athenaeus, *Deipn.* 5.198.

[52] Rice (1983), p. 64; she credits Hodges (1970), p. 183, with the suggestion that the cam is employed in this period. Landels (1978), p. 25, speculates as to its possible use much later, in the fourth century CE.

[53] Polybius 12.13.11.

wheel.[54] The round shape of the snail's shell supports this interpretation; there is no other hint as to its construction.

Ctesibius' skills as a builder of complex devices are well attested, with sufficient detail to lend credence to reports. The early third century is evidently a significant stage in the development of working artifacts. Ctesibius' devices seem to have been on public display, used at important events and widely cited. His compression effects in particular, as I shall argue in more detail in the next chapter, inspired natural philosophical explanations designed to account for them. While he left no texts behind and is not nearly as well known today as Archimedes, he has a place in the history of the philosophical reception of mechanics.

ARCHIMEDES

From the other great inventor of the third century BCE, Archimedes, few of the texts most relevant to mechanics have survived. Pappus notes Carpus of Antioch's claim that Archimedes wrote only one book on mechanics, *On Sphere-Making*; this has not survived.[55] Carpus, apparently a practitioner himself, perhaps understood 'mechanics' to refer solely to the building of devices, not to the theory of the field. Pappus and Proclus, by contrast, include Archimedes' theoretical work on equilibrium and centres of gravity in the classification of mechanics. Two works, *On the Equilibrium of Planes* and *On Floating Bodies* are contributions to the theorization of equilibrium and balance, and thus to the mathematization of the physics of devices; other lost works seem to have articulated the principles of weightlifting devices. The *Method* of Archimedes outlines a technique using a conceptual analogy to mechanical devices – the balance – as a method for solving a geometrical problem. There are also reports of a number of inventions.[56]

---

[54] Rehm (1937).

[55] Pappus 8.1026.10. Ver Eecke (1933), p. 813 n. 3, suggests a date in the first or second century CE for this mechanic, who is also mentioned by Proclus.

[56] Besides those discussed here, Diels (1915) discusses a text attributing a pneumatic flute-playing device to Archimedes.

Archimedes was born in Syracuse; he is said to have been to Egypt at least once, and to have maintained scholarly contacts with the Alexandrian mathematicians.[57] He is said to have been an old man at the time of his death in 212 BCE during the Roman conquest of Syracuse. Because Archimedes was such a prominent figure, some have raised doubts about the reports concerning his practical achievements: he seems to have been the figure to whom all inventions could be ascribed.[58] Many of the stories are reported by different sources using significantly different details. They attest to the power of the *idea* of Archimedes the mechanic: that a single person can, by sheer ingenuity, create devices that alter the balance of power. Stories show him doing the work of many men single-handedly, terrifying armies, outwitting scoundrels, refuting authoritative theories, offering to move the earth. In earlier times it took a semi-mythical figure such as Daedalus, descended from the gods, to accomplish feats of such magnitude. The third century saw it in flesh and blood. 'Archimedes' became – in Drachmann's phrase – 'a name to conjure with'.[59]

Archimedes is described by Plutarch as less interested in practical devices than in mathematical theory, applying his knowledge only at the request of the king. A traditional presentation of the sage as absorbed in pure research, and – like Thales – only turning to practical application when pressed, may underlie this literary presentation of Archimedes' disdain for mechanics; as mentioned earlier, it also serves Plutarch's literary ends.[60] There is no reason to take it seriously, or to suppose that Archimedes saw nothing of theoretical interest in practical mechanics.

One of the most famous of these stories tells of his having moved a heavy ship by means of a device. Stories differ considerably on the

---

[57] Dijksterhuis (1956), pp. 11–13. Simms (1995), p. 45, suggests that he most probably studied at the Museion in Alexandria.

[58] Simms (1995); de Gandt (2003).

[59] Drachmann (1948), p. 36. On the idea of the individual inventor, see Cuomo (2000), pp. 101–2; Zhmud (2006); Dalley and Oleson (2003), pp. 25–6.

[60] See Cuomo (2001), pp. 197–201. I thank Hans Beck for discussing the role played in Plutarch's narrative structure by Archimedes' presentation as a purely contemplative figure, serving as a foil to the picture of the active Marcellus.

details of this feat and whether it was instigated by practical necessity or was intended as a demonstration to his patron Hieron of the general principles of mechanics. Any reconstruction requires making assumptions about the size of the ship, the nature of the feat, and the technology used.[61] It has been plausibly suggested that the ship-hauling demonstration is a practical contradiction of Aristotle's denial that the proportional generalizations involved in motion can be extrapolated indefinitely.[62] Aristotle had argued that the fact that a number of haulers can move a ship does not license the inference that one hauler can move an appropriate fraction of the ship alone.[63] Later Aristotelians certainly saw the applicability of Archimedes' action to Aristotle's claim.

Some reports say the device could be worked by a single individual, others that it took several people. Plutarch and Hero mention a *poluspaston* and *trispaston*, compound pulleys; Athenaeus claims that it was moved by a windlass; another tradition, attested by Simplicius, is that the device was inspired by a *charistiōn*, a balance with unequal weighing arms.[64] It is telling that the literary sources give such poor and conflicting descriptions of the techniques. Dijksterhuis suggests that Archimedes is not talking about a particular device but is proclaiming the generality of the theory of mechanical devices.[65] Certainly Simplicius' discussion of this famous boast takes it to be a claim about the general extrapolation of the proportionalities involved in mechanics.

Inventions ascribed to Archimedes include a water screw. Some modern scholars argue that the screw was not Archimedes' own invention, but a device already in use in Egypt or Assyria; others defend Archimedes' claim as its inventor.[66] The device uses the geometry of a cylindrical helix. A drum with an internal helix will lift a continuous stream of water as it is turned, provided it is laid at the proper angle between a lower and a higher container. It seems

---

[61] Dijksterhuis (1956), pp. 14–16; Drachmann (1958); Simms (1995), pp. 46–52.

[62] Fleury (1993), p. 138, citing Mugler. Fleury situates Archimedes' feat in the context of the cranes used to unload ships.

[63] *Ph.* 7.5, 250a17. [64] Dijksterhuis (1956), pp. 17ff.; Simms (1995), pp. 52–4.

[65] Dijksterhuis (1956), p. 18.

[66] Dijksterhuis (1956), pp. 21–2; Landels (1978), p. 59; Drachmann (1963a), p. 154; Oleson (1984), pp. 23, 92–3, 291; Dalley and Oleson (2003).

most useful in contexts of irrigation, where water needs to be transferred from a lower to a higher ditch as efficiently as possible. There
are reports of it in use from the second and first centuries BCE.[67]
A fresco excavated at Pompeii (79 CE) shows a water screw worked
by human power using a treadle to turn the screw.[68]

The story of Archimedes' involvement in the defence of Syracuse
includes the invention of ballistic devices and cranes, as well as the
more dubious story about the use of burning mirrors to set fire to
ships from a distance.[69] His inventions are said to have had a
powerful effect on the Roman legions. One clear implication of the
stories is the power of a single human mind over the traditional
sources of power: Polybius reports that he fostered the idea that the
genius of one man could outsmart military might.[70] Simms suggests
that his most original contribution to warfare was his systematic
approach rather than any individual invention.[71]

We do not know the entire extent and scope of the theorization
of mechanics that Archimedes undertook. Drachmann argues that
eleven chapters that appear as a block in the Arabic manuscripts of
Hero's *Mechanics* are from lost works of Archimedes, *On Centers
of Gravity*, *On the Balance* and *On Uprights*. The last title is not
mentioned in the surviving Greek literature; it concerns a topic that
would reasonably deserve attention, especially given the close connection between mechanics and building, which is the distribution of
weight of a large block placed over varying numbers of columns.[72]
References in the Heronian text surviving in Arabic suggest that
Archimedes' work on theoretical questions raised by mechanics was
even more extensive than the Greek records indicate and considered
a wider range of problems.[73] There is positive evidence against
Plutarch's account that Archimedes scorned mechanics as being
purely practical.

---

[67] Diodorus Siculus 1.34.2; 5.37.3–4; Vitruvius, *de Arch.* 10.6; Simms (1995), p. 58;
Oleson (1984), pp. 91–3, 291–2.
[68] Dijksterhuis (1956), pp. 22–3; cf. Simms (1995), p. 56.
[69] Dijksterhuis (1956), pp. 26–9;   [70] Polybius 8.7. 1–12.
[71] Simms (1995), p. 68.   [72] See Drachmann (1963b), pp. 114–33.
[73] Heath (1921) vol. II, pp. 23–4; Drachmann (1963b).

The surviving text *On the Equilibrium of Planes* lays theoretical foundations for approaching a central topic in mechanics, by an axiomatic treatment of the notion of equilibrium.[74] Some modern scholars have contrasted the fundamental assumptions of Archimedes' theory of plane equilibrium with that of the Aristotelian *Mechanica*, in that Archimedes does not begin by considering the problem as one of the motion of heavy bodies. Rather, he begins from some very general claims about equilibrium, comparable in form to the postulates of Euclidean mathematics. He uses deductive geometrical methods to find the centres of gravity of various figures, in a context that is far removed from the practical problems of weightlifting devices.

Thus it might seem that there is a considerable divergence between the Aristotelian and Archimedean approaches to theorizing the balance. However, Pappus' report suggests that Archimedes' lost work on balances, *Peri Zugōn*, adopts the notion – central to the Aristotelian *Mechanica* – that greater circles about the same centre overpower lesser circles.[75] Knorr argues that Philo's and Hero's references to this idea ultimately derive from Archimedes' reformulation of the Aristotelian notion.[76] It seems that, in antiquity, the Aristotelian and Archimedean works were considered not as two distinct and independent traditions, but as an ongoing body of work that attempted to contextualize and better ground the original insights, providing more systematic and mathematically exact foundations.[77] While Archimedes' approach is distinct from that of more practical mechanics and closer to the tradition of geometry, it is not removed from questions of natural philosophy.[78]

Even more intriguingly, Archimedes' work might also have brought the otherwise disparate fields of weightlifting and pneumatics into relationship with one another. Pappus tells us that *kentrobarikē* – a term Archimedes seems to have invented, referring to the study of

[74] This approach is criticized by Mach, but defended by others; see Goe (1972); Cambiano (1998); Netz (2000); Russo (2004), p. 70.
[75] Pappus 8.1068.   [76] Knorr (1982), pp. 91ff.
[77] Knorr (1982), p. 115; Micheli (1995), p. 118. See also appendix, n. 12.
[78] Knorr (1982), p. 104; see Netz (2000) on the relationship between mathematical and physical in Archimedes.

centres of weight[79] – is concerned with the centre of a body's weight, and that other parts of mechanics are dependent on this.[80] Both Archimedes' work on plane equilibrium and the work on floating bodies use the concept of centres of weight. A geometrical proof of the equality of plane figures refers to the notion of a centre of weight of a triangle and makes reference to a proof in the *Mechanics*.[81] Although this use of ideas from mechanics in geometrical solutions is sometimes taken to be associated with the use of tools to produce a geometrical solution in the duplication of the cube,[82] the techniques are very different. The idea of a three-dimensional balance is used as a way to conceive of the relation of equality of plane figures, in contrast to a comparison based on calculation of areas.

Archimedes' work on floating bodies, although not explicitly connected to the discipline of mechanics, concerns the effects of displaced water. Thus it might be seen as providing theoretical underpinnings for the discipline of pneumatics. It could be that Archimedes attempted to treat both fields as following from common principles.[83] A general account of the working of weightlifting and pneumatic devices might begin from a question about equilibrium conditions or the 'resting point' of a given system, treating the workings of devices as an attempt to return to that point. This is speculation. But Fleury notes that Ctesibius' water organ exemplifies Archimedes' principle that the pressure of the column of water is equal to the volume of water displaced.[84] This raises the intriguing possibility that Archimedes' articulation of this principle was inspired by Ctesibius' inventions.

---

[79] I adopt this term from Netz (2000), who warns against using the modern 'centres of gravity'.

[80] ...τὸ δὲ κέντρον τοῦ βάρους ἑκάστου σώματος, ὃ τῆς κεντροβαρικῆς πραγματείας ἀρχὴ καὶ στοιχεῖόν ἐστιν, ἐξ ἧς καὶ τὰ λοιπὰ μέρη τῆς μηχανικῆς ἀνήρτηται, Pappus 8.1030.6 (Hultsch). See Dijksterhuis (1956); Goe (1972) for the implicit link between centres of weight and the notion of balancing at equilibrium.

[81] Archimedes, *Quadr.* 6; Dijksterhuis (1956), pp. 336ff.; Cambiano (1998), p. 294.

[82] E.g. Cambiano (1998), p. 302.

[83] For an attempt to trace the origins of hydrostatics to the Aristotelian theory of motion, see Ugaglia (2004).

[84] Fleury (1993), p. 195.

Archimedes applied an abstract version of techniques from mechanics to geometrical problems in the *Method*.[85] There, the balance supplies the central idea for a model that could overcome the difficulty involved in measuring areas of irregular figures: in Cuomo's words, connecting 'geometrical being, extension, which determines area or volume, and mechanical or physical being, which has to do with equilibrium and centre of gravity'.[86] In contrast to the practical use of devices in geometry, this text looks to mechanics to provide a conceptual model for approaching a problem in a different field. It does this by thinking of the shapes as composed of lines of minimal thickness, the centre of weight of each being its midpoint. A line through the midpoints of these lines is treated as if it were the centre of a balance, and a figure of known area is 'weighed' against the unknown figure.[87] This technique uses the notion of a physical balance to conceive a method for equalizing two-dimensional figures.

Although this is not a mechanical approach to the study of the *natural* world, it does show the conceptual power of the idea of the balance in comparing quantities. It avoids the problem of measuring an awkward quantity – an area, in this case – by setting it equal to a known quantity in the context of a balance, the archetypal device for establishing equality. In this sense, it is comparable to the technique used in the Aristotelian *Mechanica* for quantifying abstract notions such as force. The balance is used to give intuitive content to the notion of 'setting equal' two quantities that cannot, strictly, be weighed.

PHILO OF BYZANTIUM

The first collection covering the whole range of mechanical knowledge might have been that of Philo of Byzantium. The dates of Philo are unknown, beyond the fact that he was later than Ctesibius and

---

[85] Study of this fascinating text is ongoing, and no attempt is made to do it justice here. See, e.g., Netz (2000) for an accessible discussion; for the latest reports and a full bibliography, see www.archimedespalimpsest.org.

[86] Cuomo (2001), p. 110; see also Simms (1995), pp. 74–81.

[87] See G. E. R. Lloyd (1973), pp. 44–6; also Knorr (1982), p. 97, on the correct orientation of the diagrams.

earlier than Vitruvius, who mentions him. Hero – who is now widely thought to have been working around 62 CE – speaks of Philo as someone from the distant past. Drachmann surmises that, since Philo seems to have spoken to someone who had seen Ctesibius' catapults, Philo cannot have lived more than a generation after Ctesibius.[88] This would date him to the late third century, although a second-century date is possible.[89] Philo writes of the royal patronage at Alexandria, and he might have been working there.[90]

The *Mechanikē Syntaxis* appears to have been a compendium, of which only part survives. Book 4, *Belopoiika*, is devoted to siege devices and artillery-making; books 7 and 8, *Paraskeuastika* and *Poliorketika* – military defence and siege-making equipment – survive in part.[91] Book 5, *Pneumatica*, survives in a partial Latin version and longer Arabic versions, but not in Greek.[92]

The aim of the art of artillery-making or ballistics is to send a projectile as far as feasible so that it still has a vigorous impact.[93] Philo's discussion of siegecraft talks much of method and system, with the implication that Philo sees himself as describing a craft with certain principles and a degree of mathematization.[94] The most systematic mathematical principle seems to be that the dimensions of all parts of the artillery device need to be proportional to the size of the bore hole, and the bore hole proportional to the cube root of the weight of the stone. Philo writes of a *methodos* for converting measurements in due proportion to enlarge the size of a device.[95]

---

[88] Drachmann (1948), p. 41.
[89] Cf. Cohen and Drabkin (1958), p. 255 n. 2; Ferrari (1984), p. 276. Cuomo (2001), p. 63. Marsden (1969), p. 3, Prager (1974), pp. 1, 14, and Tybjerg (2005) date his work to about 200 BCE.
[90] Prager (1974), p. 14.
[91] His prescriptions for defensive architecture were apparently used: see Cuomo (2001), p. 63.
[92] See Prager (1974), p. 16, for reports on the contents of other books.
[93] Philo, *Bel.* 51.8. Marsden (1969), (1971); DeVoto (1996).
[94] Cuomo (2007), p. 52, sees Philo's notion of knowledge that 'is able to give an account of itself and can satisfactorily fit with mathematical and physical theories'.
[95] Philo, *Bel.* 55.12. See Ferrari (1984), on the importance of this technique to the field's claim to be mathematical.

This is the formula discussed above that requires cube roots. These are important enough for Philo to provide a reference table of values, since the calculation is difficult.

Such a severely practical discipline may not seem like the place to look for reflection on natural philosophy. But in contrast to many of the problems of natural philosophy of this period, a discipline such as catapult building would have provided an opportunity for systematic experimentation and repeated field trials.[96] Engineers would have been refining the exact conditions under which optimum range of fire could be achieved. There was clearly both the incentive and the funding for repeated trials and innovative approaches; and in contrast to some areas of natural philosophy, mechanics provided a context in which many different parameters involved were open to manipulation. Philo is conscious of relationships between size, tension and position of spring, length of arm, weight of missile and range and impact; he discusses the difficulties of combining forces from different sources to produce greater speed.[97] While he is not writing systematic natural philosophy and is not as concerned as some other figures to present his work as theoretically grounded, the potential contributions of ballistics to physical theory should not be overlooked.

Philo is clearly interested in placing his work within the tradition of theoretical mechanics: in the surviving ballistics treatise he refers to the principle found in the Aristotelian *Mechanica* that larger circles are more powerful than smaller ones about the same centre, and that loads are moved more easily when the fulcrum is closer to the load, because the load then moves in a smaller circle. He says that he detailed these principles in his work on leverage, apparently an earlier book of the *Syntaxis*.[98] In concert with the Aristotelian text and its reduction of various devices to the principle of the lever, Philo tells us that the catapult arm is a lever in

---

[96] G. E. R. Lloyd (1973), p. 99.
[97] For the recording of figures for weight and range of different devices by many sources, see McNicoll (1997), p. 5.
[98] *en tois mochlikois*, Philo, *Bel.* 59.11; cf. 61.14: see Marsden (1971), p. 156.

reverse.[99] He compares catapult designs according to established mechanical principles, noting that applying force further away from the fulcrum will produce a more forceful discharge.[100]

Because he is working with elastic materials such as sinew and bronze springs, he needs to use concepts that are not found in the tradition of weightlifting technology. Ideas about tension and elasticity are explored in the treatise, albeit unsystematically. He asserts that power lies in the spring, and hence that shooting far requires as much spring-cord as possible.[101] Spring-cords – twisted bundles of sinew or human hair – were slotted through upper and lower circular holes in a frame and tensioned by a tourniquet inserted through the twisted skein above and below the frame. A larger spring-cord requires a larger hole, which weakens the frame, but making the frame larger adds to the weight. Philo is scornful of those who try to overcome this problem by reinforcing a basically weak structure: the emphasis is on finding the optimum dimensions for a functional prototype, and preserving these proportions in larger models according to a mathematical formula.[102] He makes clear that range of fire increases when the tension is increased, but this relationship has its limits. A technique for gaining extra tension by over-twisting the bundle as a whole thickens and skews the bundle and reduces the power of the spring, apparently because it overstretches the sinews.[103] Thus it is critical to understand the relationship between different dimensions of the device, and also the nature of elasticity.

---

[99] ὁ γὰρ ἀγκὼν ἐστι μοχλὸς ἀντεστραμμένος, Philo, *Bel.* 59.16. On the view that Philo did not know the Aristotelian text, but that the work of Philo and Hero was based on the Archimedean tradition, see Micheli (1995), pp. 89ff.

[100] Philo, *Bel.* 59.16–22: see Marsden (1971), pp. 166–7.

[101] Philo, *Bel.* 57.1–3. On the nature of the cord, see Landels (1978), pp. 108ff., as well as Marsden (1969).

[102] Philo, *Bel.* 57.1–58.5; Marsden (1971), p. 162; (1969), pp. 30ff.

[103] Philo, *Bel.* 58,6–23. Marsden (1971), p. 164, thinks that Philo misunderstands elasticity here, wrongly blaming the over-twisting (*epistrophē*) for what is really loss of resilience. Philo improved the design by using wedges to tension the spring: these eliminated the need for an additional stretching device and could be tightened in the field: Marsden (1969), p. 42; Philo, *Bel.* 61.6ff.; Schiefsky (2005).

The question of elasticity, *eutonia*, also arises with regard to metal.[104] Philo tries to understand the physics behind metal's resilience, discussing the technique used to make Celtic and Spanish swords resilient. He does so in the face of scepticism that metal plates can be made springy, citing the importance of new research into this property of recoil.[105] In general, he claims, heating softens iron and bronze by rarefying its particles; beating, conversely, makes metals harder and brittle because it drives the particles closer together and drives out the interspersed void.[106] Gentle beating on both sides creates a three-layer effect, where the middle stays pliable.

This is less than a complete theory of elasticity, and Philo refrains from delving too far into physical theory. Still, in discussing Ctesibius' work with pistons using compressed air as a driving mechanism, Philo evidently thinks the discussion is about the nature of the air, not merely about an artificial condition.[107] We will see further evidence in the following chapter that Ctesibius' compression effects were taken to require new explanations in natural philosophy. This is new territory.

Some general principles of projectile motion are articulated, if not systematically. Philo tells us that the swiftest recoil produces the furthest projection, and the sharpest thrust effects the swiftest movement and thus the greatest range.[108] Philo says that the force pulling back a spring needs to be greater than its resistance in order to prevail over it, but he doubts that the difficulty of pull back is proportional to the power of the recoil.

The question of adding forces seems to have been an issue under discussion among the mechanics; Philo's doubts about this idea are striking. One context is the action of catapult arms. The design of the sinew spring makes the contribution of each half of the spring impossible to assess by trial.[109] He apparently supposes that the two

---

[104] Drachmann (1948), pp. 8–9, suggests that the use of metal springs, first attested in the accounts of Ctesibius' pump, did not become widespread. Landels (1978), p. 128, doubts that they are very powerful.
[105] Philo, *Bel.* 71.35. [106] Philo, *Bel.* 71.27–31.
[107] Philo, *Bel.* 77.30. [108] Philo, *Bel.* 68.18ff.
[109] For a critical assessment, see Marsden (1971), p. 175.

half-springs act in opposition on the arm, rather than that both together force it to rotate.[110] Like the Aristotelian *Mechanica*, he thinks of circular motion as composed from a simultaneous forward and backward motion in opposition to one another, but he seems to doubt that these two forces are resolved into a single composite. He doubts that the two halves of the sinew spring can each be contributing forces that add together to produce a greater effect: one power would not increase the speed unless it were greater than the other, in which case the greater would overmaster the lesser. He reasons that there must be different forces working in opposition, since they can break the arm of the device.[111] This is why he favours a bronze spring that acts on the arm from only one direction.

His view seems to be that powers acting at the same time do not produce a compound result, but that the greatest power present determines the effect. Philo tries to prove this by comparing the case of the downward motion of falling bodies. He claims that the greater weight falls faster, whether because it displaces more air by its heavier weight, or because its *rhopē* or downward tendency is greater because of the greater weight. These two alternative explanations are drawn from contemporary natural philosophers.[112] He argues that fastening two smaller weights together will not cause a quicker fall. This, he reasons, means that when two bodies are merely linked together, they do not act in concert. Elsewhere, Ctesibius is criticized for thinking that equal forces working in tandem will produce a greater speed.[113] Philo cites the case of ships towing another ship that is itself moving at the same speed. His point is that the towed ship never goes faster than the tugs, apparently demonstrating that a body can only be moved by one force at a time, whether its own or an external force. Although Philo's reasoning is not fully articulated, it is evidence of an ongoing debate amongst the mechanics of the third century about the compounding of forces.

Much of Philo's compendium has been lost. We know something about his mechanical theatre displays from Hero's comments in a

---

[110] Philo, *Bel.* 69.28–9.   [111] Philo, *Bel.* 68.29ff. See Landels (1978), p. 117.
[112] Philo, *Bel.* 69.8ff.   [113] Philo, *Bel.* 72.26–8.

work on automata-making from the first century CE.[114] Hero seems to be working from surviving texts, rather than actual devices: he criticizes Philo – described as his only important predecessor in theatrical devices – for not giving sufficient description of certain features of his standing theatrical showpieces. Hero also complains that the devices are difficult to build. He is evidently trying to reconstruct the devices from inadequate descriptions and needs to work out the details himself.

Philo's theatre-pieces, as Hero describes them, consist of a small puppet-theatre in which different scenes are shown in succession. According to Hero, the theatre is to be free-standing and mounted on a pillar.[115] Apparently the older version had only three moving parts: a device for opening and closing the theatre; a mask with eyes that opened and closed; and a device for displaying in turn a series of painted backdrops illustrating the story. In the more updated version individual scenes contain moving parts, such as a seascape with leaping dolphins. The effect is created by the turning of a wheel hidden below the horizon of the spectators: three dolphin cut-outs are attached to the rim of the wheel at equal intervals. On a backdrop representing Hephaestus in his workshop, a wooden arm holding a hammer is attached to the figure, so that a trip-hammer device located behind the scene makes the arm move up and down as a rope uncoils.

While none of the techniques seem very sophisticated individually, the coordination of the various contraptions into a single working unit must have required considerable ingenuity. Hero criticizes Philo's unnecessarily cumbersome device for lowering the figure of Athena into view, and he complains that there is no mechanism described to show how a lightning bolt is contrived to fall on Ajax.[116] The latter complaint is not about the technical sophistication of Philo's theatre, only the completeness of his descriptions.[117] This

[114] Fraser (1972), p. 426, supposes that most of Hero's devices have Ptolemaic origins.
[115] Hero, *Aut.* 21.1.   [116] Hero, *Aut.* 20.
[117] Russo (2004), pp. 123ff., suggests that Hero's technology is largely derived from Philo's, but his argument relies heavily on assumptions about the technological expertise of the Hellenistic era.

may be indicative of the fact that a good deal of craft knowledge was acquired from practitioners, not from formal treatises.

Hero presents more elaborate pieces centuries later, but this should not detract from the interest of Philo's. In an age with few working artifacts, these theatrical displays must have drawn quite a crowd.

VITRUVIUS

There is clearly much that has not survived from the Greek mechanics of the Hellenistic age. The last book of the compilation *On Architecture*, written by Vitruvius, gives some indication of the sophistication of the mechanical technology that the Romans adopted from the Greek world at the end of the first century BCE, and it is included here as a source. Vitruvius' ten-volume work on building is thought to date from the late first century BCE, possibly about 27 BCE.[118] In common with Athenaeus, who wrote a ballistics treatise that survives from about this period, Vitruvius might have been drawing on an earlier writer, Agesistratus, for his account of war machinery.[119]

The work makes much mention of the connection of architecture to natural philosophy and acknowledges methodological issues, such as that elements should be analysed before composites, or that the same principles can be seen at work in various machines. However, it does not give much account of what these principles are or attempt to sort them into a coherent system.[120] Vitruvius insists that machination is a creation of nature, seeming to mean that human devising to produce given results follows and improves on the devising already found in the natural world. He is apparently not degrading mechanics to secondary status here, but rather claiming a trades' allegiance to the divine architect.[121]

---

[118] Granger (1985), p. xiv; Whitehead and Blyth (2004), p. 30. On the arrangement into ten books, see McEwen (2003), pp. 42ff.

[119] See Whitehead and Blyth (2004), pp. 25ff.

[120] On the presence of Stoicism as cultural backdrop, see McEwen (2003).

[121] Vitruvius, *de Arch.* 10.1.4. Proclus makes the same accusation, perhaps teasingly, against the mechanic Theodorus: *Prov.* 1.2.

His theoretical framework seems to be derived from the Aristotelian *Mechanica*.[122] He does not say much about the philosophical problems involved or about the general theory of mechanics, whether in explaining how pulleys or levers allow a person to lift more weight, or explaining how air is able to force water to move upward. The most interesting discussion surrounds the idea that a number of devices work by some sort of interface between circular and straight-line motion. The stress on the role of concentric circles is familiar from the Aristotelian treatise; here, the emphasis is on the intersection between two different *kinds* of motion. In an architectural context, the fact that a lever rotates its load is, after all, less important than the fact that it moves a block *upward*; other devices such as a pulley or wheel-and-axle more evidently use circular motion to produce straight-line motion.[123]

Vitruvius presents the architect as a polymath, skilled in a number of fields that have some bearing on devices: for instance, he suggests studying music, since the tension of ropes is apparently gauged by pitch, and makers of water organs clearly need some musical training. Astronomy is needed to build timepieces.[124] Architecture is not for the dilettante: he warns his reader not to expect to understand the works of Ctesibius and Archimedes on pneumatics unless he has studied natural philosophy.[125] This is evidence to support the idea that both of these figures were theorizing the power of pneumatic devices. Vitruvius claims that the theory of matter helps in understanding the properties of building materials: why bricks are lighter, for example, or why wood from trees grown in different climates has different properties.[126] He does not make extensive use of these in his account of architecture: knowledge of this kind might have been part of the craft knowledge of builders, not codified. Some of the appeal

---

[122] *De Arch.* 10.3. See Fleury (1993), p. 324. Vitruvius' other sources include Ctesibius, Diades, Athenaeus and Agesistratus.

[123] Micheli (1995), p. 96, suggests that Vitruvius may be drawing an implicit parallel to geometry, which is also based on the constructions possible with ruler and compass, i.e. with straight line and circle.

[124] Vitruvius, *de Arch.* 1.1.8–10. [125] Vitruvius, *de Arch.* 1.1.7.

[126] Vitruvius, *de Arch.* 2.1.3.10.

to education might have been to establish social status: a background in philosophy makes the architect more cultured and less avaricious.[127] He values philosophy not only for its practical but also for its moral and aesthetic benefits.[128]

Vitruvius' collection focuses on the relatively detailed descriptions it gives of various devices, such as the inventions of Ctesibius, described above, or a grain mill with intermeshing toothed wheels.[129] Vitruvius describes a clock that is an elaboration of Ctesibius' design. It uses a similar float rising in an inflow clepsydra, except that instead of a rack-and-toothed wheel, the float turns an axle by means of a chain and a counterpoised weight. Since the axle turns once in twenty-four hours, the display could represent the turning of the heavens. Although one version of this 'anaphoric clock' is ascribed to Archimedes, there are reasons to think that it must be later.[130] Other devices such as the hodometer that Vitruvius describes use gearing to keep track of the number of revolutions of a cart's wheels along a road, enumerating revolutions by the drop of a pebble.[131]

As in Philo, Vitruvius' account of ballistics devices cites the need to keep the parts in fixed proportions to produce optimum firing power. The weight of stone to be thrown is the figure from which other parameters are to be calculated.[132] He theorizes that the law of the lever applies to the tensioning of a catapult arm: a longer arm can be pulled back more easily.[133] He seems to connect this to the fact that shorter arms are more powerful on release, although the relationship between the ease of tensioning and the power on release is not drawn explicitly.

---

[127] Vitruvius, *de Arch.* 1.1.7.

[128] See Cuomo (2001), p. 203, for a sensitive account of Vitruvius' professional boundary delineation.

[129] Moritz (1958), pp. 122ff.; K. D. White (1984), pp. 65–7.

[130] Vitruvius, *de Arch.* 9.8.8–10. See Drachmann (1948), pp. 21–6; (1963a), pp. 21–41; Berggren (1991), p. 228. Berggren agrees that it was probably based on the stereographic projection of Hipparchus, since it could show the length of daylight, given the position of the sun in the ecliptic.

[131] See Fleury (1993), pp. 205–18.   [132] Vitruvius, *de Arch.* 10.10.5–10.10.11.

[133] Vitruvius, *de Arch.* 10.10.5.

Vitruvius' conception of a machine seems to be that of a device enabling the coordination of different elements. When he distinguishes 'tool-like' from 'machine-like' devices, the basis for his classification depends on whether they are worked by a single person or a group of workers.[134] Drachmann conjectures that the distinction is really that between devices using several different powers, and those tools that use only one, although he admits that one of the examples does not really fit this analysis.[135] Vitruvius says little about the combination of forces, even where these problems are implicit in the techniques he uses.[136] Nor does he consider whether there are specific limits or numerical constraints on the capacities of tools to augment the power of the individual worker.

Vitruvius' work makes much mention of the idea of integrating mechanics into a general schema of the arts and sciences. Vitruvius' official line is that the best position is achieved by an interchange between theory and practice. However, at times his notion of understanding *devices* seems to be centred on the idea of acquaintance.[137] Perhaps echoing the Aristotelian remark about the importance of perceiving the cause, Vitruvius remarks that acquaintance provides more information and a better understanding than is available from writing.[138]

Vitruvius might have had real reasons for being suspicious of abstract theory removed from experience with building. Pierre Gros has drawn attention to an anecdote in the discussion of the use of scaling to produce larger catapults, showing that there were problems with the idea that proportional relationships could be extended indefinitely.[139] The context is an arms race when Rhodes was under attack from a colossal siege engine. An engineer, asked to build a defensive machine to counter it, denied that this was possible.

---

[134] Vitruvius, *de Arch*. 10.1.3; Granger (1985), p. 277.
[135] Drachmann (1963a), p. 142. Fleury (1993), p. 46, notes that the distinction between simple and complex is not used consistently.
[136] Fleury (1993), pp. 84–6.   [137] Vitruvius, *de Arch*. 10.8.
[138] See McEwen (2003), pp. 16–18, 157, for the preference for writing over drawing, and p. 33 for the *auctoritas* of the written account.
[139] Gros (2006).

The problem was that, while scaling formulae worked in some contexts, in other cases the larger version collapsed.[140] The solution was eminently practical: the defenders prepared the ground so that the colossus became bogged down in mud. Vitruvius had reason to keep theoretical speculation in its place.[141]

HERO OF ALEXANDRIA

Hero of Alexandria has been the centre of much scholarly controversy, some of it – that focused on the century in which he lived and worked – fortunately now resolved. It is now widely accepted that the eclipse mentioned in the *Dioptra* probably dates him to the first century CE.[142] The close relationship of some aspects of his texts to the work surviving from Philo of Byzantium has led to speculation about his lack of originality or his understanding of the material.[143] Much of this comes from the disorderly state of the *Pneumatica* collection; Drachmann, who defends Hero's abilities, explains the haphazardness of this particular work by suggesting that it was unfinished.[144] In the next chapter I shall examine more closely Diels' argument that Hero's ideas on pneumatics are largely derivative. The texts of most concern in this chapter are Hero's *On Theatre-Making*, and the *Mechanica*, which survives only in an Arabic version. This last text was only widely known from the nineteenth century, although parts had survived in Greek in Hero's *Dioptra* and in Pappus.

Hero's *Mechanica* was first edited and translated into French by Carra de Vaux in 1893 and has been discussed extensively by Drachmann.[145] There are many textual problems and difficulties of interpretation. It begins with a discussion of the *barulkos*, or 'weight-lifter', which is reproduced both in the Arabic manuscript and in

---

[140] Vitruvius, *de Arch.* 10.16.4–8.   [141] Gros (2006).

[142] In support of this, Argoud (1998), p. 127, notes that a device in Hero is said by Pliny the Elder to be a recent invention; Keyser (1992) discusses additional textual evidence; also Tybjerg (2005), p. 205.

[143] For a defence of Hero's originality, see Tybjerg (2005).

[144] Drachmann (1948), pp. 77–80.   [145] De Vaux (1893); Drachmann (1963a), p. 19.

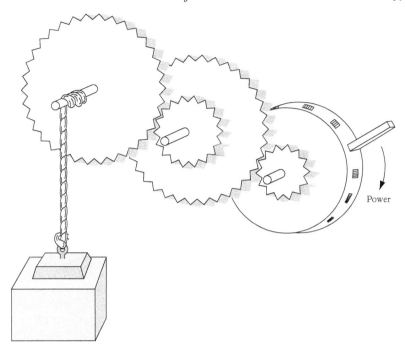

Figure 3 Three-dimensional sketch of a *barulkos*, 'weightlifter'.

Hero's *Dioptra*: this discussion seems to be misplaced, as the treatise only much later goes on to discuss more systematically the theory of the 'five powers'.[146] The discussion of the 'weightlifter' uses a physical illustration showing how to solve the theoretical problem of lifting a given weight by a given force.[147] It is, in effect, a general-ization of the mathematical relationships noted in the Aristotelian *Mechanica* and epitomized in Archimedes' ship-moving exploit. As one of the three mechanical problems listed by Pappus, it may fairly be regarded as one of the centrepieces of the claims of the field of mechanics to be a mathematically grounded discipline.

The device offered as a solution to the problem, in Hero's text, is an assemblage of large toothed wheels on the same axle as a smaller wheel,

[146] See Drachmann (1963a), pp. 22–32, which I follow here.
[147] Price (1975), p. 54, doubts its viability, seeing it entirely as a 'schoolbook example', i.e. a problem based on the theory of mechanical advantage derived from the law of the lever.

lined up in succession, so that each large wheel engages a smaller which transmits the motion to a larger wheel affixed to its axle.[148]

The construction of the device is driven by a theory that, to move a given weight by a power five times smaller than the weight, the power needs to be applied at a point proportionally further from the axle. Drachmann notes that the *Dioptra* version, unlike the Arabic version, initially poses the problem as one of holding a given weight in balance by a given power, and then adds a small amount to the power – one *mina* to five *talents* – in order to lift it.[149] Although we are given a specific quantity of the added power, this might have been a stand in for an arbitrarily small quantity. The approach to mechanics as a problem of finding equilibria is thereby connected to the tradition of mechanics as a problem of moving weights.

Hero offers another way to connect the problem of equilibrium to that of causing motion, an idea that Knorr credits to Archimedes.[150] Beginning from the notion that equal weights balanced on equal circles will be in equilibrium, Hero then *derives* the idea that a great weight can be moved by a small power, since, for two concentric circles,

> if the greater weight is on an arc from the small circle and the small power is on the arc from the great circle, and the ratio of the line from the centre of the big one to the line from the centre of the small one is greater than the ratio of the great weight to the small power that moves it, then the small power will prevail against the great weight.[151]

Motion occurs when the proportional *distance* of the smaller power from the centre is slightly more than its weight in relation to the greater weight. Rather than adding an arbitrarily small power to cause motion, one could move the weight an arbitrarily small distance away from the fulcrum. As Knorr notes, Hero is inverting the order of inference. He uses this formulation in order to connect the discussion of the five powers and of geared devices.[152] This notion of finding a

---

[148] Drawing by author using modern perspective: for the manuscript drawings, see Drachmann (1963a); also Weitzmann (1971), (1959).
[149] Drachmann (1963a), p. 26.   [150] Knorr (1982), p. 92.
[151] Drachmann's translation from the Arabic, Drachmann (1963a), p. 62.
[152] Knorr (1982), p. 92.

balance point and moving slightly away from it takes the emphasis off the role of the agent, whose additional effort cannot be measured, to a context where the inclination happens naturally. It bears some similarities to the Aristotelian explanation of the motion of a wheel.

The problem of the *barulkos* is approached in quantified terms, and illustrates the Archimedean conclusion: mechanical theory will show how it is possible to lift any given weight with any given power.[153] The discussion of the problem of moving a greater weight with a given power recognizes that the mechanical solution takes greater time to move the weight proportionally as the mechanical devices are increased. In Hero's presentation, the mathematics are understood to be general, and not limited to this particular device: indeed, as Tybjerg notes, the device itself is unlikely to be feasible in practice and is really a calculation technique.[154] In addition to the solution using toothed wheels, we are told how it could be achieved using compound pulleys. There is also an attempt to apply levers in succession to achieve the same result.

The treatise includes more general theoretical discussions, including a consideration of the power needed to move a body lying on a plane. Drachmann describes this as 'the theory of mechanics in general',[155] since it places the problems of mechanics within a broader context of the physics of motion. Hero considers the claim that it would require a force equal to the weight of a body to move it on a plane surface. Hero denies that this is so: he claims that the body can be moved by a force smaller than any known. He acknowledges that this is a theoretical possibility, not one evident in practice. He reasons from the case of a weight on an inclined plane. It takes no power to move it downward, whereas a specific amount of power would be needed to hold it in place. Even the slightest tilt of the plane in either direction is enough to make the weight slide in that direction. Thus, he reasons, when a weight rests on a level surface, the smallest power should suffice to move it.[156]

---

[153] Pappus 8.1060.2.   [154] Tybjerg (2003), pp. 449–50.

[155] Drachmann (1963a), p. 46. Unfortunately, Drachmann does not make clear whether this is Hero's own presentation of the problem.

[156] Drachmann (1963a), p. 46. See Schiefsky (forthcoming), which came to my attention too late to address properly here.

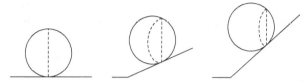

Figure 4 Sketch of a cylinder on slopes of different inclinations, to illustrate
Hero's use of the balancing point to account for the greater downward tendencies
of cylinders on steeper slopes.

Although he recognizes that the irregularities of actual bodies
impede motion, and that more power may actually be needed to
produce motion, Hero uses a methodology that deliberately abstracts
from real experience to an idealized case. He supports this method
by citing cases where surface contact is minimal, for example a flat
body resting on a cylinder or on smooth, greased planes.[157] We shall
see in Chapter 6 that some philosophers deny the generality of
mechanical theories because of problems about the minimum threshold for moving a body; Hero seems to be trying to answer this kind
of objection.

He appeals to the methods of mechanics in his demonstration that
a body is moved upward on a smooth and greased inclined plane by a
power slightly more than that equal to it. He reasons from the case
of two weights balanced over a pulley: the weight that will balance
the first is taken to be equivalent to a power, although in practice,
if there is any rubbing or stiffness in the rope, the power required
will be greater.[158] This style of reasoning appeals theoretically to the
methods of mechanics to study a problem of natural motion, using
the notion of balancing weights to think about how to measure the
elusive notion of force.

Hero also uses the methods of mechanics to think about forces
causing downward motion. He approaches this indirectly, by considering a body on a slope of increasing steepness, and he thinks in
terms of the power that would be required to keep the body at rest.
Hero puts the problem in terms of balancing a cylinder on an inclined

[157] Drachmann (1963a), p. 46.   [158] Drachmann (1963a), p. 47.

surface. He is using the idea of centres of weight of the parts of the cylinder, reasoning that the slope of the plane shifts the balancing point of the cylinder. The power required to keep the cylinder at equilibrium is proportional to the amount of the cylinder that is in disequilibrium, given the balancing point on the slope.[159]

The reasoning is 'mechanical', in that Hero appeals to the idea of a balance to try to understand the complex powers needed to keep a body at rest. Techniques from mechanics are used to try to conceptualize the causes of motion more generally, especially the elusive notions of power or force.

Hero offers a parallel treatment of the equilibrium of liquids and solids. The question whether waters will move or rest is expressed in similar terms of inclination and equilibrium. Reasons for differences in mobility of solids and liquids are noted: the parts of liquids are not so strongly bound together, whereas the roughness of surfaces of solids impedes mobility.[160] He might have been following Archimedes in trying to treat the theory that underlies problems of weightlifting technology in tandem with those of pneumatics.

After a discussion of problems apparently derived from Archimedes' work on the balance, on centres of weight and on uprights, Hero begins his second book with a treatment of the five 'simple powers'. These are the windlass, the lever, pulley, wedge and screw. The last – not included in the Aristotelian text – is described as a kind of wedge wrapped around a cylindrical centre.[161] This connects the screw to the lever, since the Aristotelian treatise shows how to consider the wedge as a kind of lever.[162]

The last book describes some more complex practical applications, including cranes, systems for safely lowering large blocks, screw presses[163] and a screw cutter. These practical problems are clearly useful for devices he describes in other works, especially

---

[159] See Drachmann (1963a), p. 48; Schiefsky (forthcoming).
[160] Drachmann (1963a), pp. 46–7.   [161] Drachmann (1963a), pp. 56–7.
[162] Since the problem of lifting a given weight with a given power is solved for axle-and-wheel, pulley and lever, but not for the screw, Drachmann (1963a), p. 91, concludes that Hero does not have a formula for calculating the power of the screw.
[163] For analysis of these, see K. D. White (1984), pp. 68–70.

On Theatre-Making.[164] There, his approach is quite detailed, apparently driven by frustration with others who neglect to specify practical details. Hero emphasizes that hidden techniques create the effect that – to the watcher – seems marvellous, but to the engineer behind the scene is nothing mysterious. The devices are mostly showpieces, with the emphasis on the illusion created for the observer. At one point it is stipulated that the dimensions of the devices should not be so large as to arouse a suspicion that there is someone inside working them. Other parts of the device are constructed so that the mechanics are invisible to the observer, either shielded by woodwork, or, at a pinch, painted so that the ropes cannot be seen.

The observer's delight is not in the cleverness of the design or the beauty and elegance of the internal workings but rather in the illusion, which would be shattered equally by the suspicion of agency as much as by observing the internal mechanisms. Believability is mentioned by Hero as a desideratum both of the appearance created by the devices, and also of his own account: believability is achieved by giving sufficient detail. These notions of believability are different, the one created by hiding the mechanisms, the other by revealing them.

Besides elaborating on the construction of standing theatre-pieces in the tradition of Philo, Hero details the construction of devices set on wheels, so that a piece moves as a whole. This seems to be his special contribution to the art. In his description of devices, Hero's approach is also focused on results rather than principles, although he describes his devices in credible and ingenious detail, and he shows considerable technical virtuosity in suggesting elaborate variations. The devices are driven by a falling weight that pulls a rope wrapped around an axle.

In the most interesting piece, a self-contained automaton, the fall of the weight is slowed by resting the weight on a miniature silo of millet or mustard seed, which trickles out of the silo when the trapdoor at the bottom is opened. This initial movement, the opening of the trapdoor, is hidden from view and the rope carefully arranged

---

[164] On this work, see Murphy (1995); Marshall (2003) offers a reconstruction of the dramatic narrative.

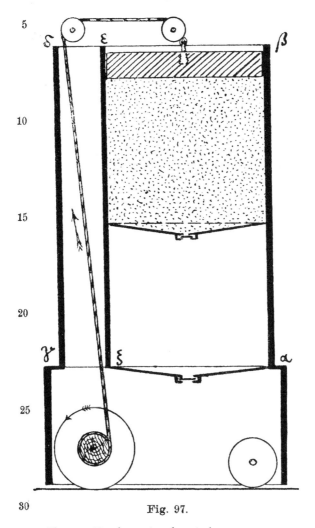

Fig. 97.

Figure 5 Hero's moving theatrical automaton.

so that there is a time gap between the opening of the trapdoor and the point where the rope reaches sufficient tension to start the device moving. The implication is that, because the trigger is released ahead of time, the human agent can be out of sight when the motion starts, to heighten the sense that the device moves by itself.

The wonder and delight seem to arise from the fact that it starts and stops moving by itself. As the level falls, a weight resting on the grains is lowered slowly, and this weight pulls a rope that, by means of pulleys, unwinds from a wooden axle and turns the wheels driving the device forward.

Hero provides details on some possible modifications of this basic design. One is an additional mechanism designed to produce a greater forward rotation from the pull of the rope. Since the motion of the device is limited by the distance that the weight falls, Hero applies the method used in the *barulkos* in reverse to increase the distance moved by the device. As the weight falls, it pulls a first rope as before; but this rope connects to an intermediate axle-and-wheel, which increases the length of a second rope that turns the axle. The axle-and-wheel transforms a smaller pull by the first rope attached to the driving weight into a larger degree of rotation of the wheels and thus a greater motion of the device.

Hero describes his devices as self-moving or self-sufficient, apparently because there is no human agent operating them.[165] At a number of points he describes the effect produced when a part of a device is moved by hand, and then he goes on to detail how this effect could be produced automatically; this does not refer to the absence of contrivance, but to a device contrived so as to run without constant intervention. His conception of *automatos*, then, centres on the idea of a device so contrived that the necessary sequence of motions will achieve the designer's aim without intervention.

Hero is perhaps best known to philosophers for a boast at the beginning of his work on war machinery, claiming that this one branch of mechanics had done more to further tranquillity than all the chatter of the philosophers. This remark is the basis for Diels' claim about his rejection of philosophical speculation.[166] This kind of defensiveness or professional self-promotion echoes Vitruvius, who

---

[165] Hero sometimes contrasts *to automaton* to a process that happens *ek peiras*, by trial, a phrase used to describe a process wherein the designer takes the device through its motions 'by hand' and sets up the operating ropes to the correct length by continuous intervention.

[166] Diels (1893), p. 107.

insists that it was the insight of the architects, not the machinery alone, that liberated Marseilles.[167] Cuomo takes Hero to be emphasizing the need for the body politic to focus its intellectual energies on the production of effective weaponry.[168] Rather than opposing theory and practice, she argues that Hero is advocating the use of theory concerned with instruments over that concerned with words, and the public rather than the private pursuit of security.[169] In the tradition of Archimedes, the man who through ingenuity alone shifted the balance of power, Hero presents the mechanic as a source of wisdom, not a mere practitioner.

Hero's theoretical interests are genuine. Cuomo notes that he uses geometry in some of his constructions, including catapults, and uses the style of geometry in his use of lettered diagrams.[170] Tybjerg shows how he exploits ambiguities in the terminology of geometrical proofs, especially the term *kataskeuē*, used of both mechanical devices and geometrical constructions, to make the transition between the geometrical and mechanical aspects of his problems seamlessly. His goal, she argues, is to be comprehensive in his presentation of the possibilities, rather than to preserve the purity of mathematical method or to sharply observe disciplinary boundaries.[171] Hero's commitment to the theoretical ambitions of his discipline is clear.

PAPPUS OF ALEXANDRIA

A text from late antiquity – about 320 CE – provides something of an overview of mechanics as it survives in late antiquity. This is book 8 of the mathematical *Collection* of Pappus of Alexandria.[172] There is some controversy whether Pappus is simply recording past ideas at a time when Greek science is in decline, or whether his work is itself

---

[167] Vitruvius, *de Arch.* 10.16.12.   [168] Cuomo (2002).
[169] Cuomo (2002). Cuomo (2001), pp. 203–5, considers Hero's creation of a professional self-image.
[170] Cuomo (2001), p. 164.
[171] Tybjerg (2004). On the view that construction problems in mathematics are mechanical, see Bowen (1983).
[172] Cuomo (2000), p. 2.

evidence of a small renaissance in interest in the sciences.[173] His work surveys the existing wisdom on mathematics, presented so as to stress its author's contribution, even though the extent of his own innovation might not have been large.[174] It is, incidentally, the work that Newton cites in the opening to his *Principia*, claiming that some of the ancients took account of mechanics in their investigations of natural philosophy.[175]

The eighth book of the *Collection* is devoted to mechanics, a discipline which Pappus tells his readers is praised by mathematicians and philosophers alike. He is not necessarily countering a view to the contrary,[176] so much as simply echoing the Aristotelian view of the intermediary position of the 'mixed mathematics'. The presentation of mechanics is structured around three classic problems,[177] a presentation that might have consciously echoed the discussion of the three great problems of Greek mathematics. In mechanics the problems are to raise a given weight with a given power, to duplicate the cube, and to find whether a wheel with a given number of teeth will mesh with another with a fixed number of teeth.[178]

In contrast to Hero, Pappus does not approach the first problem using the *barulkos*, or 'weightlifter'. Rather, he presents it in very general terms as an issue about the power required to support a weight on a plane inclined at a given angle. A gloss on this notes that this quantity is useful to mechanics needing to lift weights, since they can confidently move a weight once the power required to support it has been found.[179] The third problem, whether cog wheels with a given number of teeth will mesh, is also discussed by Hero. It is a problem that mechanics would have needed to solve in building devices such as the *barulkos*. The duplication of the cube is common to the lists of problems in mathematics and mechanics and would have been used primarily in scaling torsion devices.

---

[173] Russo (2004), p. 240; Cuomo (2000), p. 117.

[174] Cuomo (2000), pp. 90, 146, 199.   [175] Newton (1995), p. 3.

[176] Cuomo (2000), p. 95.   [177] Cuomo (2000), p. 109.

[178] Pappus 8.1028.4. Cuomo (2000), p. 109 n. 37.

[179] Pappus 8.1028.12. Ver Eecke (1933), p. 814 n. 5, regards the gloss as an interpolation.

Cuomo discusses the differences between Pappus' treatment of the case of a weight on a horizontal surface and that of Hero: rather than assume that the least force *ought* to move a weight on a horizontal plane and ask what interferes with this, Pappus begins by taking the force *actually* required to move it, and determining its relationship to the force required to move the same weight up a plane inclined at a given angle.[180] Cuomo's explanation of this is that Pappus' interest is in the geometrical problem raised by the angle of the plane; to solve this, it is necessary to give a definite quantity to the force moving the weight on the horizontal.[181]

Pappus is interested in primarily geometrical problems involving centres of weight. Indeed, as Cuomo remarks, his book contains problems with every available combination of mathematical and mechanical issues.[182] He moves between an abstract and a physical understanding of quantities he is solving for: in the middle of a proof involving the geometry of a figure on an inclined plane, he converts a lettered variable he has been using back into an actual weight in talents, and a variable for 'power' into a number of men.[183] He uses the Archimedean procedure of treating a problem of equalizing areas of plane figures as if it were a question of balancing a figure at equilibrium.[184] The emphasis on the utility of the field does not preclude a preference for mathematically elegant solutions.[185] Although modern historians sometimes draw a contrast between the pure, mathematical approach of Archimedes and the practical bent of the Aristotelian *Mechanica*, the work of Hero and Pappus indicates that the field allowed for different emphases and different ways of integrating the two sorts of considerations, and indeed of relating them to problems of natural philosophy.

---

[180] Cuomo (2000), pp. 113–16.   [181] Cuomo (2000), p. 116.
[182] Cuomo (2000), p. 121.   [183] Pappus 8.1058.17.
[184] Pappus 8.1040.26. Cuomo (2000) takes Pappus' citation of Carpus' claim that Archimedes wrote only one mechanics text as evidence that Pappus did not have access to other texts of Archimedes but was working from Philo or Hero's texts.
[185] On Pappus' concept of utility, see Cuomo (2000), pp. 123–4.

MODELS OF THE HEAVENS

There is a particularly vexed question about the nature of the celestial models that were constructed in the Hellenistic period. Reports of such models do not give enough detail for us to know how they worked, and it is also possible that some of the ancient reports mistakenly retroject devices and techniques from their own day onto an earlier time period.[186] Modern scholars differ considerably in their interpretation of such reports. Assessing the reports requires making suppositions about the kinds of technology available, and the astronomical data and theory of the motion of the heavenly bodies that were used in building a given device.

Given the paucity of literary evidence for celestial devices with moving parts from the Hellenistic era, it came as something of a surprise when Price reconstructed the workings of the Antikythera mechanism and concluded that it was a sophisticated sun and moon calculator using differential gearing to show the relative positions of sun and moon at different times.[187] This discovery shows the danger of the argument from silence: the absence of evidence in the literary record is no indication that such devices were not built. However, the inverse danger is to take this find to license unfettered speculation about the technology available in any given period. Besides questions of technology, another aspect of the interpretative controversy concerns the astronomical models on which different kinds of devices were built, given the data and the solar or planetary theories current at the time. In a context where the texts are unclear, the state of technology not well understood, and the astronomy in dispute, interpretative caution is surely merited.

The impact of cosmic devices on the philosophical imagination might not have depended on their predictive ability so much as on

---

[186] See Goldstein and Bowen (1983), for the difficulties of reconstructing the history of Greek astronomy, and the tendency of ancient sources to retroject later developments.

[187] Price (1975). Based on the style of lettering, Freeth, Bitsakis, Moussas *et al.* (2006), p. 587, conclude that it was constructed in the latter half of the second century BCE.

their usefulness for visualization, demonstration and explanation. Autolycus reasons about the points that will be apparent on a sphere rotating about a pole oblique to the horizon;[188] Ptolemy appeals to an armillary sphere in his argument that the size of the earth needs to stand in the same ratio to the sphere of the fixed stars as a point to the diameter of the sphere.[189] These passages only refer to a constructed device to understand the *geometry* of the heavens, not the *functioning* of the heavens.

Bowen argues that the predictive use of devices was a late development and shows how many literary reports of 'predictions' are suspect.[190] The claims about Thales' ability to predict an eclipse have long given rise to doubt. But even in Roman histories from the first centuries BCE and CE, Bowen argues, the idea that a successful military commander could use expert knowledge to dispel the fears of his troops at the ominous portents in the sky was a literary *topos*, and the historical accuracy of such stories is open to doubt.[191] We should be wary, then, of taking such literary reports as evidence for the kinds of devices that must have been available in the Hellenistic period to produce the predictions claimed.

Thus the philosophical reception of cosmic devices does not seem to depend primarily on their ability to predict. More important, from the perspective of mechanical philosophy, is a device's ability to suggest that the *kind* of physical and causal connections found in such models might be at work in the heavens. Many astronomers, including Ptolemy, continued to regard the planets as independent intelligent beings. Although theological commitments might support this view, it might also have seemed like the only possible way to account for their movements. Others had toyed with the idea that their movements could be accounted for by a lifeless mechanism of some kind. But the mechanical analogy could only undermine the view that the heavenly bodies must be divine intelligences if a physical device could produce *something like* the observed phenomena by

---

[188] Autolycus, *de Sphaera Quae Movetur*.
[189] Ptolemy, *Alm.* 1.6; Toomey (1984), p. 43.
[190] Bowen (2002a). [191] Bowen (2002a), pp. 109–11.

means of interconnected rotations of intersecting spheres. In other words, the devices that could inspire an idea like that of the early modern 'clockwork universe' would need to show how interconnected motions could work in coordination without ongoing intervention. The devices in question would need to be understood as – at least roughly – *isomorphic* to the heavens. This raises the problem of knowing what exactly, at any given period, the principal phenomena were taken to be.

Of the kinds of devices mentioned in Chapter 3, the spherical star map and the armillary sphere are structurally isomorphic to observed phenomena but are limited in what they can represent. They do not show the 'wandering stars' – sun, moon or planets – although the armillary sphere can be used to calculate the place and time of solar rising and setting. Astrolabes and anaphoric clocks offer roughly the same information using a two-dimensional representation of the heavens. Calculators could be constructed to show the orbits of some of the 'wanderers' relative to the earth, but without maintaining the same spatial configuration as the heavens. Only orreries attempt to show topographically the relative positions of the wanderers. The techniques required to build a device tracking the relative positions of 'wanderers' – on a geocentric model especially – would be quite sophisticated.[192] We would need to know what astronomical theories were available at the time, before being able to assess what devices could be built.

The question, then, is how to interpret reports of 'cosmic devices' from different time periods. A passage in Epicurus' *On Nature* 11 discusses a celestial device, apparently built by the mathematical school of Cyzicus. There is evidence of a school of mathematicians in the early third century in the southern Hellespont, apparently founded by Eudoxus.[193] Recovery of parts of Epicurus' *On Nature* – which is among the texts recovered from the Herculaneum library – yields new evidence about this school. Sedley has argued that this

---

[192] Keyser (1998); Oleson (1984), p. 371. See Price (1975) on the reconstruction of the Antikythera mechanism.

[193] Sedley (1976), pp. 27ff.

papyrus fragment includes 'an attack on some unnamed opponents for using mechanical instruments to illustrate their mathematical laws of planetary motion'.[194] Epicurus' attack indicates that the device was used to 'measure' times of risings and settings, and thereby to 'form an adequate mental model by means of their instruments'.[195] Epicurus questions the viability of the instrument, on the grounds that the place of the setting of the sun is not fixed but appears different as we walk only a short distance away: there is thus no reason to prefer one place rather than another as the place to make measurements.[196]

Nothing is said about eclipses in the Epicurus fragment, and only once does it refer to the motion of the moon: most of the discussion is a general diatribe against the use of intelligible models, and the detailed discussion focuses on measurement of the rising and setting of the sun.[197] Sedley reasons that the device was a planetarium, citing Archimedes' construct and the Antikythera mechanism as evidence that such devices were built in the Hellenistic world.[198] The Cyzicean device need not be an orrery to model the risings and settings of the fixed stars or of the sun, however. Reasoning that the phenomena in question at this period would probably concern sun, moon and fixed stars, Mendell suggests that it is a calculator showing positions on a dial, since the complexity of an astronomically adequate nested sphere model would have to be considerable.[199]

The report in *On Nature* is fragmentary and difficult to interpret. Epicurus' criticisms seem odd if the device in question portrays the earth as spherical, since an armillary sphere makes it evident that times of risings and settings would be calculated differently with respect to different locations. Given his rejection of the spherical-earth theory and of the finite sphere of the fixed stars, however,

---

[194] Sedley (1976), p. 35.   [195] Sedley (1976), p. 32.
[196] Sedley (1976), pp. 31, 35.   [197] Sedley (1976), p. 34.
[198] Sedley (1976), p. 37. Guerra and Torraca (1996), p. 145, seem to regard the device as an armillary sphere, attributing its invention to Eudoxus. Goldstein and Bowen (1983), p. 336, interpret the account of Eudoxus' *arachnē* or spider web as indicating a projection of lines onto the surface of a kind of sundial.
[199] Mendell (2000), p. 130.

Epicurus might have made quite sweeping criticisms of conventional representations that depended on a geocentric cosmos and a finite sphere for the fixed stars.[200] It is difficult to tell from such piecemeal and partisan criticisms what kind of devices the mathematicians of Cyzicus were using, and to what extent they understood them as models of the movements of the heavens.

Other reports claim that Archimedes built a model showing the relative positions of sun, moon and planets. Cicero mentions such devices in his *Republic* and *On the Nature of the Gods*, ascribing them to Archimedes in the former case, Posidonius in the latter. Ovid (43 BC–17 CE) refers to such a device built by Archimedes; Lactantius (*c.* 240–320 CE) and Claudian (born *c.* 370 CE), quite possibly following Cicero, echo the ascription, with some elaborations.[201] Sextus credits Archimedes with a device that represented the motions of the sun, moon and stars, without mentioning the planets specifically.[202] There are real discrepancies between sources, even on issues as non-technical as whether the device was made of wood, bronze or glass. Archimedes was one of those semi-legendary figures around whom tales gathered, and the accuracy of poets or polemicists centuries later is not guaranteed.[203]

Cicero takes the device as evidence of divine ingenuity: his response in *On the Nature of the Gods* is a version of the famous watchmaker argument for the existence of a rational designer.[204] As he describes it,

All the more remarkable, therefore, was Archimedes' discovery, since he had devised a method of construction whereby, extremely different though the movements of the planets are, the mere turning of the globe would keep them

---

[200] See Guerra and Torraca (1996), for a detailed account of Epicurus' opposition to astronomy, not only for its attempt at univocal and demonstrative explanation, but also for its use of a finite cosmic model. Furley (1996) suggests that Epicurus diverges radically from contemporary astronomical theory in defence of a flat-earth theory.

[201] Price (1975), pp. 56–7, conveniently collects these texts.

[202] *M.* 9.115. cf. Cicero *Rep.* 1.14.21–3.

[203] See Simms (1995); Cuomo (2001), pp. 197–8.

[204] *Nat. D.* 2.88; see Hunter (forthcoming), for an analysis of the argument.

all in their unequal and different orbits. When Gallus rotated the globe, the moon really followed the sun on the bronze globe by the same number of revolutions as are the days it lags behind it in the sky. Thus it happened that on the globe occurred a solar eclipse just like the real eclipse; and also that the moon passed into the tract of space covered by the earth's shadow when the sun…[205]

Unfortunately the text has a considerable lacuna at just this critical point.

Russo believes the reports claim that Archimedes built a 'planetarium', a kind of orrery showing the motion of sun, moon and planets; he takes this to imply that Archimedes must have used a heliocentric model.[206] Archimedes was certainly familiar with Aristarchus' heliocentric hypothesis: the *Sand-Reckoner* calculates the magnitudes invoked by Aristarchus' claim that the sphere of the moving earth needs to be proportionate to the sphere of the fixed stars 'as the centre of a circle is to the circumference'.[207] However, as Neugebauer notes, there is no evidence that a corresponding planetary theory was developed to complement Aristarchus' theory that the earth moves around the sun.[208]

Cicero's report tells us that Archimedes' model was able to show a solar eclipse. Scholars versed in astronomy caution that the

---

[205] Hoc autem sphaerae genus, in quo solis et lunae motus inessent et earum quinque stellarum quae errantes et quasi uagae nominarentur, in illa sphaera solida non potuisse finiri atque in eo admirandum esse inuentum Archimedi quod excogitasset quem ad modum in dissimillimis motibus inaequabiles et uarios cursus seruaret una conuersio. Hanc sphaeram Gallus con moueret, fiebat ut soli luna totidem conuersionibus in aere illo quot diebus in ipso caelo succederet, ex quo et in sphaera solis fieret eadem illa defectio et incideret luna tum in eam metam quae esset umbra terrae, cum sol … (eight pages missing); Cicero *Rep.* 1.14.21–3 (Bréguet), trans. Sabine, cited in Savage-Smith (1985), pp. 5–6.

[206] Russo (2004), p. 80. Evans (1998), pp. 78–83, also accepts the reports that Archimedes built an orrery. See Simms (1995), for a discussion of the different reports.

[207] Archimedes, *Aren.* 136.1–2. Aristarchus addresses one of the most compelling objections to the theory that the earth moves, which is that there is no apparent stellar parallax, or shift in observed positions of the constellations; he solves this by postulating that the fixed stars are sufficiently far from the earth that the radius of the earth's orbit is negligible by comparison. See Evans (1998), pp. 67–8.

[208] Neugebauer (1975), vol. II, p. 697.

astronomical knowledge needed to *predict* an eclipse accurately was
not available before Hipparchus' work in the second century BCE:
before this time, the data on the relative alignment of sun, earth and
moon were not sufficiently precise to produce a usable calculating
device.[209] The text does not claim that the device could *predict*
eclipses, however. Bowen notes the emphasis on demonstrating the
causes of eclipses: this was politically useful in quelling the fears
of worried soldiers who would otherwise take an eclipse as an evil
omen.[210] Clarifying the geometrical relationships between the light
of sun, earth and moon was also important in using the phenomena
of eclipses to estimate the sizes and relative distances of the bodies
involved. Cicero's report, if it is accurate in ascribing the device to
Archimedes, could be describing a demonstration model showing in
three dimensions how the relative positions of sun, earth and moon
could produce a shadow merely by their juxtaposition. A demonstration of this could be quite useful in showing causally how eclipses
come about *in general* without necessarily being very accurate as
to the motions of the relevant bodies, that is, about the timing of
particular eclipses.

There are greater problems with the claim that Archimedes'
model could show the position of the planets.[211] Price draws on
the techniques used in the Antikythera mechanism to suggest that
Archimedes might have built a mechanism involving gears in parallel
planes. Interlocking gears in appropriate ratios could be used to
indicate the conventional approximations for the mean periods of
the planets – thirty years for Saturn, twelve for Jupiter – for each
revolution of the sun.[212] The central gear wheel used to indicate the
annual motion of the sun would directly drive different wheels
representing the orbits of the planets: the placing of these would be
dictated by mechanical considerations, not by an attempt to represent
the topography of the heavens. The position of each planet would

[209] Neugebauer (1975), vol. II, pp. 664–9; Keyser (1998), p. 246; Evans (1998), pp. 20,
213; Bowen (2002a).
[210] Cicero, *Rep.* 1.16.25; Bowen (2001); (2002a).
[211] Evans (1998), p. 297; Neugebauer (1975), vol. II, p. 652 n. 7.
[212] Price (1975), pp. 57–8; Sedley (1998), pp. 82–3.

presumably be indicated by a dial and a pointer, showing its motion through the zodiac in solar years.

Price accepts that the kind of calculator he describes could have been built by Archimedes, although this would date a much more complex device at least a century – if not two – before the Antikythera mechanism.[213] Neugebauer notes, however, that this kind of calculating device could only display the mean positions of the outer planets – ignoring stations and retrogradations – and could not show positions of the inner planets, Mercury and Venus.[214] Moreover, a plane calculator such as Price describes would not show eclipses directly, as Cicero's account seems to imply. The suggestion that the moon moved into the cone-shaped shadow cast by the earth implies that it was a three-dimensional model of the relative positions of sun, earth and moon.

Clearly, there are problems with taking Cicero's report at face value, and we should be wary of inferring too much about the state of ancient technology from this evidence. Keyser suggests that Posidonius is the real source of the device,[215] and that the report in the *Republic* is retrojecting a later device onto Archimedes. This certainly suits Cicero's literary purposes.[216] Neugebauer is sceptical that even Posidonius possessed the astronomical knowledge to build what Cicero describes.[217]

References to other astronomical devices are even less detailed. Keyser discusses the evidence from the second letter attributed to Plato, which mentions a *sphairion* that is not functioning correctly; he concludes from the reference to functioning that this is a device with working parts, possibly an orrery.[218] From astronomical as well as philological considerations, Keyser dates the letter to the first

---

[213] Freeth, Bitsakis, Moussas *et al.* (2006) date the device to the late second century BCE, based on the lettering.

[214] Neugebauer (1975), vol. II, p. 652 n. 7.   [215] *Nat. D.* 2.34–5.

[216] Keyser (1998), p. 247. Keyser cites as parallel Posidonius' retrojection of Democritus' atomic theory onto a figure from the time of the Trojan Wars. See Boys-Stones (2001), on the Stoic tendency to look for ancient origins of all wisdom.

[217] Neugebauer (1975), vol. II, p. 652.   [218] *Epist.* 2, 312d1ff.

century BCE.[219] However, there is little to tell us what this device did. Hero of Alexandria describes a model using a glass globe and bronze sphere inside it floating on water and held in the centre, but without moving parts.[220] Drachmann notes that this, along with half a dozen entries in sequence in the *Pneumatica*, does not share the diagram lettering conventions of the surrounding entries, and he suggests that they may be an interpolation, perhaps copied by Hero from a different source.[221] The model has no internal working parts, and its purpose is obscure. Galen talks of people who imitate the revolutions of the 'wandering stars' by certain instruments, without giving specifics other than that the instruments work by themselves.[222]

There is, then, little consensus on what devices were built – by the mathematicians of Cyzicus, by Archimedes or Posidonius, or other unnamed figures – or on what techniques they used. It is clear that armillary spheres and astrolabes were available in late antiquity, and we have good archaeological evidence of plane calculators using parallel gearing from at least the first century BCE. But there is little certainty about the existence of orreries showing the relative positions and motions of sun, moon and planets.

In this chapter I have highlighted some of the most important developments in the mechanics of antiquity during the Hellenistic period and thereafter. In the next chapter I shall consider evidence that the field of pneumatics – an important if somewhat distinct part of ancient mechanics – also spurred new reflections in natural philosophy. Finally, I shall look at the philosophical reception of mechanics in antiquity and discuss evidence that there were those in antiquity who looked to ancient mechanics to help understand the organization of the natural world and the nature of organisms.

---

[219] Keyser (1998).   [220] Hero, *Spir.* 2.7.   [221] Drachmann (1971).
[222] Galen, *UP* 14.5. More on this in Chapter 6.

CHAPTER 5

Ancient Greek mechanics continued: the case of pneumatics

Texts have survived from the Hellenistic period concerning a so-called *pneumatikē technē*. I shall refer to the field as 'pneumatics', although – as scholars have noted – the English transliteration does not exactly capture the sense of the subject matter, which concerns devices worked by flowing water, compressed air or steam. As Landels aptly suggests, the German title *Druckwerke* best captures the sense:[1] although there are some anomalies,[2] the field is largely about what might be called pressure effects.

The characterization of pneumatics as delimited by pressure-driven devices is, admittedly, a simplification of a vaguely defined field, and it works better for Hero's collection than for Philo's. The latter – especially in the more extensive Arabic version – includes a number of water wheels, which do not depend on pressure differentials so much as the simple weight of water.[3] Both Pappus and Philoponus describe a branch of mechanics as being concerned with devices that raise water, perhaps by analogy parallel to the category of devices used to lift weights. However, the vast majority of devices in the *pneumatica* collections use pressure differentials to regulate the flow of water in different ways.

I have previously discussed the classical philosophical theories offered to account for 'rarefaction effects'. Some pneumatic devices

---

[1] Landels (1978), p. 201.

[2] E.g. Hero, *Spir.* 68, the *hagnistērion*. This is a wheel-driven device with no fluids or pressure-driven effects, and it is clearly out of place.

[3] The Arabic text under the name of Philo of Byzantium describes one variant in which the water falls into an inner enclosed chamber forcefully enough to produce a whistling sound: see Humphrey, Oleson and Sherwood (1998), pp. 29–30.

of the Hellenistic era work by the reverse procedure, forcing air into a smaller place than it otherwise occupies. These 'compression effects', as I call them, are credited to Ctesibius.

Although the pneumatics treatises do not say how the discipline acquired its name, the field seems to have been called *pneumatikē* because of a notion that an aery substance called *pneuma* – *spiritus* in Latin – must be involved in explaining unusual behaviour in fluids. Ctesibius is said by Vitruvius to have *discovered* pneumatics.[4] Although rarefaction effects were evidently known – and theorized – from the time of the Presocratics, the claim might have been that Ctesibius was associated with the appeal to *pneuma* to account for pneumatic effects. The account in Hero of the compression effects discovered by Ctesibius does not appeal to *pneuma* in particular,[5] but we do not know how Ctesibius himself would have accounted for them.

Even in Aristotle's biology, ejecting fluid is vaguely associated with 'pneumatic force'.[6] *Pneuma* has a history in both medical and Peripatetic thought as a substance with peculiar properties, accounting for changes in fluids such as fermentation and foaming. It plays an increasingly large role in Hellenistic medical theory as the substance in some vessels of the body, particularly the nerves, capable of transmitting impulses caused by pressure and impact. In Stoic physical theory it acquired a starring role, since in their view *pneuma* permeates everything and accounts for the properties of the permeated bodies, particularly those involving the cohesion of matter and the transmission of impact and effect from one part of the whole to another.[7]

It is not always clear which of these various accounts is at play in individual references to *pneumatikē*: they might not always have

---

[4] *qui etiam spiritus naturalis pneumaticasque res invenit*, Vitruvius, *de Arch.* 9.8.2; cf. Pliny, *HN* 7.125.

[5] Hero, *Spir.* 8.5; more on this below.

[6] δηλοῖ δὲ καὶ ἡ ἔξοδος ὅτι γίνεται ὑπὸ πνεύματος οὐδὲν γὰρ ῥιπτεῖται πόρρω ἄνευ βίας πνευματικῆς, Aristotle, *HA.* 7.7, 586a16–17 (Louis); Berryman (2002a).

[7] E.g. Plutarch *Comm. not.* 1085c; Alexander, *Mixt.* 223.25–224.26; Galen, *Plen.* 7.525.9–14.

been very well differentiated. There is ample potential for confusion, since *pneuma* could be used of breath or wind and could
mean ordinary moving air. In some philosophical theories *pneuma*
was understood to constitute a distinct substance; in other cases,
the term *pneumatikē* may be better thought of as referring to a kind
of effect or motion. It was particularly associated with the phenomena characteristic of living things and cases where matter seems
especially active.

Since I believe that mechanical devices were first developed and
subsequently inspired theoretical reflection on their capacities, I shall
sketch some of the major new fluid-moving devices of the Hellenistic
period before turning to the theories of pneumatics that attempted to
account for their capacities. Finally, I shall return to a more general
consideration of the status of mechanics in antiquity in the light of
the evidence of these two chapters.

PNEUMATIC TECHNOLOGY IN THE POST-CLASSICAL PERIOD

The surviving pneumatics treatises provide a clue to the evolution
of the discipline, since both Hero and Philo begin by detailing the
simplest techniques available. The treatises seem to be compilations,
with the order of devices, like archaeological strata, loosely reflect-
ing the history of the discipline. Early examples are as simple as a
vessel inverted in water, to contrast the trapping of air inside with
the situation where the air is allowed to escape through a hole in
the bottom. This demonstrates that air is a body, and, second, that
trapped air, although lighter than the surrounding water, can nonetheless act on the suspended water. Other devices show that air can
pull water along with it to prevent a void from forming. A small vessel
suspended from one's lip after the air has been sucked out shows that a
heavier tissue – flesh – is drawn in following a lighter material – air –
with enough power to suspend the vessel. The clepsydra shows how
water can be held suspended in air; the siphon, how it can be made to
flow uphill. In Hellenistic times increasingly elaborate devices were
constructed on the basis of these techniques.

Ctesibius' use of compression opened up a whole new range of devices, some of which were included in the *pneumatica* collections, others elsewhere. The use of valve-and-piston produced a simple pump.[8] The most famous forced-air device is perhaps Ctesibius' water organ or *hydraulis*.[9] It contained a number of pipes through which air was forced by water pressure, producing sounds of different pitch. Air was pumped into the device by hand, displacing a column of water; the continuous pressure of the displaced water forced air out continuously into the pipe chamber.

We are told in a quotation from Aristocles that Plato had a large clepsydra resembling a water organ – the 'alarm clock' story discussed earlier – but the resemblance seems to be superficial. Athenaeus affirms that the water organ was unknown to Aristoxenus, a music theorist and student of Aristotle.[10] A late source, Tertullian, attributes a device of this kind to Archimedes,[11] but Tertullian could be mistakenly ascribing Ctesibius' device to the most famous inventor of bygone days.

Ctesibius improved the design of the water clock and added some mechanical embellishments.[12] The traditional outflow clepsydra had been known since Egyptian times; a version was found in the law courts of the classical Athenian Agora. It marked time by the rate at which a full vessel empties, and it had limitations for more precise calibration of time intervals, since the rate of flow varied with the pressure of the remaining head of water. A more sophisticated version, invented by Ctesibius, measured inflow into a lower vessel from an overflowing vessel placed above it.[13] Vitruvius describes Ctesibius' construction. A valve device regulated the influx of

---

[8] Based on examination of the available literary, archaeological and papyrological evidence, Oleson (1984), pp. 74–84, 301–25, concludes that a force pump like that invented by Ctesibius was in practical use in Roman imperial times.

[9] Athenaeus, *Deipn.* 4.174bff.; Philo, *Bel.* 77.27; Vitruvius, *de Arch.* 10.8.

[10] See Drachmann (1948), pp. 7ff.; Fleury (1993), pp. 179–204.

[11] Tertullian, *de Anim.* 14.

[12] These could be classified as pneumatic, although they are not strictly pressure-driven; or as part of *gnomics*; or possibly even as sphere-making, if they show the rotation of the heavens. This report is important for its early indication of toothed wheels.

[13] Drachmann (1948), pp. 17–19; Noble and Price (1968).

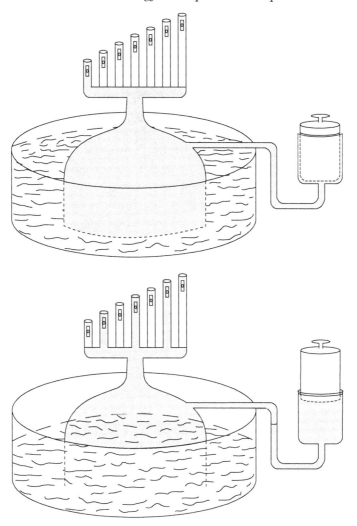

displaced water maintains constant
air pressure during pump action;
valves allow air to escape through
selected pipes

Figure 6 Sketch of Ctesibius' water organ, adapted from a drawing by James
A. Diamond.

water. The rising water level raised a float, connected to a bar by which a toothed drum was made to revolve. This rack-and-pinion in turn connected to other toothed wheels, causing other 'sideshows', *parerga*.[14] Stones fell, trumpets sounded, figures moved. Pointers marked the hour, although these needed to be reset manually to mark days and months.[15]

Archaeological evidence shows that clocks like this were in use. Noble and Price conjecture that the Tower of the Winds in the Athenian Agora contained some such inflow clepsydra, with piped water refilling an upper chamber that emptied into a lower chamber, adjusted so that the lower tank would fill in twenty-four hours. A float in the lower chamber was attached to a displayed marker, which would need to be reset by hand every day.[16] A horn of Aphrodite is also ascribed to Ctesibius: it seems to have been a wine-serving device that made a sound when the cap was released, apparently a prototype for the 'surprise vessel' collected by Philo and Hero.[17]

Other pneumatic devices are known from the surviving treatises. The first of these, that of Philo of Byzantium, forms one book of his nine-volume survey of mechanics. No Greek version has come down to us. A version of Philo's treatise that has survived in Latin contains much less material than the texts that have survived in Arabic. Carra de Vaux's 1903 edition is based on two Arabic manuscripts, one at Oxford and one at Istanbul. While there is considerable overlap with a Latin manuscript,[18] the two Arabic manuscripts include more devices: their authorship is not certain, and de Vaux emphasizes that the text he presents as Philo's may include later interpolations.[19] Hero's treatise, from the first century CE, survives in Greek and describes many similar devices. It contains a lengthy theoretical introduction that is independently interesting.

---

[14] Drachmann (1963a), p. 202.   [15] Vitruvius, *de Arch.* 9.8.4–6.

[16] Noble and Price (1968), pp. 345–51. They ascribe the device to Andronikos of Kyrrhos and date it to the second half of the first century BCE.

[17] Athenaeus, *Deipn.* 11.497d. See Drachmann (1948); Prager (1974); Ferrari (1984), p. 265.

[18] It was first published in 1870 and re-edited by Schmidt in 1899.

[19] De Vaux (1903), p. 35.

The two treatises between them record a number of different techniques for creating pneumatic effects. One involves suspending water in a situation where air cannot enter to replace it. Some devices are elaborations of the simple clepsydra. 'Surprise vessels', for example, are multi-chambered vessels from which different liquids can be made to flow at will by unstoppering different holes. The trick is to keep one's guests in suspense as to whether they will be served wine or water. Other versions heat and cool the trapped air, to produce movement: a vessel is first heated so that air is bubbled out through a side arm immersed in water; as the air in the vessel cools, water is drawn up to refill the void. In another, a candle trapped in a vessel consumes air and draws up water.

Another version of this is the siphon, a bent tube through which water will continue running once started, again to prevent a void space forming. Sometimes the siphon itself is the trick: a carved animal figure with an internal siphon can seem to drink water. A particularly useful variation of this is the intermittent or self-starting siphon, called a *diabētēs*. An outflow pipe is covered by an overturned cap; this permits water to enter the space between the cap and the outflow pipe. When water reaches the top of the outflow pipe the siphon will start and will continue emptying until the water level reaches the bottom of the cap. This device permits a steady water source not only to create an intermittent outflow, but also simultaneously to vary the water level – and hence the pressure – in the holding tank.

A different effect uses pressure to force out air. A stream flowing into an airtight holding tank can force out enough air to create sound in suitable pipes or whistles. The sound may emerge through carved figures, such as birds, which thus seem to sing. Besides incoming water, heat can also be used to drive out air, whether to produce sound alone or to move some other object. Hero's famous steam-driven sphere spinning on its axis – sometimes misleadingly referred to as a 'steam engine' – is of this variety.[20]

A device combining various effects is the self-regulator, wherein an arrangement of interconnecting pipes, floats and a shut-off valve

---

[20] Hero, *Spir.* 2.11.

maintains a constant water level in a bowl. The basic version involves a storage tank connected by pipes to a serving vessel. When water is removed from the serving vessel, the liquid refills to its former level. The storage tank is airtight and has a hidden bent pipe connecting it through the base to the serving vessel, and a visible refill pipe pouring into the serving vessel from above. Water will not pass through the refill pipe when the level in the storage tank is as high as the top of the bent connecting pipe, because there is nowhere for air to enter as replacement. But once some water is removed from the system, the refilling commences. If the system is airtight, the refilling will stop at a certain point (see Figure 7). In one of Philo's versions the storage tank is hidden behind a wall and can be refilled manually; in another, a storage tank in the roof of a pedestal dispenses water through a lion's mouth. Other versions are used to keep a constant level of oil in lamps.

The 'trick' is that the device responds to its environment, refilling the water that guests remove or 'sensing' when the level of the oil lamp is low. Otto Mayr drew attention to the creation of self-regulating or feedback systems, a type of device whose significance he thinks went unnoticed by the ancients.[21] A device apparently 'senses' when the water level is lowered and reopens the valve to refill it. This feedback system is a kind of device for which anthropomorphic description comes easily. Because it is designed to respond to external changes by restoring its initial state, it is readily described as 'perceiving' when a change has occurred that requires correction, or as 'striving' to retain an equilibrium state.

The idea of an interactive serving device is dressed up in the Arabic version of Philo's collection, so as to hide the entire workings inside a copper figure of a servant, within whose body multiple reservoirs and pipes are hidden. When a heavy bowl is placed in the servant's left hand, the weight of the bowl moves the arm downward and opens a connection between pipes; as air can then enter, water is correspondingly released through pipes leading out to an amphora in the servant's right hand, which fills up the bowl. The diagram of the

---

[21] Mayr (1970).

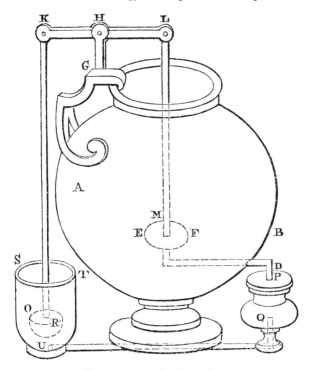

Figure 7 Water-level regulator.

piece, reproduced by de Vaux, suggests that a life-like representation was part of the effect. Although the technology is not new, the presentation in a self-contained and free-standing figure containing all the resources needed within it seems only to occur in the Oxford manuscripts and may be a later interpolation.[22]

Not all techniques depend on pressure and the void. Some use the introduction or removal of solid barriers to regulate the flow of water: taps and valves open and close passageways, blocking the flow. A tap might be a vertical cylinder in a sleeve with a hole drilled through horizontally so that when the hole aligns with the bore of a pipe, water flows through. Another device regulates flow by a flap-valve opened by a copper rod pushing back as the tap rotates. In

[22] De Vaux (1903); cf. Drachmann (1948), pp. 59–60; Berryman (2007a). See Prager (1974) on the history of the Greek text.

Hero's self-regulator, water flow is cut off when a float drops and, because it is attached to a rigid lever arm, a valve opens permitting water to flow through (Figure 7).

Controlled or intermittent water flow is used to work various devices, whether by varying water level or exploiting the differential weight of the water. The coordination of various otherwise simple effects can produce a fascinating complex device, with parts apparently responding to one another. Some devices explicitly imitate organisms: a bird or a horse that 'drinks' by means of an internal siphon, birds built around whistling pipes, a bird with wings that are lifted by the rising of a float. A drinking bird with sound effects, is described as seeming to be thirsty.[23] Particularly when these effects are dressed up with animal images and props to create a narrative context, the result can be a charming and even rather compelling imitation of animate reactions. The 'owl-and-birds', for example, coordinates the turning of an owl with the singing of birds: to the watchers' eyes it would seem as though the whistling of the birds were attracting the owl's attention, whereas in fact the same inflow of water produces both results in tandem.[24]

In another device Heracles shoots a serpent, which hisses; although both actions result from the release of the same trigger mechanism, the device is constructed to seem to the watcher as though the serpent hisses *because* it has been shot.[25]

Hero describes devices depending on fire to create the pressure; solar and wind power are occasionally pressed into use; one device is even worked by inserting a coin. Many devices require an agent to trigger them, whether by beginning the flow of water or lighting the fire, but the operation seems to be understood as independent of the agent: Hero describes the forcing upward of water in a pump as *automaton*, although an agent initiates the process.[26]

A number of new techniques were developed in the Hellenistic period, then, and simple techniques were elaborated into complex showpieces; the understanding of 'pneumatics' as a distinct field,

---

[23] Hero, *Spir.* 136.10–14.   [24] Philo, *De Ing. Spir.* 60; Hero, *Spir.* 16.
[25] Hero, *Spir.* 40.   [26] Hero, *Spir.* 70.10.

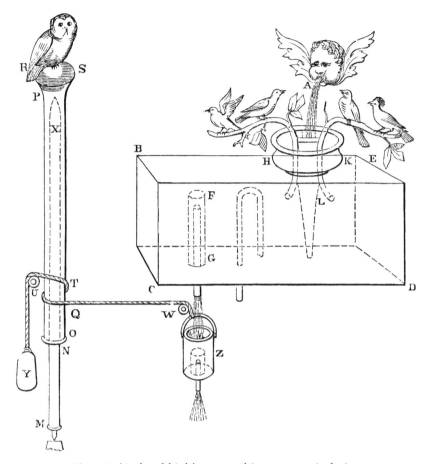

Figure 8 'Owl-and-birds', a water-driven pneumatic device.

described in technical manuals, seems to be Hellenistic. The *explanation* of pneumatic effects is a vexed question, both amongst the ancient sources and amongst modern interpreters. To gain a clearer picture of the evidence, it is necessary first to consider a view that has shaped scholarship on the subject for more than a century.

ANCIENT GREEK PNEUMATIC THEORY

I have already discussed the major theories of rarefaction effects and argued that these can be traced back to the fourth century. As in the fourth century, devices are said to work, rather vaguely, 'because there can be no void',[27] or 'by the tendency toward the void'.[28] In 1893 Hermann Diels advanced a bold conjecture that has dominated twentieth-century understanding of ancient pneumatic theory. Diels proposed that ancient pneumatic theory, which he took to be a single position broadly shared by Philo of Byzantium and Hero of Alexandria, centres around a notion he calls *horror vacui*, which he traces back through Philo to Strato of Lampsacus.[29] His reconstruction is based on Hero's introduction, which is taken to represent a unified view. He supposes that all theorists who take there to be forces acting against an extended void space in nature are largely in agreement,[30] and that they take the existence of this 'aversion' in nature to be explanatory.

Diels' article inaugurated an unfortunate tradition of treating ancient Greek phrases about 'motion towards a void' or 'by the void' as evidence of a common *theory*. The use of the medieval Latin tag *horror vacui* has caused confusion, since the phrase is often read as if it were a technical term for an explanatory theory[31] and seems to imply that void itself was thought to be explanatory of the movement, 'attracting' matter to it, or else that matter had a quasi-intentional aversion for void. Diels seems to read Hero's demonstrations of this effect, for example, as proving a theory and

---

[27] *nec fit hoc nisi quia locus vacuus esse non potest*, Philo of Byzantium, *De Ing. Spir.* 8.
[28] τῇ πρὸς τὸ κενούμενον ἀκολουθίᾳ: Galen *Art. Sang.* 1.3; cf. Galen, *Nat. Fac.* 2.6; *Ven. Sect. Er.*; Diels (1893), p. 105 n. 3. πρὸς γὰρ τὸ κενὸν ἡ φορά. Theophrastus, *Vent.* 5.33–5.
[29] See Drachmann (1948), pp. 90–1, for some problems with Diels' conjecture, which is defended by Gottschalk (1965) and Lehoux (1999). The multiplicity of sources is recognized by more recent scholarship, such as Tybjerg (2003), p. 446 n. 12, and the new edition of Strato in preparation by R. W. Sharples.
[30] This tendency is also echoed by Prager (1974), p. 18, who – while he disagrees with Diels on specifics, sees a dichotomy between Strato, Ctesibius and Philo on the one side, and the 'anti-vacuist, anti-atomic and ultimately anti-observational dialectics of "classic" Greece'. I suggest that the picture is more complex.
[31] As Edward Grant pointed out, even the medieval philosophers who coined the term *horror vacui* understood it as *explanandum*, not *explanans*: Grant (1981); cf. Prager (1974), p. 23.

not merely showing that there is *an effect to be explained*.[32] This simply muddies the waters.

Hero – as he tells us – borrows from various sources; they seem to have had very different views of the nature of matter. Rather than crediting matter with an aversion, he mentions several different accounts of the effect in question. In the most prominent discussion, the structure of matter is compared to that of grains of sand on a beach with air pockets between; by analogy, the particles of matter enclose void pockets. Hero claims that there is no amassed void space in nature, although one can be created artificially, and he details a respectable account of why it is that an artificially created void space tends to refill: the motion of bodies is quicker in a void, because nothing opposes or hinders them, until the bodies are touching one another.[33] This parallels a classic atomist argument, found in Lucretius and, I have argued, in earlier atomists.[34]

However, when it comes to the motion of water in a siphon, Hero's claim is not that a void forms artificially and then refills because of the quicker motion of the atoms, but that the air pulls the water along *because of the continuity of the water*.[35] This could only be compatible with the particle theory mentioned above if there were some additional cohesion of the particles when they are in contact, and that is not impeded by the presence of scattered void spaces.[36] It is hard to see how a 'continuity' account could be reconciled to a particle theory, especially as he had mentioned no interlocking barbs on the particles, such as atomists posit. Rather, Hero seems to be quoting a different account altogether of pneumatic effects

---

[32] Diels (1893), p. 107: 'Wie die Sandkörner Luft zwischen sich enthalten, so enthalten die Molekeln der Luft selbst Leeres zwischen sich. Daher die Elasticität, daher der horror vacui. Erstes Experiment: Saugt man aus einer enghalsigen kleinen Flasche die Luft aus, so bleibt sie an die Lippen hängen. Das Leere zieht das Fleisch an. Zweites Experiment.'

[33] *Spir.* 8.14–16.   [34] Berryman (1997), (2002c), (forthcoming 1).

[35] διὰ τὴν συνέχειαν, *Spir.* 34.26 (Schmidt).

[36] Drachmann, defending Hero's coherence, denies that the reference to the 'continuity' of water is meant to refer to 'glueing' at all, but merely to show that the water in the siphon cannot have pockets of air interspersed with water.

here – one found in some Peripatetic texts[37] and in Stoic theory – where 'continuity' or *sunecheia* is explanatory, since it prevents the formation of void.

Hero adds a third kind of explanation for the case of the person starting a siphon by suction. In this case, the Platonic explanation is pressed into service. The reason why wine is drawn up into a siphon when the person sucks out air from one end is that the person intaking air becomes fuller and that this presses on the surrounding air, setting up a sequence that creates a void at the surface of the wine, so that it is driven up into the siphon from below.[38]

There are occasional traces of the idea that void has an attraction. Besides saying that bodies *drift* in to refill a void because they encounter no resistance, claiming that the continuity of matter *pulls* bodies along to prevent void from forming, and claiming that circular currents *pushing* from behind create the conditions for upward movement, Hero is not above claiming outright at one point that *void draws* matter in to refill the emptied place.[39]

A fifth apparent account of the motion of matter against its natural tendency is found in the account of the *diabētēs*, an enclosed siphon where water is drawn up and then down through a central spout. The explanation stresses the greater length of the downward spout and says that the attraction comes about because of the greater depth of the spout.[40] There is a reference here to the idea of weights held in balance.[41] This might not have been intended as a complete explanation: the idea that the quantity of water in the upward and downward arms of the siphon is in equilibrium or imbalance appears elsewhere, but in conjunction with a claim about continuity of matter.

---

[37] I argue this in Berryman (1997) and Berryman (2002b).   [38] Hero, *Spir.* 36.23ff.

[39] ἐπισπωμένου τοῦ κενοῦ τὴν σάρκα πρὸς τὸ ἀναπληρωθῆναι τὸν κενωθέντα τόπον. Hero, *Spir.* 8.19–21 (Schmidt). See Prager (1974), p. 21, on the possible misreading of the text at *Spir.* 36.11.

[40] *Spir.* 42.14. A similar account of a siphon later shows that the greater downward position of the pipe is credited with drawing water: *Spir.* 146.11–12.

[41] Hero, *Spir.* 30.12–15; Drachmann (1948), p. 93, notes that Hero subsequently denies that weight is relevant.

Although most of the explanations cited above focus on rarefaction effects, a distinct phenomenon is involved when air is unnaturally compressed into a smaller space than it would normally occupy. Compression effects were not considered by the classical theories of matter; with Ctesibius' devices, however, they entered into the discussion of the nature of matter. While he certainly followed Philo in claiming that there is a natural elasticity or *eutonia* to certain materials, Hero did not stop at simply characterizing a macroscopic phenomenon but offered a theory of the microstructure of matter to account for these effects.

Aristotle had discussed an atomist argument to the effect that if a certain quantity of steam, for example, is able to condense into a kettleful of water, this must be because there were void spaces before into which the particles of matter condense. This type of explanation requires that the void spaces in air be considerable, that is, the kind of space one might expect to find between freely moving atoms in mutual collision, not merely the unfilled spaces remaining between close-packed particles that are in contact. Because Hero claims that the particles of air *are already in contact*[42] before they are compressed, he cannot be relying on the account that Aristotle cites. He says that the particles are squeezing against one another in a way that is *para phusin*, not according to nature.[43] Since the bodies are already in contact, the idea must be that the particles are deformed so that they can pack closer together. Round elastic particles can pack closer together if they are compressed so as to fit into the empty spaces, becoming in effect a cubic array. The volume of the particles does not change, but a change in shape from spherical to cuboid allows for closer packing, and hence a change in the volume occupied by the whole array. Apparently, in violation of atomist strictures, Hero is claiming that the particles fill up the void gaps by changing in shape.

---

[42] τὰ δέ τοῦ ἀέρος σώματα συνερείδει μὲν πρὸς ἄλληλα, *Spir.* 6.23–4 (Schmidt).

[43] παρὰ φύσιν τῶν σωμάτων πρὸς ἄλληλα θλιβομένων· ἀνέσεως δὲ γενομένης πάλιν εἰς τὴν αὐτὴν τάξιν ἀποκαθίσταται τῇ τῶν σωμάτων εὐτονίᾳ, *Spir.* 8.5–7 (Schmidt).

The problem is not only to explain the closer packing of a given volume of compressed air, but to account for the sudden and violent expansion of the air to its former volume when the pressure is released. Hero says that when the non-natural pressure is removed, the particles return to their former arrangement: this happens because of the elasticity, *eutonia*, of the particles. The particles themselves are unnaturally deformed under pressure; they spring back forcefully. Nothing in the atomist account of compression would account for this sudden force upon release, instead of a gradual drift back into the unoccupied space; previous accounts of the refilling of the void are all unconvincing when it comes to these new compression effects. Moreover, no previous natural philosophers had offered an account of elasticity: classic atomism, indeed, denies that individual particles could deform.

Readers of Hero seem to have misunderstood the account.[44] It is, I suggest, a new theory of matter, developed to explain the sudden and violent tendencies of Ctesibius' compression effects that can shoot a stream of water upward or fire a catapult. Just as the elasticity of sinew, horn and steel is considered by Philo in the context of ballistics, the elasticity of air particles is offered to account for the newly discovered 'spring of the air'. I shall return to the significance of this in Chapter 6.

THE STATUS OF MECHANICS REVISITED: NATURAL OR ARTIFICIAL?

The brief survey here and in Chapter 4 has considered some of the devices and theories developed by the most famous mechanical inventors of later antiquity. It does not claim to be exhaustive. Some early treatises on the lever and balance survive in the Arabic tradition, for example, and it is possible that these are based on other Greek originals that have been lost.[45] Other surviving Greek texts

[44] See, e.g., Sambursky (1962), p. 90, who thinks the particles were loose-packed, and spring back to their original *position*, not their original shape. This reading cannot take account of the role of *eutonia*. Furley (1989), p. 158, thinks *eutonia* is borrowed from the Stoics and is used to explain why particles are not always in contact.

[45] Duhem (1991), pp. 47–74.

describe devices or apply available techniques to practical prob-lems.[46] I have paid little attention to texts documenting the spread of engineering in public use, although the very extent of civil engineering in the Roman world could have contributed to a sense that human technology could imitate nature.[47] For example, a Latin poem from the late first century BCE celebrates the virtues of the water-driven flour mill in freeing people from toil;[48] Seneca records the building of stage devices that rise upward by them-selves, or devices that amaze the ignorant by falling apart or collapsing suddenly without an evident cause.[49] A number of stories of automata in Roman literature are associated with imperial glory: Suetonius records a silver Triton raised *per machinam* out of a lake and sounding a horn during a mock sea battle. It was staged by the emperor Claudius, who forced the builders of unsuccessful automata to compete in gladiatorial contests.[50]

The intention in outlining some of the major *philosophical* devel-opments in the Greek mechanics tradition is both to indicate the extent of involvement with natural philosophical questions by the mechanics, and also to set the stage for consideration of the reception of this body of work in natural philosophy But before examining the detailed evidence for the reception of Hellenistic mechanics, it is worth returning to the question of the status of mechanics in antiquity. Did the field of mechanics remain at that time, as some have claimed, insulated from natural philosophy? Were its products considered to be achievements of art working outside or against nature, mere trickery or a deceptive art? Or were there ancients who thought of mechanical creations as phenomena for natural philoso-phy to explain, and thus potentially as a way of investigating nature?

---

[46] For a discussion of Oreibasius' surgical stretching devices, see Drachmann (1963a), pp. 171–85; for Athenaeus, see p. 191.

[47] E.g. Manilius 4.259ff.

[48] Antipater, *Anthologia Graeca* 9.418; Oleson (1984), pp. 26, 370–85.

[49] Seneca, *Ep.* 88.22.

[50] Suetonius 5.21. Cf. Vitruvius, *de Arch.* 10.3, for machinery used in theatrical performances and gladiatorial shows: he notes the difficulty of producing these on time without cost overruns.

This question is an important one, since the assumption of the separation of mechanics from the natural philosophy of antiquity has dominated at least the history of science literature.

Mechanics is not the only discipline whose status in late antiquity might have been underestimated. Cuomo talks of a 'marginality thesis' concerning the impact of Greek mathematics. She challenges the widespread belief that Greek mathematics, including its branches such as mechanics, had little social, cultural or economic impact in late antiquity.[51] Her historical study of the social context – far beyond what I have been able to undertake here – has proved valuable in correcting the picture of the status of mathematics in the milieu of Pappus of Alexandria, in particular. This also helps to evaluate the reception of a more applied field such as mechanics. Cuomo's evidence of the prominence of engineers and architects and of the importance and prevalence of disciplines with a mathematical basis belies the idea that the late ancient Greek world marginalized mechanics. Her work indicates that – whatever the prejudice against the practical expressed by particular authors – this should not be taken to represent *the* ancient view of mechanics.[52]

There may be some justice to Diels' remark that the mechanics – among whom he includes Ctesibius and Philo as well as Hero – were dismissive of theoretical speculation.[53] However, I believe that this classic assessment is overstated and does not adequately represent the degree of permeation between mechanical practice and natural philosophical theory in late antiquity. Although in most texts of ancient mechanics the degree of theoretical sophistication lags far behind the practical, this does not diminish the reality of the attempt made by some to integrate the findings of mechanics within theoretical natural philosophy. And while some ancient Greek sources themselves draw a sharp division between the purity of mathematical theory and unsophisticated, untheorized mechanical practice, this is by no means a universal view. The distortions in the presentation of

---

[51] Cuomo (2000), pp. 2ff. See also Giannantoni (1984). Cuomo borrows the term from Sabra, who used it of Islamic science.
[52] Cuomo (2000), p. 92.   [53] Diels (1893), p. 107.

the figure of Archimedes are a case in point of the power of ideological propaganda. Modern tendencies to read technology as mere derivative application of theory, and not as the locus of experimentation or as a heuristic, make it easy to accept these distorted presentations at face value.

I have tried to show that there does seem to be some effort in the mechanical tradition to draw on natural philosophy to explain its discoveries. The theory of the lever in the Aristotelian *Mechanica* accounts for its effects in terms of the geometry of the circle; Archimedes' more abstract and mathematical approach begins from questions about equilibrium of balances and the stability of bodies in a fluid medium. As mentioned in the previous chapter, Archimedes' theory of the pressure of displaced water might have been developed as a response to Ctesibius' use of water pressure to work devices. Philo's and Hero's discussions of the elasticity of matter were probably inspired by Ctesibius' compression effects as well as by the use of spring in swords and torsion-driven ballistic devices. The coordination of different forces to a single result is a theme in a number of mechanics texts.

Moreover, the presentation of the mechanics tradition draws on the methods of the best scientific work of the day.[54] Geometry served as the standing example of a science and its method as the pattern to imitate: there are some indications that mechanical treatises tried to work within this genre by first laying out general principles and then explaining – in the form of individual 'proofs' or 'problems' – the construction of various devices, along the lines of geometrical demonstrations.[55] In Hero's text individual discussions follow the style of mathematical *problēmata*, in which a figure to be constructed is specified in the opening sentence, sometimes in the hypothetical: 'if we want such a result', or 'if a device of such a kind is used, the following effect occurs'. The construction is sometimes formulaically announced[56] and the instructions given in the hortatory, often

---

[54] Asper (unpublished) details the syllogistic structure of the Aristotelian *Mechanica*, imitating the presentation Aristotle stipulates for scientific knowledge.

[55] Netz (1999); Tybjerg (2004); Russo (2004), p. 185.

[56] ἔστι δὲ ἡ κατασκευὴ τοιαύτη, Hero, *Spir.* 66.7–8 (Schmidt); 70.12; 136.13–14; cf. also *Spir.* 80.5; 84.8–9; 88.3; 116.12; etc.

beginning with the positing of a certain figure, labelled as in geo-metrical figures.[57]

This use of the structure of a demonstrative science might remain somewhat superficial. For example, the introduction to Hero's *Pneumatics* presents a compendium of various physical the-ories that explain the effects to be demonstrated and looks little like the careful articulation at the beginning of Euclid's *Elements*.[58] The degree of theorization of the construction of devices might not have been extensive and might have been limited to the problem of building devices to a given scale, not to the causal theory underlying their operation. Where Philo of Byzantium complains that many have not been able to grasp the *theory* of device building, he likewise refers to the mathematics involved in copying a successful device on a different scale of magnitude.[59] Philo even doubts how far 'mechanical methods' (*tais ek tōn mēchanikōn methodois*) can help in determining correct proportions for mechanical devices. As with the correction of optical illusions, only experience can really determine these.[60] Pappus concedes that there is much to mechanics that is not theoretical. While study of principles is deemed necessary for the inventor, the person desiring merely practical skills is instructed to focus on those alone. Because the study of causes falls to natural philosophy and not to the *mathematica mixta*, it might not have been considered problematic to view mechanics as a 'theoretical' study that nevertheless did not engage with fundamental causal explanations.

It is not always clear whether the devices described in ancient technical manuals were in fact based on experience, or whether they were theory-driven extensions of the techniques that had been developed in simpler devices. Modern scholars sometimes doubt the viability of descriptions found in Hero or Philo or Vitruvius.

---

[57] For a detailed account of the norms and practices of Greek mathematics, see Netz (1999). For the close connection between geometry and mechanical construction, see Bowen (1983); Tybjerg (2004).

[58] Netz (1999), pp. 92–5, suggests the *Elements* really begins with an introduction laying out its central terms, and that the perception of the introductory section of the *Elements* as axiomatic in structure is partly a function of modern typography.

[59] *Bel.* 2; cf. Biton 53.   [60] Philo, *Bel.* 4.50–1.

Were Ctesibius' piston catapults really practicable? What kind of ship could Archimedes have realistically towed single-handedly? Did Vitruvius' hodometer work, or was it merely imaginary? Could Hero's more elaborate automata be constructed, using the materials and techniques available? Questions such as these arise because of the nature of the materials and the techniques for cutting and planing and grinding: pistons would need to be perfectly regular; toothed wheels exactly cut to mesh; surfaces smooth; materials light yet strong.

The question is not whether given mechanical techniques were available, but whether the engineering could have been perfected to make them work as well as is claimed. Hero knows how the components of his devices work under the best of circumstances: toothed wheels will mesh in a certain way; the relationship between loads and powers can be calculated; the power required to move a body on an almost frictionless surface is said to be minimal. Using the best theories of the quantitative proportionalities involved, Hero is willing to speculate about what could be accomplished if the shortcomings of the material could be eliminated. When Archimedes offers to move the earth, he is relying on his theory, and ignoring certain practical constraints. It seems that some of the mechanics were sufficiently confident in their grasp of the theory to speculate ahead of practice, while others, such as Philo and Vitruvius, were suspicious of this approach and pointed to its failures. Natural philosophy, we will see, raised other objections to the extension of theory.

Another issue concerning the status of mechanics is its perceived association with wonder and surprise, and whether this was thought to exclude its results from natural philosophy. I suggested earlier that they were not so excluded, and that the trope of wonder or surprise has been mistakenly overstated in the light of later classifications. In ancient mechanics the 'surprise' factor – the sense that devices move themselves as if they were alive, or that effects come from nowhere – is partly fostered by hiding the causal processes and partly brought about in a way that depends on violating expectations. Mechanics is surprising because it places parts in combinations not typically found

in nature – or considerably more complex than those readily observ-
able in nature – and produces effects we do not expect.

However, as I stressed earlier, this is not a reason for thinking
that mechanics was taken to work contrary to nature, or that the
element of surprise classifies it as magic. Rather, its workings ultimately depend on certain combinations of relatively familiar interactions: 'to those who perceive the cause', there is nothing especially
remarkable. Devices produce effects by the sheer combination of
individual interactions, none of which in isolation are remarkable,
but in coordination, with careful sequencing and a showy presentation,
can be very startling. And where the individual interactions are
less familiar – such as the movement of water uphill in a siphon –
the devices isolate and highlight an effect that could occur in nature
and thus show what nature can do.

In sum, negative assessments of the degree of theorization of
ancient Greek mechanics need to be reconsidered. Whatever the
limitations of the discipline, it is clear that a considerable body of
work developed and its theoretical foundations were given serious
thought. The common view that ancient mechanics was purely
practical is based partly on a misguided Platonizing tendency in
authors such as Plutarch, and partly on a mistaken view that the
tradition Galileo is rejecting goes back to ancient Greek thought.
The question of the philosophical reception of ancient Greek
mechanics should be approached as an open one, not a topic the
ancient Greeks would have ruled out of court on *a priori* grounds.
Evidence for that reception will be considered in Chapter 6.

The philosophical reception
of mechanics in antiquity

In outlining the history of the discipline, I have already indicated a number of ways in which specific theories and concepts provoked philosophical responses from the mechanical theorists themselves. I shall now consider evidence from ancient Greek natural philosophers – including philosophically inclined medical theorists – concerning the reception of ideas from mechanics.

On a number of specific issues, natural philosophers engaged with the implications of mechanical theory and took seriously the question of its relationship to natural philosophy. There is, moreover, some evidence of a commitment, in a few ancient thinkers, to the use of mechanics as a *heuristic*. There are reports in late antiquity of those who considered whether the natural world might be understood to 'work like that': to function in ways that could be illuminated by appeal to the working artifacts that were available at the time. This latter evidence tends to cluster in three areas: the functioning of organisms, the motion of the heavenly bodies, and – at a more general level – the operation of causality in nature as a whole in relation to a directing intelligence.[1]

The existence of complex working artifacts exhibiting regular, pre-programmed causal sequences in their operation showed vividly what could be achieved by material arrangement alone. This, in turn, threatened some of the classic arguments for teleological explanations,

---

[1] Price (1964) notes that the two most common points of analogy between artifacts and nature, in the history of mechanistic thinking, are the heavenly bodies and animals. The third point of comparison could arise in the context of either of these.

which are typically based on the impossibility of adequate explanation of the phenomena using the resources of materialism alone. Sometimes the ensuing discussion was framed around the need for intelligent direction to produce an orderly result, in contrast to the possibility of complex causal chains unfolding reliably without ongoing intelligent direction. Sometimes the issue was posed as a question whether mere structural rearrangements of parts could explain the complex processes in nature, challenging the need to treat qualitative change as irreducibly different in kind, and the need to posit irreducible powers to guide natural processes. In late antiquity mechanics not only presented new ideas on specific topics in natural philosophy; the machine analogy also challenged the arguments of teleologists about the divide between living and non-living, between human and divine art.

The evidence presented here is scattered, and less than conclusive as to the extent of the impact of mechanical technology on ancient natural philosophy. I do not mean to suggest that the philosophical reception of mechanics was comparable to that in the early modern period. Little is known of the proponents of this approach: there are shadowy figures, including unnamed doctors, the mechanic Theodorus, the unknown author of the *de Mundo*, and other anonymous opponents. Still, their ideas were considered important enough to be discussed by Galen and Alexander, and by Neoplatonists, including Plotinus, Proclus, Simplicius and Philoponus. There are reactions to a mechanical conception of nature in some Christian writings of late antiquity.

In the post-Aristotelian context, the interpretation of teleology in nature seems to have acquired a higher 'metaphysical mortgage' than it perhaps had in Aristotle himself.[2] Stoicism, Galenic medicine and Neoplatonism tended to present teleological explanations as grounded in the nature of things, requiring the existence of explanatorily basic properties. It is against *this* understanding of teleology that a 'mechanical hypothesis' can be most clearly formulated.

---

[2] The phrase is from Solmsen (1960), p. 92, who uses it in a different context. Interpretation of Aristotle's teleology is of course a vexed topic: see Berryman (2007b) for a development of this contrast.

If machines showed us a way in which apparently goal-directed processes could be realized by structural arrangements of the material components, without ongoing intelligent direction, the argument for ascribing certain kinds of teleological properties to natural things would be undermined.

It is important to remind ourselves that in the modern period too the impact of mechanical technology and the machine analogy on natural philosophy took different forms. Mechanics can serve as a heuristic: steering speculation away from certain kinds of answers towards others; providing a touchstone or point of reference for deciding which properties can be ascribed to matter, what kinds of causal connections to expect, what kinds of powers to attribute; indicating how design might be realized in matter without ongoing intelligent direction; or suggesting what relationship to anticipate between properties of a whole and the properties of its parts.

Discussion of 'mechanistic' thinking in antiquity has, to date, focused principally on the atomists, or on the question whether Aristotle's physics contains elements of a 'mechanics'. Some scholars have noted the importance of mechanics for medical theories, but only a few have thought there was much to say about the impact of mechanics on post-Aristotelian natural philosophy more broadly. By collecting here a miscellany of scattered evidence – from a long time span and a variety of intellectual contexts – I hope to make a case for renewed attention to the impact of Hellenistic mechanics on ancient Greek natural philosophy. This is offered, not as a definitive account, but as an invitation to further consideration of the question.

MECHANICAL THEORY IN NATURAL PHILOSOPHY

Scholarly literature has certainly noted, in very general terms, that mechanics contributed to the development of empirical methods. Ernst Mach challenged the Baconian view that the ancient Greeks did not benefit from experience or experiment, pointing to Greek mechanics.[3] Sambursky noted the application of mathematics to the

---

[3] Mach (1907), p. 4. See von Staden (1975).

study of motion in 'statics'[4] and recognized the methodological value
of systematic field trials, improvement of prototypes and formal-
ization of results in Hellenistic ballistics.[5] Clagett recognized the
presence of experimentation in the Greek pneumatics tradition, as
well as in statics and applied mechanics.[6] Edelstein noted the importance of Philo's articulation of an ideal of progress through systematic experimentation and cumulative refinement of technique.[7] These
scholars challenged negative assessments of the role of experiment
and experience in Greek science.[8] But even among defenders of
Greek science, the role of mechanics is not always given its due,
sometimes because of a tendency to divide the field along modern
lines, sometimes because its contributions are assessed in terms of
their closeness to modern theories rather than their contribution to
the thought of the day.

The claims of mechanics are not always taken at face value by
natural philosophers. Still, the reasons given for rejecting such claims
are very specific and speak against the existence of a *prima facie*
separation in kind that would limit the ideas of the mechanics to
artificial contexts and render them irrelevant to natural philosophy.
That is, the conclusion is not that certain relationships apply only in
art and not nature, but that specific claims made by mechanics
concerning the generality of their results are rejected.

The perceived relationship of mechanics to other disciplines is
indicated most clearly by taxonomy. Aristotle's inclusion of
mechanics alongside astronomy, optics and music is echoed in a
number of ancient works: not only writers on mechanics, but
philosophers in the Aristotelian and Neoplatonist traditions and
the Stoic Geminus endorse this classification.[9] In late antiquity the
Aristotelian *Mechanica* was considered part of Aristotle's corpus, if

---

[4] Sambursky (1956), pp. 3–4, 238.   [5] Sambursky (1956), p. 236.
[6] Clagett (1957), pp. 29–31. Philo's *Pneumatics* has been described as the first
surviving experimental treatise: see Prager (1974), p. 1.
[7] Edelstein (1967), p. 403.
[8] Most famously Koyré: see G. E. R. Lloyd (1987), pp. 215ff.
[9] Alexander, *in Metaph.* 251.23; *in Top.* 22.22; Proclus, *in Euc.* 39–41; Philoponus, *in
Cat.* 119.6; *in A Po.* 119.22ff.; Olympiodorus, *Prol.* 7.33.

not one of the more studied texts in the Neoplatonist curriculum.[10]
The *Problemata* ascribed to Alexander of Aphrodisias alludes to a
whole class of 'mechanical contrivances' working by similar principles.[11] Aristotelians occasionally use mechanics in organic contexts:
the *Problemata* collection in the Aristotelian corpus makes use of the
principle of leverage to explain erection in male organisms, perhaps by
analogy to the puppets Herodotus describes that had moving phalluses
worked by strings. Testicles are compared to counterweights moving
an external appendage as if it were a lever.[12] The pseudo-Alexander
Problemata also refers to the Aristotelian *Mechanica*. There, the motion
of long hair is explained by comparing it to the motion of a lever,
which moves more when it is further from a fulcrum.[13] Although
not particularly far-reaching, these two passages at least show
that the Aristotelians recognized no prohibition on applying ideas
from mechanics to natural things. The idea that the limbs work
by leverage has precedent in Aristotle and is a commonplace in
discussions of animal motion.

One perceived peculiarity of mechanical devices was to show
how a mover with one kind of motion could produce a result
different in kind.[14] Aristotle himself recognizes this feature, referring to a cart or an automaton to illustrate the idea that animal self-
movers can transform one kind of cause into an effect of a different
kind.[15] However, as Sambursky notes, Aristotle is equivocal in his
recognition of this possibility, arguing that the soul must be moved
with the motion it imparts.[16] A. C. Lloyd identifies a common
assumption in ancient theories of causation, which he calls the
'transmission theory of causation', based on the view of causation

---

[10] E.g. Simplicius, *in Cat.* 4.26; Olympiodorus, *Prol.* 7.33; Bottecchia Dehò
(2000), p. 7.
[11] [Alexander] *Pr.* 1.95.7. The devices mentioned here are from different branches of
the discipline.
[12] *Pr.* 4.23, 879a15ff.   [13] [Alexander] *Pr.* 4.63.3
[14] For the idea that the distinctive contribution of mechanical devices is to show how
a mover can cause a motion different from that which it has itself, see Sambursky
(1962), p. 105.
[15] Aristotle, *MA* 7, 701b2ff.   [16] Sambursky (1962), p. 105.

as the transfer to another body of a property already possessed by the mover.[17] Mechanical devices were seen to violate this stricture, showing how to turn straight-line motion into circular, or vice versa; how to transmit motions in different planes or in reverse direction; or how to use the downward fall of water to produce effects as varied as the whistling of birds or the pulling of ropes. Sambursky aptly describes Philoponus as displaying a 'mechanistic attitude' when he challenges Aristotle's claim that the soul is moved by the same kind of motion it imparts, citing a cart and *sphaira* as examples.[18]

Assumptions of mechanical theory, particularly the ideas associated with the workings of balance and lever, found their way into some discussions of the natural philosophers. Archimedes' work on the mathematics underlying notions such as heaviness and balance seems to have helped to consolidate the understanding of the category of 'mechanics' as a field not limited to the artificial, but concerned with the movement of heavy bodies in general. Although these discussions do not always wear their mechanical origins on their sleeves, the derivation can be inferred.

Mechanics also complicated the treatment of weight. The Aristotelian *Mechanica*, because it recognizes that weights at different distances from a fulcrum have a different effect, distinguishes the notion of weight or *baros* from that of downward tendency or *rhopē*. Wolff suggests that Hipparchus' theory of the relationship between *baros* and *rhopē* echoes the distinctions made in the Aristotelian text;[19] Hipparchus' theory in turn inspired Galileo's impetus theory.[20] Certainly Simplicius, in his discussion of the truth of Hipparchus' theory, appeals to the case of a weight in a balance to argue his point.[21] Indeed, there is other evidence that Hipparchus was familiar with the views promulgated in the Aristotelian text, if it is true that – as Wolff suggests – Hipparchus' explanation of the relationship between the forces

---

[17] A. C. Lloyd (1976).   [18] Philoponus, *in de An.* 106.25; Sambursky (1962), p. 106.
[19] Wolff (1988), pp. 493–7.   [20] Noted by Krafft (1970a), p. xv.
[21] Simplicius, *in Cael.* 265.29–266.1.

acting on a projectile merely adopts one of the alternatives offered in the *Mechanica*.[22]

Alexander of Aphrodisias cites Archimedes' work on centres of weight and the equilibrium of solids:[23] he introduces a problem from this work into the discussion of the resting of the earth at the centre of the cosmos.[24] Proclus claims that the idea that weights in balance produce movement and rest has precedent in Plato's *Timaeus*.[25] Although this may be reading quite a bit into Plato's text, it speaks to Proclus' interest in integrating mechanical theory into natural philosophy. Proclus' surviving commentary on Euclid's *Elements* shows his commitment to the importance of the *mathematica mixta* and his belief that the study of these fields is part of Platonic natural philosophy. Proclus not only includes equilibrium theory squarely within Platonic theory: his reference to the production of both *motion* and *rest* implies that he takes the theory of the balance and the theory of the lever to be connected. Far from marginalizing mechanics, he is granting it a philosophical pedigree.

The impact of mechanical theory can be seen in discussion of problems involving circular rotation. The theoretical discussions of the power of mechanical devices connect that power to circular motion: both the issue of its complex composition, and the different trajectories of different points moving at different speeds on the same radius. Explanation of the power of the lever requires treating circular motion as compound, in tension with a commonplace philosophical doctrine. The tension is not easily resolved by treating mechanical action as distinct from nature: as noted above, the *Mechanica* applies its results to natural cases, while Vitruvius takes the art of building machinery to be derived from nature, in particular from studying the revolution of the spheres.[26] The nature of circular motion was

---

[22] Wolff (1987), pp. 101–2; (1988), p. 495, following Krafft (1970a), pp. 75ff., who notes the terminological similarities.

[23] Simplicius cites Archimedes a few times in his commentaries, although not the work of Pappus or Hero. Philoponus mentions Pappus once.

[24] Simplicius, *in Cael.* 543.30.   [25] Proclus, *in Euc.* 41.

[26] *De Arch.* 10.1.4. Thorndike (1929), p. 187, takes this remark as 'a feeble effort to introduce the factor of astrological influence'.

contested in natural philosophy. Xenarchus, an Aristotelian working in the late first century BCE, doubts the simplicity of circular
motion because the parts of the celestial sphere nearer the pole
move more slowly than parts closer to the equator.[27] This parallels
the concern in the *Mechanica* about the motion of points on a
radius.

Debate about this issue was partly inspired by Aristotle's argument for the fifth element, which requires the simplicity of circular
motion as a premise. Xenarchus argued that any argument based on
the simplicity of circular motion would apply equally to the cylindrical helix. Proclus rejects the claim that the cylindrical helix is
simple on the grounds that it is analysable into two different components.[28] There are criteria available under which the helix counts
as simple – the curve is homoiomerous, each part able to be superimposed on any other – but the reason for counting it as compound
stems from the view of the mathematical form as a product of two
motions.[29] Again, this approach to considering lines as products of
motions might echo discussions in mechanics.

Although there were dissenters such as Philo, mechanical theory
held that forces causing motion produce a compound result, and
not that the greater force predominates. Galen discusses the view
that two forces acting obliquely to one another will produce a
compound result dependent on the relative strengths and directions
of the components. Where one force is much greater than the other,
he says, the smaller is not destroyed, although it is not apparent in
the composite.[30] A strong wind at sea does not destroy the power of
the rowers but merely makes their efforts unapparent. We see this
most clearly in the case of a bird that is able to hover in a strong
wind: it is taken as evident that a good deal of effort is required to
remain in one place.[31] Forces are inferred to be acting on a body
that is standing still.

---

[27] Simplicius, *in Cael.* 24.21ff.   [28] Proclus, *in Euc.* 105–6.

[29] On difficulties in understanding Proclus' discussion of whether the circle is also
complex, because it is composed from non-uniform motions, see Morrow (1970),
p. 86 n. 40.

[30] ἀφανίζεσθαι, Galen, *UP* 3.70.11ff.   [31] Galen, *MM* 4.402.12ff.

The principle of composition of motion was accepted by other figures, including the astronomers Sosigenes and Geminus.[32] Simplicius quotes Sosigenes' explanation of the use of the parallelogram to find not only the direction but also the speed of the composite motion.[33] He emphasizes that the resultant speed is not reached by adding the two components: it is less than the sum but is nevertheless composed from them. Philoponus, commenting on Aristotle's denial that sideways motion is opposite to upward motion, explains this remark using a parallelogram for the addition of motions.[34] Instead of impeding one another, the two separate motions work together to produce a motion along the diagonal: they do not interfere with each other's motion *per se*, only the goal that each motion had separately.

However, there does not seem to have been a more general agreement on a mathematical model for composing 'powers' or 'forces'. Qualities such as hot and cold were regarded as 'powers', but there were different views as to whether and how they could be given a quantitative treatment. Philoponus argues that amassing qualities increases their efficacy, so that putting together two similar parts would more than double the power of the whole.[35] He cites as evidence the fact that a piece of wood will burn more quickly in a large flame than in a small one, to suggest that qualities are proportionally more efficacious in larger concentrations.[36] Another case brought to support this view concerns the addition of weights: he claims that two equal weights added together will have more than twice the weight, whereas dividing a weight in half leaves each part with less than half the weight of the whole. This is regarding weight as a *quality* inherent in the body, rather than a *quantity*; his point seems to depend on a general doubt that the relationship between whole and parts is necessarily linear. We will see other qualms about

---

[32] Simplicius, *in Cael.* 501.3–8; Proclus, *In Euc.* 106; Micheli (1995), pp. 61–2.

[33] Simplicius, *in Cael.* 500.22–501.11.

[34] Philoponus, *in Ph.* 842.20–8; Sambursky (1962), pp. 88–9.

[35] Philoponus, *in Ph.* 420.7; Sambursky (1962), p. 67.

[36] Philoponus, *in Ph.* 420.18–20.

whether the quantitative claims of mechanics can be accommodated to qualitative change.

Sambursky explains this passage by reference to the doctrine of natural motion, which makes the weight of a body equivalent to the form, like the soul of an organism, accounting for its natural tendencies.[37] In such a context there would be no reason to anticipate a simple mathematical relationship to hold between the weight of a whole and the weight of its parts. This is in contrast to the treatment of weight fostered by mechanics, with its use of a balance to compare weights to one another or to the powers that can hold them in balance. Mechanical theory suggests that force and weight should be treated as quantities.[38] However, other examples suggest that the issue is not peculiar to weight, but that it is regarded as a general rule – and the explanation of the paradox of the heap – that qualities are more effective *en masse*.[39]

In the context of mixtures of different parts blending into a new whole, it is easier to see why the contribution of the parts to the whole might not seem to be straightforwardly linear. Philoponus reiterates and develops Aristotle's idea that the 'powers' of dissimilar ingredients are only present in potential in a mixture.[40] Aristotle had used the notion of potential in explaining how a genuinely new compound is created, not merely a juxtaposition of the ingredients. That the powers of the ingredients are present 'only in potential' explains how a genuinely new fusion can have been created without disabling the powers of the ingredients from in some way contributing towards determining the properties of the resulting mixture.[41] One suggestion as to why the contribution of the parts to a whole in cases of similar ingredients might not be straightforwardly linear also uses this idea that the parts are only present 'in potential' in a whole. Thus we should not expect to be able to assess the power that each part would have taken separately by considering

[37] Sambursky (1962), p. 67.
[38] Sambursky (1962), p. 83 notes that Ammonius explicitly classifies *dunamis* or force in the category of quantity: Ammonius, *in Cat.* 55.4–9.
[39] Cf. Themistius *in Ph.* 207.32–208.11.
[40] On this, see De Haas (1999).   [41] Aristotle, *GC* 1.10.

only the power that each contributes while part of a whole or vice versa.[42]

This issue comes up in one of the most far-reaching discussions concerning the projection of the proportional relations between parameters involved in motion. Archimedes' claim that he could move the earth was apparently regarded as a statement of the ability of mechanics to be able to move any given weight with a given power, and indeed to be able to calculate the mechanical devices required to do so. Since he was thought to have said this in the context of hauling a ship single-handedly, his assertion was taken as a direct challenge to Aristotle's 'ship hauler' problem. Aristotle had asserted that the fact that a given number of men can haul a ship does not license us to conclude that a single man can haul the ship a proportion of that distance alone, or haul it the entire distance himself in proportionally more time. The commentators on Aristotle's *Physics* discuss Archimedes' assertion as a response to this passage, and they offer different explanations of why a general claim made by mechanics cannot be true.

The most extensive discussion is in Simplicius' commentary, which shows the argumentative context against which the relevant passage of Aristotle was read in late antiquity. Simplicius challenges Archimedes' claim that he could move the earth, objecting that it is not possible for any given power to move any given weight.[43] Simplicius' objection is not about the practicality of building a suitable device to the appropriate scale, but about the claim that the interrelationships between power, weight, distance and time are linear and open to indefinite extension. He takes Archimedes, that is, to be making a natural philosophical claim about the indefinite extrapolation of the mathematical relationships found in mechanics. Simplicius defends Aristotle's claim that we cannot extrapolate from the fact that a hundred haulers move a ship to the claim that one hauler could move a hundredth part of the ship alone, rejecting the assumption that linear relationships between quantities can be projected indefinitely.

[42] Sambursky (1962), pp. 67–8.   [43] Simplicius, *in Ph.* 1110.2–5.

Simplicius apparently sees Archimedes' mechanical theory as requiring the assumption that the properties of a whole are a sum of the properties of the parts. Because parts only exist in the whole in potential, he reasons, the kinds of inferences offered by mechanics do not hold.[44] Simplicius seems to treat the existence of limits as an instance of a more general phenomenon, and one that denies the truth of a certain kind of materialism that treats composites as mere aggregates.

Simplicius' argument focuses on the idea that there are boundaries for certain changes to occur.[45] He elaborates on the parallel Aristotle draws to the claim that there is a least amount of millet that will make a sound when it falls.[46] This case is compared to that of the ship, which has a minimum threshold of force to make it move at all. By extension, Simplicius argues that there is also an upper boundary of weight beyond which it is not possible to move the ship any distance, nor by any corporeal power.[47] He resists Archimedes' attempt to use devices to multiply the weight that can be moved with a given power, because he thinks there are minimal limits to the force required for moving a given weight. Simplicius is not challenging the existence of proportionalities between power, weight, distance and time, which were indeed recognized by Aristotle.[48] The challenge is to Archimedes' claim to be able to extend these proportional relationships indefinitely.

This is a different response to the 'ship hauler' problem from that of Philoponus, who depends directly on the fact that parts are only present in the whole to explain this phenomenon.[49] That is, rather than suggesting that the relationships hold only within fixed limits, he is denying that we should expect to find direct proportionality holding within any domain. The contribution of a part to a whole is compared to the contribution made by dissimilar letters to a word, not to the contribution of similar parts in a composite whole.

---

[44] Simplicius, *in Ph.* 1109.5–13.   [45] On this doctrine, see de Haas (1997), (1999).
[46] Aristotle, *Ph.* 7.5, 250a20.   [47] Simplicius, *in Ph.* 1110.10–12.
[48] De Gandt (1982), p. 100.
[49] Philoponus, *in Ph.* 881.4–16; Sambursky (1962), pp. 67–8.

One factor that may support this emphasis on the whole rather than the contribution of each part is suggested by Themistius (fourth century CE). In discussing a case where the addition of an extra person might enable the ship to be moved, or an extra weight might tip an equilibrium, Themistius emphasizes that we should not attribute the effect to the added part, but to the whole.[50]

Themistius also discusses Aristotle's problem, indicating that there is a good deal of investigation of the issue.[51] He notes that the proportions sometimes hold, in such cases as men moving architectural blocks, but in other cases they do not.[52] He tries to find an explanation for the lower limit to the relationship between the number of haulers and the distance hauled, reasoning that subdivision of masses changes other factors such as the shape. He also notes a geometrical difference in the relationship of total area to surface area, connecting the differences in shape and surface area to the amount of surface contact. This move is perhaps an attempt to explain the validity of Aristotle's insight without directly challenging Archimedes' claim, showing that additional factors need to be recognized.

There are two somewhat different strategies here. One is to deny that wholes are sums of parts, and to reject any expectation of a linear relationship between the properties of the parts and the properties of the whole. The other is to admit those relationships within a restricted domain, but to suppose that there are boundaries for their application. The latter idea – most prominent in Simplicius' response – is linked to the doctrine of *minima naturalia*.[53] This notion, which originated in a passing remark of Aristotle's, was reinforced by an appeal to phenomena indicating that there were sharp boundaries for the supervenience of given qualities. Philoponus, who was interested in the extent of quantitative relationships between the properties of components and the properties of a resulting composite, points to chemical changes wherein the

---

[50] Themistius, *in Ph.* 207.10ff.
[51] Themistius, *in Ph.* 208.12ff.; Sambursky (1962), p. 66.
[52] Themistius, *in Ph.* 207.12–13.   [53] On this see De Haas (1997); Murdoch (2001).

relationship between changes in the matter and changes in the resulting qualities – 'form' – is not simply linear.[54] Heating honey changes
the matter gradually, but produces a sudden 'point-like' change in the
colour and fluidity of the honey. He argues that the properties of the
resulting composite cannot be regarded as a *product* of the properties of
the parts, because of the existence of sharp boundaries for the supervenience of certain properties. Rather, these phenomena support the
view of forms as ontologically independent entities that accrue to
suitable material conditions.[55] He thus offers empirical reasons for
thinking that any quantitative correlations between cause and effect
might hold in limited domains but cannot necessarily be extrapolated.
The problem of thresholds thus speaks in favour of the Neoplatonist
approach to natural philosophy, on grounds internal to natural philosophy, not merely *a priori* metaphysical commitments to the causal
priority of form. Galen's notion of 'indescribable' properties, which
Copenhaver links to the tradition of 'occult qualities', likewise seems
to recognize that some qualities seem not to be accounted for by
the properties of the elements composing things.[56] A fundamental
assumption of mechanical theory is thus at odds with the metaphysical
picture of the matter–form relationship needed to account for the
properties of composites.

These responses to mechanical theory raise some fundamental
issues about the nature of the universe and the methodology for
studying the natural world. The Neoplatonist response, portraying
the existence of limits as part of the larger metaphysical structure of
the universe, is not, of course, the only possible response to the
evident exaggeration in Archimedes' claim. Some mechanics treat
friction as a factor that can be effectively eliminated from discussion by constructing idealized contexts in which it is minimized.
Themistius alludes to the quantity of surface contact, but the

---

[54] Philoponus, *in Ph.* 97.21ff.; cf. De Haas (1997), (1999); Berryman (2002e), (2005).
   On the notion of 'latitude' of forms, see Sorabji (2002); on the related notion of
   'fitness' or 'suitability', see Todd (1972), Sambursky (1962), (1963).
[55] The traditional translation of *epigignomai*, 'supervene', does not exactly correspond to its current technical meaning in contemporary philosophy.
[56] Copenhaver (1984); Hutchison (1982); Henry (1986); Anstey (2000).

commentators do not mention Hero's methods for eliminating thresholds from consideration.

In summary, the evidence shows that late antique natural philosophers acknowledged and engaged with some implications of the weightlifting branch of mechanics for natural philosophy. Some of the promising ideas that were developed within mechanics seem not to have been taken up in natural philosophy, such as the idea of motion along an ideally smooth surface. Nonetheless, natural philosophers did not reject ideas and techniques from mechanics out of hand because of any view about the 'unscientific' status of mechanics. The reasons for doubting the generality of the mathematical proportions associated with the law of the lever, within Neoplatonist philosophy at least, seem to have stemmed from general concerns about 'bottom-up' explanation, not the status of mechanics as an art. Its inability to account for qualitative changes – what we might call chemical changes – caused doubts that mechanics could serve as a model for natural philosophy more generally.

THE THEORY OF PNEUMATICS IN NATURAL PHILOSOPHY

There is less need to make a case that ancient Greek natural philosophers paid attention to pneumatics, since so much discussion of void and of devices working by its power is found even during the classical period. As I have argued, the major theories of rarefaction effects were all articulated by the classical period. The most interesting developments in late antiquity were the discussion of void by John Philoponus, an Aristotelian commentator of the sixth century CE, and the changing view of matter developed to account for the new compression effects discovered by Ctesibius.[57]

David Sedley has drawn attention to the significance of Philoponus' recognition of the 'force of the void' and its implications for the theory of place. Philoponus is impressed by the ability of

---

[57] See Sorabji (1987), (1990), for the background to Philoponus' revisions of Aristotelian doctrine.

devices to control the movement of fluids merely by the threat of a void,[58] and in his *Corollary of Void* he tries to work out the philosophical implications of rarefaction effects.[59] Although he offers several arguments for a new theory of void, the 'power of the void' evidenced by pneumatic effects is one of the most compelling of these.

Philoponus cites the effect in the course of his argument against Aristotle's view of place as the surrounding surface of the enclosing body. Philoponus argues that there must be a notion of space that is independent of the bodies within it, in order for certain effects to occur. He takes this space to be 'void in its own nature', always occupied by body, but nevertheless not reducible to the quantity of the bodies occupying it. His point is that the logical arguments against the void offered by Aristotle do not suffice to explain how nature acts to prevent a void from forming. There must be a real danger of void space occurring before there can be any force to prevent it opening up.[60] In other words, there needs to be some independent notion of space that *could* become void – logically if not physically – and Aristotle's idea of a containing surface cannot supply this.[61]

Philoponus indicates that these effects are well known in his day: he writes of the 'much-bruited' (*poluthruletos*) power of the void[62] and says that 'to prevent a void' is a common explanation.[63] Sedley is surely right, however, to note the importance of Philoponus' new distinction between the *physical* impossibility of the void, as demonstrated by pneumatic devices, and the *conceptual or logical* impossibility addressed by the Aristotelian arguments.[64] The recognition that there are physical forces moving bodies against their natural motion to prevent void's occurrence shows that there must be a real danger of void occurring. Only something that *could be* void can

---

[58] Sedley (1987). *Contra Proclum* 491.4–5.
[59] He recognizes that compression, as well as cooling, can condense air; Philoponus, *in GC* 93.10ff.; Sambursky (1962), p. 91.
[60] Philoponus, *in Ph.* 570.16–17; 573.19–21.   [61] Philoponus, *in Ph.* 571.14–16.
[62] Philoponus, *in Ph.* 570.17.   [63] Philoponus, *in Ph.* 571.14.
[64] Sedley (1987), p. 146.

account for these.[65] The argument, once stated, is so compelling that it is even worth asking whether all previous Aristotelians simply missed this consequence, as Aristotle clearly did.[66] Philoponus undoubtedly has more than one reason for adopting a new position on the nature of place. Still, one of his strongest arguments rests on the need to account for the rarefaction effects found in pneumatic technology.

Another idea from pneumatics and ballistics that seems to have been adopted from there into natural philosophy is the elasticity or *eutonia* of matter. This began to be used as a technical term in the third century BCE, both in Stoic natural philosophy and in mechanics. Of course philosophers before that time recognized that some bodies both bend and spring back to their original shape: Heraclitus talks about the bending of a bow; weapons makers had been exploiting the elasticity of wood for centuries. But there is surprisingly little discussion of this springiness *as a fundamental property of matter*. Discussions of materials such as sponge, sinew or horn in the fourth century focus only on their capacity to deform, not their capacity to recoil and resume their former shape. And the natural philosophical theories of the fourth century offer little that might account for this property.[67]

Vegetti has rightly noted that the probable source of the Stoic Chrysippus' attention to *tonos* as a property of body and soul is the contemporary use of *tonos* in spring catapults. It is surely no coincidence that the theories of Chrysippus were developed at a time when the mechanics were so prominently exploiting a property with the same name in their ballistic devices. Vegetti focuses on the notion of

---

[65] Philoponus, *in Ph.* 572.2–6.

[66] Sambursky (1962), p. 7, notes that Philoponus' account of void space echoes that of Aristotle's early successor, Strato of Lampsacus. It is possible that the implications of pneumatics were recognized even in the third century. While I am inclined to accept this view, Strato's void theory is too vexed a topic to discuss briefly.

[67] Sambursky (1959), p. 3 n. 21, claims that 'elasticity' had been known since the fifth century, possibly referring to a report of Anaxagoras' view that the *eutonia* of the cosmic whirl snatches up rocks from the earth and sets them on fire to become stars. Here the term seems to mean simply 'force' or 'power', and not specifically elasticity. Sambursky's evidence from 'Aristotle' comes from the *Problemata*.

tonos as a kind of tension: a *neuron* or tendon that is capable of exhibiting good or bad tension, *eutonia* or *atonia*.[68] He does consider another way that the term *eutonia* came to be used that does not depend on the contrast or the notion of tension so much as the peculiar property of elasticity. However, he contrasts the property of elasticity of matter to its impulsive or forceful character, rather than seeing the two properties as connected.[69]

Earlier natural philosophies had little room for the property of elasticity. The atomist tradition regarded matter *per se* as rigid and considered all recoil as a case of the rebounding of atoms striking one another. Elasticity could not be attributed to the atoms themselves, since these are by definition impassive and unchanging. Lucretius discusses a case where jets of water or flame shoot upward under pressure,[70] but his point is merely to note that bodies can be thrust forcibly upward, despite their natural downward tendency. He says nothing about the conditions that create this violent upward thrust, treating it as merely one case amongst others where bodies are thrust upward. The idea that the atoms themselves could deform is ruled out categorically.

Continuum theories, by contrast, do not regard matter as fixed in shape. However, elasticity is a phenomenon distinct from fluidity or deformability, since the latter imply no impulse to return to the original shape. The concept of elasticity presupposes that subjecting certain materials to deformation creates a tension resolved by the return of the material to its original shape. This idea is somewhat inimical to the Aristotelian treatment of shape as accidental to homoiomerous tissues. How, then, to account for the fact that matter seems to 'remember' its former shape and displays a marked tendency to return rather forcefully to that previous configuration?

Aristotle's discussion of the properties of different materials in *On Generation and Corruption* or *Meteorology* 4, where he discusses such complex properties as fissibility or viscosity, certainly talks about bodies that can change shape, but he does not talk about the phenomenon of springing back. He mentions that a sponge can be

---

[68] Vegetti (1993), p. 65. [69] Vegetti (1993), p. 73. [70] Lucretius 2.194ff.

deformed, for example, and that some squeezed bodies do not retain their shape. However, he gives no account of this;[71] the pliability associated with reeds or metals is not associated with any tendency to resume their original shape.[72] Aristotle does recognize a property he calls *tasis* in organisms. In *Historia Animalium* and *Parts of Animals*[73] he ascribes this property to bodily tissues and organs: the stomach, heart, sinews, bladder, marrow, eyelid, oesophagus, midriff, limbs.[74] However, this term seems to refer to flexibility, and not to recoil.

Elasticity seems to have attracted attention in the third century, in a way that is not found in fourth-century texts. One treatise in Aristotle's corpus, thought to date from the early third century, describes the lungs as *eutonos* in a context of expansion and contraction.[75] The context of the passage is the ability of certain materials to expel other bodies on account of their elasticity. The ability of the lungs to expel air forcefully is explicitly compared to catapults, whose springs need to be pliable to shoot further. The implication is that the force of the recoil is linked to the degree of deformation. Catapults seem to have drawn attention to this property of matter.

Evidence in Philo of Byzantium and Hero of Alexandria shows, I argued previously, that the elasticity of matter was discussed both in cases involving solids such as sinews and sword metal, and also in the case of air. The capacity of some materials to return to their original shape after deformation suggests that matter – continuous homoiomerous masses – retains a memory of its own shape or arrangement through deformation. Particle theories such as that of Hero can account for this best and do indeed suggest a specific mathematical limit to the extent of deformation possible, since it depends on the potential for closer-packing of a given array.[76] But whatever the

---

[71] *Mete.* 4.9, esp. 386b3, 387a15; cf. *GC* 2.2, 330a4.

[72] *Mete.* 4.9, 385b28ff., 386b17ff.

[73] References at *Pr.* 5.14, 882a18, *Spir.* 5, 483b14–17, I take to be after Aristotle's time.

[74] *HA* 1.16, 495b23; 3.5, 515a31, 515b16; 3.15, 519b14; *PA* 2.6, 652a19; 2.13, 657b15; 3.3, 664a32; 3.10, 672b26; 4.10, 690a18; cf. *PA* 2.1, 646b19.

[75] [Aristotle] *Aud.* 800b16; Gottschalk (1968) favours Strato's authorship.

[76] If, that is, the particles are of uniform size and already packed close enough in a regular formation. Cf. Vegetti (1993), p. 70.

theory of matter used to explain this property, it is clearly important in the suggestion that matter is able to transmit impulses by wave-like motion. Matter, to act as a mere conduit for such signals and yet to retain its original tension and shape, would need to have some such elastic properties.

Chrysippus, the major Stoic natural philosopher of the third century, used *eutonia* and *tonos* as a technical term for a property of matter in general, important in explaining its ability to transmit impulses and convey complex forms by physical contact. The older use is still retained: Chrysippus attributing to Zeno the claim that *neura* – probably sinews – are strong when they have *eutonia*, weak when they have *atonia*.[77] But other passages give *eutonia* a more specific unifying function, which seems to draw on the idea of elasticity, particularly the tendency of a mass to regain its shape despite being acted upon.[78] The Stoic idea that the *eutonia* of matter allows it to transmit wave-like impulses without lasting deformation also seems to draw on the idea of a material capable of regaining its original shape after impacts and thus able to continue to transmit numerous and conflicting impulses without losing its form.[79]

Claiming that all action is by contact and that coordination nonetheless exists between distant bodies, the Stoics needed to develop new ways to talk about the transmission of information by local action, and some way for bodies apparently distant to communicate with one another by means other than physical relocation. This problem was not entirely unprecedented: on at least one reading, Aristotle's account of the transmission of colour through a transparent medium depends on motions transmitted through a medium by a body remaining at a distance and transmitting information without material relocation.[80] But Stoic physics made this problem far more pervasive and demanded a systematic account of the ability of matter to transmit impulses without dislocation, by

[77] Galen *PHP* 5.2.413; discussed in Hahm (1977), p. 154.
[78] Plutarch, *Comm. not.* 1085c–d.
[79] Nemesius 70.6–71.4; Alexander, *Mixt.* 223.35; *Mantissa* 131.8ff.
[80] The controversy between Sorabji and Burnyeat is laid out in, e.g., Burnyeat (1992); on Strato's theory of sound, see Alexander, *in Sens.* 126.19ff.; Gottschalk (1968).

means of its tension. Although the specifically Stoic uses of *eutonia* go beyond the discoveries of the mechanics, and the details of the account are a little unclear, it seems to be no accident that this property of matter entered philosophical discussion in the third century.

PNEUMATICS AND MEDICAL THEORY

Pneumatic theory in the Hellenistic period shared with medicine a focus on the explanation of fluid motion. Practitioners of both disciplines engaged in natural philosophy, and medical theories of the organism were known to a number of philosophers.[81]

A central problem in medicine since the Hippocratic writers had been to account for the movement of fluids around the body. Fluids – whether the traditional 'four humours' or the airy *pneuma* that became central to the theory of the soul – were understood to affect health and to be subject to blockages and excesses. Blood was not thought to circulate, but rather to work like an irrigation system, nourishing the tissues; *pneuma* was thought to communicate, whether by transmission of pressure or material, with the central organ. Certain organs – heart, kidneys, uterus, lungs, head – were understood to be able to draw and expel particular fluids as appropriate, sometimes extracting their proper fluids from mixtures, or drawing them upward. Thus the means for directing the movement of fluids throughout the body was of paramount importance to physiology.

With the distinction between veins and arteries by Praxagoras of Cos, and the theory of Erasistratus and Herophilus that the nervous system was responsible for motor and perceptual functions, the movement of fluids was increasingly understood to take place through hollow vessels throughout the body. *Neura* or nerves were thought to contain *pneuma*: central passageways are visible in larger

---

[81] On reactions to medical doctrine in Hellenistic philosophy, see, e.g., von Staden (1996); Sedley (1998), pp. 68–72; Nutton (2004), p. 147; on Philoponus, see Todd (1976); (1984); Marcus Aurelius, *Meditations*. 2.2.

nerves such as the optic nerve, and this was assumed to be true of smaller nerves also.[82] According to the theory of Erasistratus, tissues were entirely composed of a triple braid of vein, artery and nerve, branching out into imperceptibly small vessels. Vegetti has suggested that this conception might owe something to Hellenistic ballistic devices.[83] Or perhaps the independent development of ideas in medicine and mechanics led to a new emphasis on the role of *pneuma* and *tonos* in philosophical debates.

Even for those who rejected or modified aspects of this account of physiology, a central question remained about the body's ability to distribute fluids to the appropriate organs. Because the distribution does not follow the downward direction of natural motion, and because different organs seem able to extract and assimilate specific fluids, the explanatory resources of natural philosophy were taxed. The body seemed to be able to distribute blood and nutriment to the tissues from the central organs, to draw bile from the gall bladder, attract semen into the uterus, extract urine from the blood stream into the kidneys, expel wastes, and – for those who accepted this account of the role of *pneuma* – to move *pneuma* throughout the body in a complex sequence wherein the inhaled breath underwent various transformations and acquired new functions.

With the medical focus on explaining the fluid movement within the body, it is perhaps not surprising that pneumatic phenomena were used in comparisons to the functions of organisms. As I indicated in an earlier chapter, the Hippocratic tradition, especially as expounded by Galen, rejected philosophical attempts to 'explain away' attraction. Galen thinks there are two kinds of attraction, the unselective tendency into empty spaces and the selective attraction of organs for their own juices. He denies that any substructure can account for attraction but rather supposes that substances have irreducible attractive, retentive and expulsive powers. The Galenic idea that each organ has its own powers inherent in its qualitatively

[82] On this, see especially von Staden (1989).
[83] Vegetti (1993), p. 72; (1998), p. 95; von Staden (1998).

different matter means that no further investigation could find common causes of different powers.

To Galen, the hypothesis that organs have special powers, *dunameis*, is important for recognizing nature's forethought. Nature's ability to change material qualitatively is required to provide each organ with its powers: organs have their own particular homoiomerous matter,[84] so that fashioning a brain or heart involves transforming matter qualitatively to give it the natural powers of that organ. They cannot be specified non-teleologically, that is, in terms of material properties that do not make reference to the function of the organ in question. Galen thinks he can show empirically that rival approaches are explanatorily inadequate; he takes their failure to legitimate his hypothesis that powers are explanatory primitives.

The ability of artificial models to replicate the phenomena found in bodies seems to have encouraged the idea that organisms might be understandable in terms of features common to inorganic bodies. Some of Galen's rivals, as he notes with disapproval, try to explain the fluid dynamics of the body in terms of the material features and structures of bodies, rather than the unique matter of each organ.[85] Filters and sieves are thought to explain how fluids separate out;[86] the position of an organ is enough to account for the 'attraction' of vapours, given the natural tendency of vapours to rise.[87] Erasistratus, one of Galen's chief targets, is accused of relying on the 'refilling of emptied spaces'. This idea of an automatic, passive tendency of spaces to refill also relies on structure: there must be vessels of fixed dimensions ready to be filled, unlike veins, which collapse when they are empty.[88] The idea that empty spaces tend to refill is a constant theme in discussions of pneumatic technology, the mantra of those who suppose that no special attractive powers are

---

[84] Or in some cases is a composition from more than one homoiomer (*Nat. Fac.* 1.6).

[85] *Nat. Fac.* 2.3.80–1.   [86] *Nat. Fac.* 1.15.57–8.   [87] *Nat Fac.* 1.13.33.

[88] *Nat. Fac.* 1.16; 2.1; 2.6. For an excellent overview of this debate, see Furley and Wilkie (1984), pp. 32–9. There is of course more to say in explaining *why* matter refills empty or emptier spaces, as I argue in Berryman (1997), 147–57; my earlier account is critiqued by Lehoux (1999). See also Berryman (2002d).

needed to understand organisms any more than siphons or valves or water pumps.

Pneumatic technology in the Hellenistic period surely provided greater resources for showing the fluid motions that can be achieved by structural rearrangements alone. Lonie noted that Erasistratus' account of the heart closely parallels the water pump invented by Ctesibius.[89] Lack of evidence makes it difficult to assess whether the doctors took such technological comparisons to be sufficient to understand the movement of fluids in the body, but Galen's polemics in defence of powers indicates that there were some who tried to explain the workings of the body by structural arrangements alone.

The question of fluid distribution is not the only question on which the parallels between organisms and non-organic working artifacts were noted in Hellenistic medicine. Von Staden has pointed to a number of linguistic parallels between the surgical device of Andreas of Carystus and the war machinery of Philo of Byzantium. He argues that these similarities show that third-century authors saw the body in mechanized terms.[90]

In *On the Natural Faculties* Galen presents this debate about the appeal to mechanical techniques in medicine as being closely parallel to the debate between teleological and materialistic approaches to natural philosophy more generally. In another work, to be discussed below, he suggests that the appeal to mechanics was understood to constitute a *third* and distinct explanatory option in medical theory. Although we cannot assume that medical theories were entirely taken up by the philosophical schools, the medical interest in mechanics is important supporting evidence for the reception of mechanics in natural philosophy.

---

[89] Lonie (1973); developed further by von Staden (1996); (1997); (1998); cf. also Longrigg (1993), pp. 207–9; Vallance (1990), p. 71. Russo (2004), p. 147, suggests that the inspiration went the other way around, and that the heart inspired the valve-based pump.

[90] Von Staden (1998), p. 163: he sees the cross-fertilization of ideas between mechanics and medicine as working in both directions. Cf. Vegetti (1993), (1998); Nutton (2004), pp. 135–9.

WORKING ARTIFACTS AND THE NOTION
OF A SELF-MOVER

We have already seen that some doctors did take the fluid dynamics within organisms to be illuminated by analogy to pneumatic devices. But another defining function of animals could inspire a comparison to working artifacts, namely their capacity for locomotion. To see how this analogy might work, it is necessary to step back a little from the historical evidence and examine the notion of a 'self-mover'.

When Aristotle developed his idea of a self-mover – a definitive characteristic of animals – he made it clear that this is not to be understood as the capacity to originate motion in the absence of any pre-existing change.[91] What animals do – and plants, pots and projectiles cannot – is to turn some other kind of change into local motion. Most changes in nature are initiated by something moving in place. The self-motions of animals represent exceptional turning points in the causal order. Unlike rocks or artifacts, animals can start to move without being directly pushed or pulled. They can move in response to qualitative changes within the body: the heat produced by desire following perception of the desired object. Projectiles merely continue the motion they have been given; tools directly depend on the agent working them. Self-movers, by contrast, start moving when they are not being pushed or pulled by another body. This is a distinctive kind of motion, but it is not uncaused.

I suggest that a version of the notion of a self-mover applies to what I call 'working artifacts'. We do not know why some fields were considered part of mechanics and others not: it is not obvious that the field had any rigorous definition or sharply delineated conceptual unity. My proposal – and it is speculative – is that the unifying factor was simply the perception that certain devices have in common that they *do* something. Not all devices found in the *mechanica* tradition were working artifacts – and there might have been working artifacts that are not discussed in those treatises – but

---

[91] Aristotle, *Ph.* 8.7, 260a26ff.; 7.2, 243a35. See Gill and Lennox (1994); Berryman (2002a); (2007a).

I offer this phrase as an attempt to capture the spirit of the classification of a particular group of complex devices.[92]

The notion of 'working independently' here admits of degree, because the extent to which the subsequent motions of the artifact are different in kind from the triggering cause admits of degree. A hand turning a wheel in a horizontal plane, for example, may cause a figure to revolve in a vertical plane; a continuous stream of water may force air out of an airtight tank through whistles, producing a sound that is not that of falling water. In the two cases, the difference between cause and effect is what distinguishes the working of the artifact from a simple tool or projectile. The construction allows horizontal rotation to be translated into straight-line motion, or downward flow of water to create whistling.[93]

Various factors contribute to our *psychological* willingness to view a device as working independently. In the *hagnistērion* and owl-and-birds devices, for example, the cause and effect are spatially separated and the intermediary links hidden in a 'black box'; this screening of causal connections works on the perceptions of the naive observer, as does the dressing up of devices so as to resemble organisms. But other features of the construction of devices that increase our perception of their independence do so in a way that is not merely illusory. These include spatial distance of the triggering cause from the effect; difference in kind between cause and effect; a time lag; use of an inanimate trigger such as flowing water.

A new degree of complexity is attained by devices that can turn one kind of input into multiple outputs, and by those that can coordinate more than one kind of causal process. An even clearer case for the designation 'working artifacts' exists for devices that continue working without ongoing external input. This is true of wind-up devices, which contain within themselves a stored power

---

[92] I suggest this, despite the fact that the components to mechanical devices, such as levers, are mere tools. These simple components transform the agent's action into something else; and they can be combined into complexes that achieve greater degrees of independence of the triggering cause.

[93] The transformation of circular to straight-line motion was taken to be paradigmatic by Vitruvius, above; cf. Philoponus, *in de An.* 106.27ff.

source, which needs only to be released by an external trigger. Ancient wind-up toys of various kinds move for a time after their release, as twisted cords slacken or a weight falls, pulling a coiled rope; a self-starting siphon hidden inside Hero's owl-and-birds is able to turn the flow of water on and off, effectively using the stored water to initiate a further reaction once the water level reaches a certain point. A device on wheels that moves itself as a whole, rather than merely producing a change in some part, offers the closest parallel to the definitive capacity of animals to initiate locomotion in the absence of something pushing or pulling them.

Working artifacts are never completely independent, but in increasingly complex kinds of devices the responsibility for the effect seems increasingly to lie with the device rather than the instigating cause. I suggest that this is not simply a psychological tendency to ascribe quasi-agency to a device, but a real recognition of the extent to which the internal construction of complex working arti-facts governs the resultant motion. For a working artifact to be described as a self-mover, then, it would need to be able to react to an environmental trigger in ways that are to some significant degree determined by the construction of the device, not only by the instigating cause. The triggering cause of course provides the occa-sion for the change,[94] but other features of the subsequent change are a function of the construction of the device. While projectiles certainly continue moving even after the agent is no longer in contact, the trajectory of their subsequent motion is a direct function of the impetus given them by the initiating agent. As with tools, the direction, extent and kind of effect are determined by the triggering cause. Self-movers, by contrast, respond to an initiating change in varied and sometimes complex ways that are determined by the construction of the device in direction, extent and kind.

In *On the Motion of Animals* Aristotle elaborates an account of the animal ability to initiate pursuit as a result of the qualitative change brought about by seeing the object of desire. This is not how

---

[94] Some ancient devices, such as Hero's robot, are designed to include a time lag. This does not affect the point.

working artifacts typically work. Occasionally, qualitative change is important in the initiation of local motion, as when heating creates steam that is used to move the device. More often, though, the trigger involves something moving locally. Working artifacts do not exactly do what animals do, nor do they meet Aristotle's technical definition.

Nonetheless, I suggest that the notion of a self-mover is a non-technical notion, and that some of the working artifacts in the *mechanica* collections might reasonably seem to observers to qualify as self-movers. The extent, direction and kind of motion they exhibit are determined by the construction of the device, not by the instigating cause. An automaton converts the instigating cause – an agent opens a trapdoor, for example – into a downward fall of millet, the unwinding of ropes, and the sideways motion, to a degree and in a direction determined by the construction of the device. The instigating cause provides the *occasion* for the movement, but little more. As in animals, motion is not uncaused, but the construction of the device has more control over the subsequent change than the instigating cause. Hero's description of his devices as 'automatic' depended on their ability to exhibit complex sequences without ongoing intelligent direction. The device and not the mover determines how it moves.

The kinds of working artifacts available in antiquity vary, and the degree to which they might seem like autonomous self-movers would also vary with the capabilities of the devices. A preliminary typology distinguishing tools and working artifacts might go as follows:

Manipulated artifacts:
> Agent driven, no moving parts (puppet)
> Agent driven, moving parts (marionette)
> Agent driven, effect continues after instigating cause ceases (arrow)

'Simple powers':
> Agent driven, effect different in kind from instigating cause
> (lever, screw)

Working artifacts:
> External drive, simple output (water wheel)
> External drive, complex output (water organ)
> External drive, internal wind-up-and-release (owl-and-birds)

External trigger, internal drive, responsive output (water level
   regulator)
Wind-up drive, external trigger, simple output, stationary
   (catapult)
Wind-up drive, external trigger, complex output, stationary
   (Philo's theatre)
Wind-up drive, external trigger, complex output, mobile (Hero's
   automaton)

One could, most probably, find intermediate cases for any of these
categories, and other categories that are not listed here. How should
a siphon be classified? What counts as 'wind-up' here, or is there
a more inclusive category? Is the idea of different 'kinds' of effects
merely subjective, or could it be subjected to a more rigorous
analysis? Although many questions remain unanswered, I suggest
that the notion of a self-mover – a complex that determines the
extent, direction and kind of its change, if not the occasion – can be
lent a certain clarity, although it admits of degree. It is reasonable to
anticipate that the more complex 'working artifacts', at least, would
be taken to share with animals in this notion of self-moving.

MECHANICAL ANALOGIES FOR THE FUNCTIONING OF ORGANISMS

The reason for clarifying the concept of a 'self-mover' was to give
some precision to the idea that complex working artifacts might seem
'like' organisms, especially animals. Aristotle's analysis shows that
self-motion is, not unreasonably, taken to be one of the defining
characteristics of animals. Although working artifacts do not exactly
match Aristotle's definition, since they do not typically initiate local
motion in the absence of a locally moving cause, they might reasonably be seen as self-movers nonetheless, since many devices exhibit a
considerable degree of determination over the motions they exhibit
in response to a triggering cause.

   Above, I discussed the outlines of the discipline of mechanics in
the lists of Pappus and Proclus, which *classified* an entire field of

mechanical devices as 'imitating living beings'. In turn, the almost universal use of animal and human figures to 'dress up' the devices in the *pneumatica* and theatrical automata literature supports this idea that their interest lay in this ability to do *something like* the kinds of things that animals do. Here, I shall consider evidence that the existence of devices with some version of the capacity for self-motion was taken to illuminate the problem of explaining animal functions.

The history of comparisons between organisms and puppets is a long one. Comparisons to marionettes, operated directly by strings, predate mechanical technology. Although puppet analogies are sometimes described as 'mechanical', I suggest that this is misleading, since the marionette analogy merely relocates agency from the organism itself to another being that is outside it. The marionette is not a self-mover: as with a tool, not only the occasion but also the direction, kind and extent of its motion are largely determined by the agent working it. The most plausible candidates for a pre-Hellenistic mechanical model of an organism may be the comparisons Aristotle twice draws between organisms and 'automatic puppets'. While I argued earlier that Aristotle himself does not understand these mechanistically – inasmuch as he attributes the workings, in the case of the organism, to a theoretical substance with stipulated powers that are not susceptible to the kind of investigation and manipulation characteristic of mechanics – these references do seem to have licensed Aristotelians to consider such analogies.

We have already seen that a number of doctors were interested in the explanation of pneumatic effects by structural arrangements. Galen objects that nature's ability to change material qualitatively is required to provide each organ with its powers. Hankinson argues that these powers are 'place-holders' and that Galen is committed to the search for physical accounts of their operation: that he is conscious of the charge of 'Molière explanation', or of positing 'explanations' that merely put a name to the phenomenon. Hankinson suggests that the criticism of the explanations offered by the mechanists is that they are 'not fine-grained enough to account for such selectivity'.[95]

[95] Hankinson (1998a), pp. 396–400.

Galen's criticism of those who try to give efficient-causal accounts of the powers seems to accuse them of denying the phenomena in question.[96] He ultimately comes back to the objection that they think of Nature as rather like a human sculptor reshaping wax but unable to alter its inner nature.[97] Explanation in terms of the fashioning of passageways, however cunningly contrived, is in Galen's eyes inadequate because the 'powers' seem to accrue to the organ as an organic whole, and not to be explicable in terms of the arrangement of parts. Nature, unlike the sculptor, can effect qualitative change. Organs seem to have their own particular homoiomerous matter,[98] so that fashioning a brain or heart involves transforming matter qualitatively to give it the natural powers of that organ. Thus he would be resistant to attempts to specify the functioning of the powers non-teleologically, that is, in terms of material properties that do not make reference to the function of the organ in question.[99] I suggest that Galen's objection to the 'mechanists' is not just the crudeness of their accounts, but that their explanations are 'bottom up' and do not seem to take account of the irreducibility of qualitative change.[100]

The issue is not only about the existence of design in nature, but also about the kinds of techniques available to nature in designing organisms.[101] At one point Galen seems to endorse a 'mechanical model' as a way to show how a designer might build a device that can continue a sequence of motions without ongoing supervision, just

---

[96] E.g. *Nat. Fac.* 2.13–15, esp. 2.15.60.

[97] Galen, *Nat. Fac.* 2.82; *UP* 17.1; Berryman (2002d).

[98] Or in some cases are composed from more than one homoiomer: *Nat. Fac.* 2.13.

[99] Copenhaver (1984) on 'indescribable properties'.

[100] This may seem question-begging, if the account is merely that structural explanations are inadequate because they do not allow qualitative change, and that qualitative change is needed because structural arrangements are inadequate. I take it that there is an empirical point lurking here about the adequacy of 'bottom up' explanations, and that the justification is similar to Philoponus': the properties of composites are too varied and complex to be accounted for by the properties of parts, especially since very similar combinations of ingredients can be seen to take on radically different qualities, while the functional properties of organs are too idiosyncratic to be accounted for by the properties of the ingredients.

[101] On Galen's teleology more broadly, see De Lacy (1972); Hankinson (1989), (1998a); von Staden (1997); Schiefsky (2007b).

like celestial models.[102] But while he endorses this aspect of the machine model – that it can show how an intended result can be realized without making the parts themselves rational – he does seem to reject the systematic use of the 'machine model'. Galen criticizes Aristotle's use of the comparison to the functioning of puppets in explaining generation, because he thinks it endorses the view that external shaping – rearrangement of parts – rather than qualitative change could be adequate. He accuses Aristotle of treating the seed merely as the beginning of motion, just as puppets (*thaumata*), because of their construction (*kataskeuē*), need only such an initial motion to keep going for some time. Galen's objection is that qualitative alteration and not just local motion is needed in order for organs to acquire the power of attracting their proper fluids and repelling foreign matter.[103] This is not Aristotle's point, but it indicates why Galen rejects the comparison to devices.[104]

In his account of the development of the foetus, Galen shows that there are doctors taking the machine model quite seriously as a way to account for the existence of preprogrammed causal sequences. In contrast to the atomists, who attempt to account for generation from completely purposeless motion, he considers more seriously the idea that organisms function in the same manner as *thaumata*, theatrical devices:

---

[102] ὥσπερ γὰρ οἱ τὰς τῶν πλανωμένων ἀστέρων περιόδους μιμούμενοι διά τινων ὀργάνων ἀρχὴν αὐτοῖς κινήσεως ἐνδόντες αὐτοὶ μὲν ἀπαλλάττονται, τὰ δ', ὡς εἰ καὶ παρὼν ἔτυχε καὶ διὰ παντὸς ἐπιστατῶν αὐτοῖς ὁ δημιουργός, οὕτως ἐνεργεῖ, κατὰ τὸν αὐτὸν οἶμαι τρόπον ἕκαστον τῶν ἐν τῷ σώματι μορίων ἀκολουθίᾳ τέ τινι καὶ διαδοχῇ κινήσεως ἀπὸ τῆς πρώτης ἀρχῆς ἐνεργεῖ μέχρι παντὸς οὐδενὸς ἐπιστάτου δεόμενον, *UP* 14.5 (Helmreich).

[103] καίτοι γε οὐ τῆς ποιότητος αὐτῷ μεταδίδωσιν ἐκ τοῦ σπέρματος ὁ Ἀριστοτέλης, ἀεὶ δ' ἀρχὴν κινήσεως ἐνδίδωσι μόνην, ὥσπερ τοῖς θαύμασιν ἐμφυλάττοντα τὴν ἑαυτῶν κατασκευὴν ἐκ μόνου τοῦ λαβεῖν τὴν τοιαύτην ἀρχὴν ἐπὶ πλεῖστον ἐξαρκεῖ κινούμενα. καὶ μὴν οὐ διὰ κίνησιν, ἀλλὰ διὰ ποιότητος οἰκειότητα καὶ ἀλλοτριότητα τὸ μὲν αἱρουμένας τε καὶ κατεχούσας ἔστιν ἰδεῖν τὰς φύσεις, τὸ δ' ἀποστρεφομένας τε καὶ διὰ τοῦτ' ἐκβαλλούσας, *Sem.* 1.5.24–5 (De Lacy).

[104] The difference may be that Galen takes *kinēsis* to refer to local motions only.

Such is the argument of Epicurus and those who hold that everything happens without design; but this is not convincing. It would then be necessary either that the construction of the foetus moves towards the accomplishment of an excellent purpose without the aid of reason or design, or that what happens is like the case of those who engineer theatrical devices (οἱ τὰ θαύματα κατασκευάζοντες): they provide the first impetus of the motion and then depart, so that their devices continue to move – by design (τεχνικῶς) – for a short space of time. It could be that in the same way the gods, once they have constructed the seeds of plants or animals in such a way as to be able to perform this enormous transmission of motions, no longer act themselves ...[105]

The members of this school draw a comparison to theatrical devices that are constructed in such a way as to continue to move once their maker has departed: the puppet-master provides the origin of motion and then disappears. The sequence of motions is an automatic result of the design of the device, where 'automatic' means that no ongoing intelligent direction is involved. While Galen thinks this approach is an improvement over the views of the atomists, he thinks it would be remarkable if material processes could transmit such a complex sequence of motions without going astray.

The concern about a *sequence* of motions also appears in the discussion of Aristotle's theory of generation of animals by Alexander of Aphrodisias and Simplicius. Alexander seems to take Aristotle's analogy to automatic puppets as intended to show not only that one thing can move another through an intermediary with which it is not in contact, but also that an ordered and goal-directed *sequence* of changes can occur without choice or deliberation.[106] Alexander explicitly rejects a dichotomy thought to exist between goal-directed sequences involving deliberation and choice, and those that happen at random. He explicitly refers to the 'machine model' to make plausible the third alternative, namely that the organism can be

[105] *Foet. Form.* 4.688–9. Translation by Singer (1997), p. 194, slightly modified. I discuss this text in Berryman (2003).
[106] D. Henry (2005), pp. 12–13, rightly points to the importance of the mechanical analogue in illustrating the idea that a causal *sequence* can be produced without intelligent direction, and notes a passage in the Aristotelian *Mechanica*, 848a20–37, which echoes this account of the particular feature of mechanical devices. See Hankinson (1996) for discussion of metaphors for causal sequences.

designed so that the sequence of changes happens automatically within it, and yet it produces the intended result.[107]

Simplicius, who reports Alexander's position, recognizes that the problem is about the ability of natural things to produce a determined end by means of a *sequence* of changes. What happens in the puppet – *neurospastoumenos* – is that it preserves an order and series – *heirmos* or *diadochē* – in generation and arrives at the definite end, without there being awareness in it.[108] He remarks that it would be strange if natural things came to be like that spontaneously. Simplicius agrees that the analogy to the puppets is illustrative of this ability;[109] what he questions is Alexander's account of how such complexes come about. The commentators agree in imposing a subtle change of meaning onto the analogy to the puppets introduced by Aristotle. While Aristotle uses the comparison to make a point about the possibility that the source of motion can be something no longer in contact, Alexander and Simplicius understand the comparison to point to the possibility that a complex can be so organized that a series of changes can, without deliberation, bring about a determinate result.

Hellenistic medicine perhaps reinforced the traditional use of the marionette analogy because of new evidence that we are, in fact, 'pulled about' by means of the nervous system, whose very name, *neura*, is the word for puppet strings.[110] By late antiquity there was a well-established branch of the discipline of mechanics explicitly devoted to making models that imitate living things: Pappus talks of devices like Hero's that seem to imitate living things by strings and cords;[111] Proclus echoes his claim.[112] The passages in Galen and Simplicius suggest that this kind of imitation is not understood

---

[107] Simplicius, *in Ph.* 310.36–311.30.
[108] *in Ph.* 314.3–5. I thank Richard Sorabji and Devin Henry for drawing my attention to the importance of this passage: for a full discussion, see D. Henry (2005).
[109] Simplicius, *in Ph.* 314.1–5.   [110] Von Staden (1989), (1996).
[111] οἱ δὲ διὰ νευρίων καὶ σπάρτων ἐμψύχων κινήσεις δοκοῦσι μιμεῖσθαι, ὡς Ἥρων Αὐτομάτοις ..., Pappus 8.1024.26 (Hultsch).
[112] τὰ δὲ διὰ νεύρων καὶ σπάρτων ἐμψύχους ὁλκὰς καὶ κινήσεις ἀπομιμουμένων, Proclus, *in Euc.* 41 (Freidlein).

as merely deceptive and illusory, but rather that these devices are understood by at least some interpreters to imitate the definitive functions of living things, by means of comparable causal connections.

A peculiar twist on the traditional puppet motif occurs in Stoicism, because of the way the Stoics conceived of divine influence on nature as diffuse and corporeal. Marcus Aurelius makes frequent use of the comparison to puppets worked by strings. The term he uses is etymologically connected to *neura*, the term used first for the sinews that move an animal's limbs and, later, the nerves.[113] Marcus Aurelius uses the puppet image to claim that our impulses pull us around.[114] This is sometimes paired with the claim that the pulling is caused by involuntary impressions made on us by perception or *phantasia*.[115] Stoic theory distinguishes the involuntary causal impact of impressions from the assent to those impressions, a distinction that is meant to leave space for rational agency in the act of withholding assent. Marcus Aurelius is concerned to raise an ethical complaint against this pulling, in that it is common to animals, unlike the free and god-like control of the self by the mind. He also suggests, rhetorically, that it is slavish or perhaps futile and meaningless.[116]

Although *neurospaston* is a traditional term for a puppet and does not necessarily mean an automaton, at least one source in late antiquity applies this term to what is clearly a wind-up device.[117] Automatic puppets were clearly available in Marcus' time; the discussion of their application as models for organisms was probably known to him through Galen, his court physician.[118] It is possible that Marcus Aurelius compares the unfree agent to an automatic puppet in order

[113] He does once use a Latin term, *sigillaria*, for puppets, but more often uses derivatives of the Greek *neurospasteō*.

[114] *hormētikēs neurospastias*, *Med.* 6.28; cf. 2.2, 3.16.

[115] *Med.* 3.16, 6.28, 7.29.   [116] *Med.* 3.16, 2.2, 7.3.

[117] Synesius, *Aegyptii sive de providentia* 1.9.36. This text, discussed further below, is written rather later than the *Meditations*, but cf. ps. -Aristotle, *de Mundo* 398b12ff., discussed below. Murphy (1995), p. 5, regards *neurospasta* as marionettes with vulgar connotations, although her sources are mainly from the fourth century BCE.

[118] Cf. Nutton (2004), p. 227. There are clear Galenic echoes at *Med.* 2.2.

to make the point that the non-sage's actions are preprogrammed by the causal sequences in nature.

Tertullian (second–third century CE) reports an unusual mechanical analogy for the soul itself, when he claims that some earlier philosophers compare the soul to a hydraulic organ.[119] His understanding of the comparison emphasizes the idea of a complex device, not so much coordinating a variety of inputs into a single output but rather translating a single kind of input into sundry outputs. In his *de Anima* Tertullian draws an explicit analogy between a water organ and the model of the soul he finds in Strato, Heraclitus and Aenesidemus. The point Tertullian is making concerns the unity of the material substance of the soul even in the face of the diverse and diffused nature of its operations: the same substance is apparent at work in all the various pathways of the body. The idea that a single mode of operation can have diverse results is surely central to any mechanistic approach, while the claim seems to be that because the air is united in substance, it is able to take one form of pressure acting on it and turn this into a number of diverse effects.

The Hellenistic discovery of a single system anatomically continuous with the brain and responsible for the operation of all five senses as well as locomotion bears well the analogy to a machine with a single central control and a diffuse network of passageways leading off it and transmitting the effects through the passageways connecting the brain to the external world. While Tertullian does not spell this out, there is independent evidence that one of his sources, Strato of Lampsacus, did take the material to be directly responsible for the transmission of effect by physical means such as tension that could be likewise interrupted.[120] It is plausible that Tertullian took his predecessors' reliance on physical transmission of effect as the grounds for his analogy between their model of soul and a pneumatic device. While this is a fairly clear instance of explicit analogy to a

---

[119] Tertullian, *de Anim.* 14.

[120] Given that the water organ is a third-century invention, the 'Heraclitus' in question might not be the Presocratic figure. For Strato's psychology, see Repici (1988).

pneumatic device, there is little said about the implications of the 'mechanism' beyond the idea that a single process motivates different results through the effects on a single medium.

In the Neoplatonist commentators, the relationship of mind or soul to body is often described in terms of tools or devices. This comparison, after all, has its roots in the Platonic and Aristotelian heritage. Plato's *Alcibiades* talks about the soul using the body as an instrument;[121] Aristotle's account of the action of desire on the body uses an analogy to a rudder, and a comparison to *automata*.[122] The idea of leverage is repeated in Neoplatonist accounts of Aristotle's views of the soul–body relationship.[123] While the idea of using a tool suggests that the agent is in contact, the automatic puppet account, as it appears in *Generation of Animals* especially, suggests a detached device-maker.[124] Sallustius, a fourth-century Neoplatonist, updates the idea of the soul using a body as an instrument, turning it into a comparison to a device-maker, *mēchanopoios*, who is not inside the machine. He draws on the machine as a model that allows the soul to claim full control without being itself altered by short-comings in the body.[125]

Christian authors from the same period seem to have taken a particular interest in the machine analogy. One of the most interesting versions of this is that of Gregory of Nyssa (fourth century CE), who proposes a mechanical analogy and presents the criticisms of it by his teacher Macrina. Gregory is interested in the evidence that the soul is immortal and has a genuine, immaterial rationality. He takes the point of the machine analogy to be that of suggesting how human beings might work without rationality, by purely material means.

---

[121] Plato, *Alc.* 129dff.
[122] Aristotle, *MA* 7, 701b2ff. For the view that Aristotle's theory of soul retains the idea that the body is an instrument, see Menn (2002).
[123] E.g. Simplicius, *in Ph.* 1259.12ff.; Philoponus, *in de An.* 106.8–9; cf. Aristotle, *Ph.* 8.6, 259b17ff.
[124] Philoponus, *in GA* 77.16ff.
[125] Ὀργάνῳ δὲ χρωμένη τῷ σώματι οὐκ ἔστιν ἐν τούτῳ ὥσπερ οὐδὲ ὁ μηχανοποιὸς ἐν τοῖς μηχανοποιήμασι, Sallustius, *de Deis et Mundo* 8.4.1ff. (Rochefort).

The discussion of the production of human-like effects – sounds, for example – shows a detailed acquaintance with pneumatic devices.[126] He argues, in essence, that our very ability to formulate this hypothesis undermines the argument.[127]

Gregory's interpretation of the argument focuses on its theological implications rather than its usefulness as a model for natural philosophy.[128] He does not, ultimately, reject the claim that our devices *imitate* the functions of organisms, perhaps including rationality, but rather points to the capacity to *create* them as evidence of human reason:

> We see many such things contrived by the makers of machines, in which they arrange matter skillfully to imitate nature. Their contrivances do not show similarity to nature in appearance alone, but also sometimes in motion, and in representation of a kind of voice, when the mechanism reverberates in its sounding part. In such cases indeed the phenomena do not lead us to suppose that an intelligent power brings about in each machine the appearance, form, sound, or motion. If we should say that the same also happens in the case of this mechanical instrument of our nature, we might say that no intelligent essence is infused in us according to the peculiarity of our nature, but some kinetic power resides in the nature of the elements in us. Such activity would be a result.[129]

Here, a mechanical analogy is considered full-blown: while it is primarily directed to the functioning of an organism, it is clear that it could apply *a fortiori* to nature as a whole. Not only organic functions but also intelligent behaviour can be imitated by an unthinking mechanism. Devices had been built that do *something like* the kinds of things that organisms do; and it was at least a conceptual possibility that we are just like them.

The issue that Gregory is concerned about is the existence of an immortal and separable soul, conceived as rationality. The machine

---

[126] Gregory of Nyssa, *de Anima et Resurr.* 46.36.36.

[127] *De Anima et Resurr.* 2: I thank Stephen Menn for directing me to Gregory. This passage is also discussed in Schiefsky (2007a).

[128] On the fusion of Platonic, Aristotelian and Stoic elements in Gregory's philosophical background, see Zachhuber (2000), p. 151.

[129] Gregory of Nyssa, *de Anima et Resurr.* 46.33.11. Translation by Roth (1993), pp. 40–1.

analogy serves to raise the possibility that we might be composed entirely from unintelligent material nature, merely programmed to look as though we are acting rationally. Macrina's response to this challenge is not to offer evidence that any given human being is rational – to solve the problem of other minds – but rather to suggest that the human ability to create such devices – devices that imitate purposive behaviour – itself demonstrates the existence of human intelligence, in at least some humans. We first study processes in nature to learn the capacities of materials and then conceive devices that exploit these capacities. The very fact that we can build devices that imitate the functioning of organisms shows not that we might work like machines, but that we have access to an immaterial rationality. Given the evident assumption that rationality is immaterial, the point seems to be that an immaterial cause is needed to account for the causal action of at least some human beings, those capable of craft activity. Thus – presumably – since machines are arrangements of matter, the human craftsman is not a machine.[130]

Macrina suggests that the materialist position amounts to a claim that the matter could organize itself into working artifacts.[131] The implication seems to be that the attempt to deny the need for an additional immaterial soul to account for human capacities – by building the capacity for goal-directed activity into matter itself – should entail matter's being able to produce functioning artifacts automatically. Those who erase the distinction between natural and artificial, that is, need to explain why artifacts are not self-organizing. As both Epicurus and the Stoics are mentioned as philosophical targets, this counter is presumably a critique of the Stoic idea that rationality is spread throughout all matter as well as a critique of non-teleological materialism. In contrast to the Cartesian move of looking inward to establish our awareness of the activity of mind, Gregory seems to be relying on the external evidence of rationality in our ability to engineer effects. Gregory turns the 'machine analogy' on its head and finds proof of *human* intelligence in the building of the device.

---

[130] Compare Proclus' argument against Theodorus, above.
[131] Gregory of Nyssa, *de Anima et Resurr.* 46.37.33.

WORKING ARTIFACTS IN ASTRONOMY

There are references to mechanical devices in later Greek astronomy proper. Unfortunately the picture is somewhat muddied by a controversy that may not be about the use of mechanics for producing physical effects, but about the use of instruments to produce geometrical objects. Duhem notes, in his work on the idea of 'saving the appearances' in astronomy, that Adrastus of Aphrodisias and Theon of Smyrna appeal to ancient geared mechanisms to justify a planetary theory in which the planets trace epicycles on a circle concentric to the earth. He claims that they thought 'a hypothesis appeared compatible with the nature of things if a competent craftsman could embody it in metal or wood'.[132] Duhem takes Theon's appeal to devices as being used to justify a literal, physical reading of the epicyclic hypothesis.

There had long been a question whether the planets, or the fixed stars, were to be regarded as divine bodies moving freely in the aether, or as passive bodies carried in their paths by solid spheres. This question concerned the *causal* account of the heavens. Independent of this question, however, was an issue over how to regard the geometrical pathways traced by the planets. Were they to be seen as created by an eccentric orbit, or by a concentric orbit with epicycles, or by some other geometrical form? This seems to have been the main question preoccupying astronomers, and it did not imply a particular view of the underlying physics involved. Questions about the *geometry* of the planetary path could be asked by those who took the wanderers to be ensouled beings as well as by those who took them to be carried on intersecting spheres.

Nor is there a necessary connection between the building of cosmic models and the assumption of a given view about the causation at work in the cosmos. Ptolemy, who held that the stars exercise individual volition,[133] presents his work on the planets in

---

[132] Duhem (1969), p. 15. See G. E. R. Lloyd (1991), for a critique of Duhem's distinction between realist and instrumentalist theories in antiquity.

[133] See, e.g., Neugebauer (1975), vol. ii, pp. 922ff.; Sambursky (1962), pp. 143–4; Taub (1993), p. 121.

such a way as to be convenient for making models (*organopoiia*). He does not think that the difficulty or simplicity of constructed models *for us* necessarily reflects on the complexity or simplicity of the heavenly spheres themselves, because of the subjectivity of human judgements about simplicity.[134]

All that the description of a model demonstrates is a possibility. It is a further question whether that possibility is geometrical – that an apparently irregular trajectory can be produced by the intersection of regular motions – or mechanical, with the added implication that all of the motions involved can be produced by mechanical means, perhaps a single driving mechanism.

Theon of Smyrna (second century CE) certainly refers to sphere-making (*mēchanosphairopoiia*) in his explication of the system of interacting spheres. Aristotle is quoted as endorsing the account of Callippus and Eudoxus and apparently adding the notion that there need to be counteracting spheres in order to reverse the direction of the spheres that in concert produce the retrograde motion of the planets. This seems to be so that the addition of extra spheres to produce retrogradation does not interfere with the transmission of celestial motion to the next-lowest planet.[135] Theon takes Aristotle to be conceiving of the Eudoxan model as mechanical:

One had to suppose that between the spheres carrying the planets there were other obviously solid spheres that by their own motions counteracted those of the carrying spheres, rolling them back through their contact. This is similar to the effect of the so-called drums in artificially constructed spheres that have a certain motion of their own which, by the gearing of the cogged wheels, *reverse and rewind* the spheres fixed beneath them.[136]

---

[134] Ptolemy, *Hyp.* 2.70.19ff.; Sambursky (1962), pp. 140–1; Taub (1993), p. 112.

[135] Aristotle, *Metaph.* 12.8, 1074a1–14.

[136] ὑπέλαβον δεῖν εἶναι μεταξὺ φερουσῶν ἑτέρας τινάς, στερεὰς δηλονότι, σφαίρας, αἵ τῇ ἑαυτῶν κινήσει ἀνελίξουσι τὰς φερούσας ἐπὶ τοὐναντίον, ἐφαπτόμενας αὐτῶν, ὥσπερ ἐν ταῖς μηχανοσφαιροποιίαις τὰ λεγόμενα τυμπάνια, κινούμενα περὶ τὸ κέντρον ἰδίαν τινὰ κίνησιν, τῇ παρεμπλοκῇ τῶν ὀδόντων εἰς τοὐναντίον κινεῖν καὶ ἀνελίττειν τὰ ὑποκείμενα καὶ προσυφαπτόμενα, Theon 180.15 (Hiller); translation after Sambursky (1962), p. 138, revised. I thank an anonymous reviewer for noting the difficulty

Although Theon does refer to machinery, this need not mean that, as Sambursky assumes, he is presenting a 'concrete physical picture' based on mechanical devices, since there is no account of how the independent motions of the different spheres are to be produced.[137] A criticism by Proclus of the reference to physical models seems to recognize this problem: if the astronomers suppose that there are real circles attached to the spheres, 'the astronomers destroy the continuity of the spheres to which the circles belong. For they attribute separate motions to the circles and to the spheres ...'[138] Proclus takes the account to be *ad hoc*, not grounded in a real causal explanation. It may be that Theon's focus is really on techniques for producing regular geometrical objects, and that he only appeals to mechanics to make a limited point. His interest seems to lie in showing how apparently irregular movements can be produced by interactions of regular geometrical objects, not how the physics of the heavens should be conceived.

John Philoponus (sixth century CE) compares the motion of the cosmos to that of cosmic models: one similarity he sees between the heavens and *sphairai* is that both possess the ability to transmit motion to other bodies that is different in kind from the motion of the mover.[139] Likewise, in his polemic against Proclus, Philoponus is concerned with the question whether the motion of the heavens needs to be due to the nature of the material from which it is composed, as Aristotelian theory suggests. Philoponus suggests rather that cosmic fire could be carried round by the motion of the outer spheres containing it, just as water is carried around by

in Sambursky's rendition of the last line and for challenging my earlier reading of this discussion. Cf. Dupuis (1892), p. 291.

[137] Sambursky (1962), p. 139; at p. 134 he describes even Aristotle's model as 'fitted together like the wheels and cogs of a clock'.

[138] εἰ δὲ καὶ εἶναι καθ' ὑπόστασιν, τὴν συνέχειαν ἀφανίζουσιν αὐτῶν τῶν σφαιρῶν ἐν αἷς εἰσιν οἱ κύκλοι, χωρὶς μὲν τούτους κινοῦντες, χωρὶς δὲ ἐκείνας, Proclus, *Hyp.* 7.54.1 (Manitius), translation by Sambursky (1962), p. 148. Cf. Proclus, *in Ti.* 56.28: see G. E. R. Lloyd (1991), p. 263.

[139] Philoponus, *in de An.* 106.28ff. The similarity only needs to be in genus – local motion produces local motion – but not in species, as straight motion can produce circular, *de An.* 107.13–15.

devices.[140] Wolff notes the parallel to other passages where Philoponus rejects the Aristotelian strictures against employing non-natural motion to account for the motion of the heavens.[141] Like Lactantius, Philoponus uses the analogy between devices to suggest that the heavenly bodies are passive, moved by something else. Christian authors would probably be more sympathetic to comparisons that attribute passivity to the heavens, rather than regarding them as divinities.[142]

These analogies drawn between the heavens and the cosmic devices of late antiquity seem to make only specific points. Sometimes the issue is divine action, illustrating the idea that a designer could leave a device to run by itself. Theon and Philoponus use devices to show how one body can be carried around by the motion of another, which gives it an opposite motion, or at least a motion not natural to the material involved. Krafft suggests that there might have been only limited use of mechanics as analogue for the cosmos, because the classification of mechanics as 'violent and unnatural motion' means that a 'mechanics of the heavens' would appear to be a contradiction in terms.[143] I have argued that no such generic distinction between natural and artificial is maintained in ancient mechanics. Moreover, some of the specific discussions applying cosmic models to our understanding of the operation of the heavens concern the mode of action of God on the cosmos, which could certainly involve forced motion.

Perhaps the cosmic devices available had limited utility as models of causal explanation in astronomy. In the first place, it is not clear whether there was anything like a modern orrery, a device purporting to be an isomorphic representation of the heavens.[144] Moreover, the kinds of techniques used to coordinate the motion of several wheels turning at different speeds in devices do not obviously translate into physical structures that can be assumed to exist in the

---

[140] *Contra Proclum* 492.20–493.5, cited in Wolff (1987), p. 97.
[141] Wolff (1987), p. 97.   [142] Sambursky (1962), p. 132; p. 147.
[143] Krafft (1970a), p. xvi.
[144] I thank Jim Evans for discussion of the practicalities of building a geocentric orrery.

heavens. Aristotle's attempt to model the heavens used an outer turning sphere to impart movement to other spheres in turn; quite how this motion was transmitted was left a little vague, especially where some spheres have independent motions, at different speeds and in different directions. Geared devices work from a central driving rotation. Calendrical devices do not have the same topography as the heavens and do not map readily onto a physical model of the heavens.

This point is made by a Latin author, Martianus Capella (fifth century CE), in his *Marriage of Philology and Mercury,* where he challenges those who use armillary spheres[145] as a way to understand the heavens themselves. He makes two objections. The first is methodological: since the earth is more genuine than a copy, he says, one should not look to a copy to understand the original.[146] The second is a substantive point of disanalogy between models and the heavens: armillary spheres require an axis and pivots to work, and there is nothing comparable to these in the rarefied aether. His point is a just one. In contrast to the functioning of organisms, where mechanical devices offered new models of the causal processes that were possible without ongoing intervention, ancient mechanics seems to have contributed less to cosmological speculation. Although this is the area where some scholars have identified 'mechanical' thinking in antiquity, the depth of the appeal to mechanics to understand the workings of astronomy seems actually less than in the case of organisms.

MECHANICAL ANALOGIES IN COSMOLOGY

Even if cosmic models were not regarded as particularly illuminating in the context of ancient Greek astronomy, there is another way in which devices might have been used in cosmological speculation.

---

[145] *sphaera aenea, quae cricote dicitur, de Nupt.* 8.815.

[146] *nihil solidius terra sit, de Nupt.* 8.815. Kuhn (1957), pp. 37–40, notes that models such as the two-sphere universe do in fact allow one to 'read off' some of its implications: Columbus' miscalculation of the length of his voyage is a famous example. Cf. Evans (1998), pp. 79–80.

This would work at a more general level, used not to account in detail for the motions of the heavenly bodies, but rather to illustrate a broader point about the functioning of the heavens in relation to the divine. As a model for the existence of complex causal sequences producing a determinate result without ongoing intelligent direction, working artifacts suggest a way to think about the relationship between nature as a whole and a directing intelligence.

In a post-Newtonian context, the idea that the universe might run 'by itself', according to a determinate sequence, is often expressed in terms of the unfolding of laws of nature governing the operation of everything within it. In a context where this thought is hard to formulate, an analogy to a mechanical device provides a way to conceptualize the possibility that apparently intended results could be brought about by automatic material processes, without ongoing intelligent direction. Such a view of the functioning of nature under-cuts some ways of conceiving of the functioning of teleology in nature, at least where it is thought to require quasi-intelligent powers or natures directing the ongoing selective responses of organisms to environmental changes. We have already seen this debate in Galen's reaction to the mechanical analogy in medicine. Other texts from late antiquity echo similar themes at a cosmic level.

First, it is necessary to note a potential confusion. In looking for evidence that ancient authors considered whether the universe as a whole might work 'like a machine', there is no one term or phrase that, alone, is sufficient evidence of the presence of a mechanistic conception of nature. Otto Mayr, for example, takes use of the Latin phrase *machina mundi* as evidence of the view that the world is a machine.[147] Mayr cites Lucretius as the first to use the term *machina mundi*; he interprets Lucretius as claiming that the cosmos is a machine. If this were true, it might well reflect the understanding of the cosmos in Epicurus, the Greek atomist on whom he draws. But, as I suggested earlier, the context does not support this reading.

Cicero, the other source whom Mayr cites for evidence of a mechanistic world-picture in the Hellenistic period, draws an

---

[147] Mayr (1986), p. 39.

analogy between the heavens and Archimedes' heavenly models in the passages discussed above. However, he uses them only to address the idea that the cosmos was created. His Epicurean spokesman Velleius attacks Plato's idea of a divine craftsman creating a cosmos, asking what kinds of tools and levers were employed.[148] It is the building of the world that is thought to require devices, not its functioning: the devices used here are hand-operated tools used by the divine craftsman. In another passage Cicero talks about Archimedes' model of the cosmic spheres in order to reaffirm the existence of a designer.[149] The examples show that he is concerned to argue only for the existence of intelligence behind the design. In *Tusculan Disputations* Cicero's spokesperson claims that it is only by sharing in divine intelligence that Archimedes is able to imitate the action of the god in *Timaeus*, who created the world.[150] Thus Archimedes' construct – rather than depersonalizing the operation of the cosmos – is used to provide yet stronger evidence of divine intelligence.[151]

Other authors make more systematic use of working artifacts as models for the cosmos. The pseudo-Aristotelian *de Mundo* endorses a 'machine analogy' for divine action in the universe, in order to distance the divine from management of the details. The text compares a designer god to an engineer – amongst many other conflicting analogies – in that he has the ability to accomplish many effects by releasing a single trigger.[152] The divine activity that can produce different effects from a single action is compared to someone moving several parts in turn by one string; each part of a complex whole responds in different ways, according to its own constitution.[153] The

---

[148] *Nat. D.* 1.8. Cf. Steel (2007), pp. 13–14, discussed in Chapter 2 above.

[149] *Nat. D.* 2.35.   [150] *Tusc.* 1.63.

[151] See Hunter (forthcoming). Cf. Gregory of Nyssa, *in Sanctum pascha* 9.257.27.

[152] The date and authorship are still debated: see, e.g., Mansfeld (1992); Keyser (forthcoming).

[153] ... ἀλλὰ τοῦτο ἦν τὸ θειότατον, τὸ μετὰ ῥᾳστώνης καὶ ἁπλῆς κινήσεως παντοδαπὰς ἀποτελεῖν ἰδέας, ὥσπερ ἀμέλει δρῶσιν οἱ μηχανοτέχναι, διὰ μιᾶς ὀργάνου σχαστηρίας πολλὰς καὶ ποικίλας ἐνεργείας ἀποτελοῦντες. Ὁμοίως δὲ καὶ οἱ νευροσπάσται μίαν μήρινθον ἐπισπασάμενοι ποιοῦσι καὶ αὐχένα κινεῖσθαι καὶ χεῖρα τοῦ ζῴου καὶ ὦμον καὶ ὀφθαλμόν, ἔστι δὲ ὅτε πάντα τὰ μέρη, μετά τινος εὐρυθμίας. Οὕτως οὖν καὶ ἡ θεία φύσις ἀπὸ

effect produced in each part by the initial trigger depends on the construction of a device: the engineer only releases the trigger and does not directly control the subsequent reactions.

This text, replete with Stoic and Platonic ideas, suggests that divine intervention in the cosmos is from a distance, since it is not appropriate for a great ruler to be constantly engaged in the minutiae of administration. The claim is not consistently maintained, and competing images of divine action are invoked. The larger aims of the passage include addressing the problem of evil by removing a god from direct intervention in the working of the cosmos.[154] It seems that the degree of divine management of cosmic matters became an issue in late antiquity, and that the 'machine analogy' played a part in these debates.

Sextus Empiricus (second century CE) records a reference to the Archimedean sphere by some unnamed Stoics, who use it to prove the existence of the gods. Like Cicero, they argue that if the presence of order demonstrates the presence of divine and intelligent direction, then the greater the evidence of order, the stronger the evidence of the gods.[155] Constructions that move automatically are more marvellous than others,[156] so if Archimedes' device suggests that the heavens are self-moving, this implicitly displays the greater art of a maker who is able to make a device *that runs by itself*. Here, the specific virtue of mechanical devices, as opposed to other technology that merely exhibits forethought, is recognized.

τινος ἁπλῆς κινήσεως τοῦ πρώτου τὴν δύναμιν εἰς τὰ συνεχῆ δίδωσι καὶ ἀπ' ἐκείνων πάλιν εἰς τὰ πορρωτέρω, μέχρις ἂν διὰ τοῦ παντὸς διεξέλθῃ κινηθέν· γὰρ ἕτερον ὑφ' ἑτέρου καὶ αὐτὸ πάλιν ἐκίνησεν ἄλλο σὺν κόσμῳ, δρώντων μὲν πάντων οἰκείως ταῖς σφετέραις κατασκευαῖς, οὐ τῆς αὐτῆς δὲ ὁδοῦ πᾶσιν οὔσης, ἀλλὰ διαφόρου καὶ ἑτεροίας, ἔστι δὲ οἷς καὶ ἐναντίας, καίτοι τῆς πρώτης οἷον ἐνδόσεως εἰς κίνησιν μιᾶς γενομένης, *de Mundo* 398b12ff. (Lorimer). See Furley (1955), p. 390na.

[154] Later, however, the text allows divine goodness to be reflected in detailed interventions: the pious youths who were carrying their aged parents on their shoulders to escape the eruption of Etna were spared as the lava flow parted around them.

[155] Sextus Empiricus, *M.* 9. 111–14.

[156] τά γε μὴν αὐτομάτως κινούμενα τῶν κατασκευασμάτων θαυμαστότερά ἐστι τῶν μὴ τοιούτων, *M.* 9.115 (Mutschmann).

Stoic sources are problematic in this regard, because they begin from a metaphysics within which the ongoing intelligent direction of the universe is diffused throughout living and non-living things. The Stoics would not have any use for a model whose sole purpose was to suggest that things could exhibit apparent order without design, because of their commitment to the universality of design and purpose and to the ubiquity of the material substance that implements and embodies this intelligence.[157] Although I have argued above that Marcus Aurelius does use a machine analogy in the context of human volition, the idea that any part of the cosmos could run 'by itself' without ongoing intelligent direction would be an empty one.

The Stoic appeal to a cosmic machine analogy may make most sense if it is regarded as an *ad hominem* response to others appealing to the machine analogy to undercut the argument for divine design. The Stoics would not be *initiating* the use of the machine analogy, but turning it against their opponents. At least one Christian critic responded in kind. Lactantius (third century CE), draws on Archimedes' sphere in order to show the errors of Stoic immanent teleology. He takes the mechanical analogy to show that attributing design to the world need not make the world itself intelligent or animate.[158] He argues that the Stoics are wrong to take the motions of the heavens as evidence that the stars are living, rather than that their motions are imparted to them by God's design.

The comparison to Archimedes' device here is implicitly used to support the possibility that a sequence of regular and orderly motions could have been produced in a non-living thing by design. He needs to show that there is an alternative to supposing that the motions of the heavens are either actively guided by intelligence on

---

[157] For example, Seneca (first century CE) uses analogies to technology in an unsystematic way, and alongside organic analogies. A siphon analogy is embedded in the comparison to organisms (*Q Nat.* 2.6; 6.14); he uses an organic analogy to explain why water emerges continuously from springs and why rivers flow (*Q Nat.* 3.15). He doubts that the capabilities of artifacts merit comparison: natural forces are better able to create an upward flow than any artificial method (*Q Nat.* 2.9).

[158] Lactantius, *Div. inst.* 2.5.13, cited by Mayr (1986), p. 206 n. 28.

an ongoing basis or happen by chance. Here the possibility of a machine designed to operate without intelligence, yet in a fashion that exhibits design, is used to argue for a particular view of God's relationship to the cosmos. Although Lactantius does not go on to exploit the implications of this model for the study of the natural world, he clearly draws the analogy between cosmic simulacra and the heavens in order to further the idea that the complex and interconnected motions of the heavens could be constructed to exhibit order without ongoing intelligent direction.

Another Christian writer, Synesius of Cyrene (fifth century CE), a student of Hypatia, takes up a similar, if more modest, use of the machine analogy. Rather than think of the cosmos as a whole as a machine, Synesius appears to use the analogy as a way to conceive of divine intervention in the cosmos: he puts into the mouth of an Egyptian sage the idea that divine intervention occurs on an occasional basis, in the same way as power is imparted to theatrical devices, *ta neurospasta organa*. Although he describes the devices as tools, *organa*, it is clear from the context that he is describing working artifacts of considerable complexity. The claim is that the impulse imparted does not last to infinity but continues after the person giving the motion to the device has stopped, for as long as the imparted force remains strong.[159] Synesius' character is focusing on the theology here: he is using the analogy to show how the gods can infuse a persisting harmony into a world that functions independently of them.

Although these two Christian sources have some sympathy with this appeal to mechanics as a way to conceive of divine action, it met with criticism in the Platonic and Aristotelian traditions. The idea of a cosmic craftsman has a natural home in the Platonic tradition, and there is some evidence that Platonists of late antiquity resisted the attempt to interpret Plato's *dēmiourgos* as too much like an engineer. Plotinus (third century CE) attacks the idea that construction techniques might suffice to explain the natural world. He rejects the idea that 'levering' – *to mochleuein* – can account for the production of the

---

[159] Synesius, *Aegyptii sive de providentia* 1.9.36.

natural world, because it will not be able to produce the variety of shapes and colours found.[160] In contrast to those who think that the *dēmiourgia* of nature is like that of wax-modellers, Plotinus objects that craftsmen can only make use of existing colours and cannot produce new ones. The techniques of craftsmen are limited to reshaping and structuring material: they cannot turn straw into gold. The Neoplatonist tradition accepted Aristotelian arguments against the irreducibility of qualitative change, and, like Galen, was concerned to preserve the notion of qualitative transformation in order to account for the functions of organic natures in particular.

Proclus (fifth century CE) also complains about investigators' use of devices to try to understand the processes of the natural world; he mentions alchemists as well as astronomers. In a passage noted by Sambursky for its defence of holism in nature, Proclus lumps together the mathematicians who try to show how the apparently anomalous motions of heavenly bodies can be produced from simpler ones with those who try to predict nature using calendrical devices.[161] A similar complaint about the audacity of trying to provide information about the heavens ahead of time is echoed by Pliny, who regards the heavens as divine.[162] Proclus tells us little about the procedures that are used to 'hunt down' the works of nature, or why he objects to this.

Proclus directs an entire treatise – preserved only in Latin – against the work of a mechanic named Theodorus: Proclus' response indicates that the comparison to a machine was used to argue for necessitation, apparently in the form of causal determinism.[163] Theodorus suggested that the world works like a mechanical device, all things depending on the single driving motion.[164] Some language in the initial presentation suggests that a comparison is being drawn to a theatrical device, although reference is made at the end to some

---

[160] *Enn.* 3.8.2; cf. 5.9.6.   [161] Proclus, *in R.* 234.9–22. Sambursky (1962), p. 60.

[162] *HN* 2.9; 2.10. See Bowen (2002a).

[163] Proclus, *de Providentia*; I thank Paul Keyser and Jan Opsomer for the reference. See Borger (1980); Ziegler (2001).

[164] Proclus, *de Prov.* 1.2.

kind of astronomical calculator.[165] Proclus tells us little about Theodorus' account, but evidently the latter saw the potential of mechanical devices to model the idea that complex causal sequences follow automatically from a single cause. Theodorus seems to be a theoretically trained mechanic as well as a philosopher, since Proclus makes a light reference to one of the classic problems of mechanics, 'to move a given weight with a given force'.[166]

Carlos Steel reads the initial references to a theatrical context as metaphorical and suggests that the device used in comparison is a clock.[167] Given the state of technology, however, the initial discussion is better taken to refer literally to a theatrical *machina*, in order to make the point about deterministic causation by sequential consequences of a single motion. Theodorus apparently uses the same term that other philosophers use when they point to mechanical devices as a model for complex causal sequencing.[168] The reference to astronomical devices at the end makes a different point about our capacity for foreknowledge based on calculation. This is the ambition Proclus criticized in his *Republic* commentary.

Proclus' criticism of Theodorus' programme includes a reference to the presence of 'powers' in organisms.[169] The argument here is compressed, but it is perhaps invoking a Galenic reading of the Aristotelian idea that organic nature requires internal powers of self-maintenance. The idea may be that these specific internal powers cannot be accounted for by structural rearrangements of the parts,[170] but rather – as Plotinus argued against the proponents of 'leverage' – must be produced by qualitative alterations, giving rise to irreducibly teleological powers specific to the organism. The Aristotelian view of the organism as a self-maintaining unit is defended: the irreducibly teleological role of natures gives organisms a special kind

---

[165] *parapēgma*, *de Prov.* 12.65.8. Cf. Steel (2007), pp. 3, 91 n. 279, who notes other references to *parapēgmata* in Proclus.

[166] *De Prov.* 4.25.25; Steel (2007), p. 81 n. 117.   [167] Steel (2007), pp. 13–14.

[168] *eirmon* in Latin: *de Prov.* 1.2.8. See below on the use of automata as models for organisms; Steel (2007), pp. 11–12.

[169] *De Prov.* 3.11. See Steel (2007), p. 76 n. 48.

[170] See Galen's criticism of the Erasistratean materialists, above.

of unity and cohesion that cannot be accounted for by thinking of them as parts of a greater interconnected whole. Proclus' concern might have been that the mechanical view of causal sequencing as material interconnections driven by a single mechanism misses the explanatory autonomy that must be accorded to organisms.[171] A machine model of the universe would tend to erase the explanatory boundary between organism and environment, since it accords no special causal priority to the natures of substantial individuals.

Proclus suggests a different critique of the machine analogy at the end of the treatise. He argues that the possibility of constructing calculators shows the existence of incorporeal ideas in the mind of the craftsman, thus – presumably – showing that not every kind of cause can be accounted for by the machine analogy.[172] The argument seems to be that a machine is material, so – if machines cannot include incorporeal ideas – no machine could construct a machine. As in Gregory, the very nature of design is used to show that we, as artisans guided by incorporeal ideas, could not be machines.

The machine analogy seemed to have some play in the cosmological debates of late antiquity, both as a way to think about divine intervention as an occasional rather than ongoing causal intervention, and as a model for complex causal sequencing. Although the philosophers recording these analogies were often those rejecting them, there was clearly some interest in this way of viewing causal transmissions. Mechanical devices do seem to be exploited to make a more general point about the relationship between complex causal sequences and ongoing intelligent direction, a point equally applicable to the case of the heavens or to aspects of the natural world. Just as the author of *de Mundo* appealed to a machine in order to suggest that a god designed the world to run by itself, Lactantius rejects the idea that the regularities of the heavens entail the presence of intelligence internal to the bodies exhibiting those regularities. The machine analogy is used to support the idea that complex

---

[171] *De Prov.* 3.11: I take this to be the point of the reference to Aristotle's claim that organic processes can go against fate. Cf. Steel (2007), p. 76 n. 50.

[172] *De Prov.* 12.65.

ordered sequences could be brought about – in designed complexes –
by material interactions and thus speaks against those who suppose
that teleology requires us to posit ongoing intelligent direction. The
same issue of causal sequencing can be seen in the texts comparing
working artifacts to organisms.

Along with the idea that the cosmos as a whole is a kind of device
constructed to run without ongoing intelligent direction comes
the possibility that we ourselves are part of that matrix. Gregory
and Proclus explicitly respond to this possibility; Marcus Aurelius'
reference to non-sages as puppets implicitly depends on a similar
point. Thus, Christian, Stoic and Platonist alike contrast their
notion of the rational capabilities of human beings to the mechanical hypothesis. The *rejection* of the machine analogy had a particular importance for those concerned to mark out the possibility
of a specifically human capacity to transcend the capacities of
the natural world and to stand in a particular relationship with
the divine.

These responses show the limits to the potential of the machine
analogy as a guiding heuristic in investigating organic nature. I hope
to have demonstrated that, against the background of Hellenistic
mechanics, the machine analogy could clearly be formulated.
Although we know more about the philosophical position of its
detractors, it evidently existed as a hypothesis in late antique natural
philosophy, distinct from both the anti-teleological materialism of
the atomists and the irreducibly teleological powers of a Galen or a
Neoplatonist. While this hypothesis does not seem to have had a
large following, it evidently attracted some attention. The specific
reasons why it was rejected by the philosophical schools deserve
attention, since they are evidently more interesting and more specific
than a separation in kind between art and nature.

Ancient Greek mechanics offered working artifacts complex
enough to suggest that the natural world might work in similar
ways. The rejection of the mechanical hypothesis can tell us much
about the interpretation of teleology in late antiquity, about the
conception of causal sequences, and about the conception of the
relationship between matter and form. Mechanics built devices that

worked, raising new possibilities about what results could be achieved by structural arrangements of matter. Ancient Greek natural philosophers did not simply ignore these attempts at devising nature. There were those in late antiquity who considered a mechanical hypothesis and wondered whether organisms, the cosmos as a whole, or we ourselves, might 'work like that'.

Conclusion

To resume: this argument for the existence of a 'mechanical hypo-thesis' in ancient Greek natural philosophy began with a conceptual examination of the meaning of the terms 'mechanical' or 'mechanistic'. I distinguished the use of the term 'mechanical' as a systematic description of perceived features of a view from the idea that the thinkers in question were explicitly motivated by their own conception of mechanics in formulating a view. Some ancient Greek thinkers can be described as 'mechanistic' in the latter sense, inasmuch as they did appeal to the field of mechanics to understand the natural world. This history has received less attention than it deserves.

A tendency to describe the ancient atomists as 'mechanistic' seems to have deterred scholars from looking for the impact of ancient Greek mechanics on late antique philosophy. Historians of science, meanwhile, have mistakenly concluded from some remarks of Galileo's that, in antiquity, mechanics was systemati-cally excluded from natural philosophy. In the other direction, a few histories of technology think that 'mechanistic conceptions' can be found as far back as Homer. I set aside some misconceptions before studying the impact of ancient Greek mechanics on natural philosophy.

Tracing the history of mechanics, I argue that there is little evidence of it – in any sense of the term – from before the fourth century BCE. Branches of the field were clearly developing in the fourth century. Nonetheless, there is little definitive evidence of what the term *mēchanikē* meant to Aristotle. The claims that the field was 'systematized' by Archytas might be a retrojection, stemming from the fact that his method for finding cube roots came to be important in the building of catapults. Although it is tempting to draw on the earliest surviving text of mechanics – the Aristotelian *Mechanica* – for evidence for the fourth-century history of the discipline, this intriguing text is more likely to be from the early third century, and not by Aristotle himself. Aristotle's work makes only occasional use of such principles, a fact that cannot easily be explained away by a distinction in kind between nature and art. Aristotle's own awareness of quantitative co-variations between various parameters associated with forced motion, though important in their own right, need not have been associated with a *mēchanikē technē*. While some branches of mechanics were clearly developing in the fourth century, the field does not seem to have fully acquired the coherence and intellectual authority it later found. Aristotle, who perhaps formulates the first unambiguously mechanical analogy, ultimately rejects it as adequate to account for the natural world.

The early Hellenistic period – and the Alexandrian court in particular – seems to have been a time when mechanics flourished. We do not know exactly when the different branches of mechanics first came to be understood as falling under a single field, nor why: other than the fact that all its devices clearly *do* something, the field is somewhat heterogeneous. I suggest that this might have been part of its strength: the field of mechanics was driven by experience of what matter can be made to do. Only gradually and partially were its devices unified under theories of their operation.

Even if ancient Greek mechanics never became a theoretically unified discipline, its contributions to natural philosophy were significant. Its best theorists – the author of the Aristotelian *Mechanica*, perhaps Ctesibius, Archimedes, Hero of Alexandria, Pappus – seem to have been responding to the devices built by their contemporaries, offering new evidence of the capacities of matter and its motions. Its theories sometimes extrapolated beyond experience – as when Archimedes offered to move the earth, or Hero offered theoretical devices that might never have been built – projecting theories that were nonetheless grounded in experience. Other mechanical theorists were more sceptical.

The contributions of mechanics to the development of mathematical techniques for quantifying motion are among its historically most prominent ones. In particular, by providing a way to quantify the elusive notion of force, the theory of the balance and lever gave inspiration to the mathematization of motion and its causes. However, it is not the only way in which mechanics contributed to natural philosophy. The 'power of the void' demanded – as Philoponus saw – a new account of matter and the impossibility of void. The exploitation of elasticity in catapults and swords – and Ctesibius' use of the elasticity of air in his pistons – highlighted a property of matter that had not received philosophical attention previously. Pneumatic devices offered intriguing evidence of cases where bodies could be held or moved despite their natural tendencies: siphons and pumps showed how water could be made to go uphill. 'Self-moving' devices, particularly devices with internal wind-up mechanisms, showed that devices could be built that imitate the defining function of animals, namely to start moving when they are not directly pushed or pulled by other bodies. And automata showed how apparently intended results could be produced by sequences of material interactions working without ongoing intelligent direction. Organic nature might not be so different after all.

The defenders of irreducibly teleological elements in the natural world – natures, qualitative transformations producing irreducibly distinct powers – were evidently resisting attempts to assimilate all change to structural rearrangements of the kinds found in craft production: the gods could not, they tell us, create the world by leverage alone. When Galen complains that mechanical arrangements such as those found in pneumatics could not adequately account for organic physiology, he is rejecting a research programme in medicine that seems to go back to the third century BCE. Wind-up devices offer a new model for divine action on the cosmos, showing that causal sequences can be preprogrammed to unwind in a determinate sequence, requiring only intermittent intervention, not ongoing direction. Teleologists concede the point, responding that it shows even greater evidence of divine forethought to be able to design such a mechanism. Although the mechanical hypothesis might have been on the losing side in late antiquity, there is evidence of its impact on natural philosophy.

Despite the evidence I have pointed to, there was nothing like the systematic interest in mechanics that occurred in the early modern world. There may not be one single explanation for this. Other 'intermediate sciences' in late antiquity – astronomy and optics – took refuge in a certain insulation they enjoyed from the seemingly insoluble problems in natural philosophy over the motion of the heavenly bodies or the physicality and directionality of vision.[1] It was only with the resolution of these obstacles that these sciences could be integrated into natural philosophy. It is plausible that there was some similar intellectual obstacle to the integration of the methods of mechanics more fully into natural philosophy.

The most intriguing philosophical reason for limiting the applicability of mechanical theories to nature arises over the issue of projectibility of quantitative co-variations. The Neoplatonists developed a theory of minima and the suitability of matter in order to address a problem inherent in their metaphysics of causation. Viewing forms as constantly emanating their causal influence, they needed an explanation of the fact that these causes are not producing uniform effects in all things at all times. The idea of minimal thresholds for the suitability of matter provided this explanation, offering a reason to challenge Archimedes' claims for the indefinite extension of the 'law of the lever'. Mechanical theory seemed to Neoplatonist philosophers to make false assumptions about the relationship between matter and form in falsely extending linear quantitative relationships beyond their appropriate domain.

Mechanical devices were also used to reconsider conceptions of divine action. The comparison between devices and the workings of the heavens was used to work out different conceptions of divine action and the responsibility of the divine for the functioning of the cosmos. Mechanics might also have been perceived as impious

---

[1] The meaning of 'saving the phenomena' in astronomy has been much discussed: see Duhem (1969); G. E. R. Lloyd (1991). For the 'insulation strategy' in optics, see Berryman (forthcoming 2).

inasmuch as its models were used for prediction: Pliny and Proclus hint at a charge of *hubris* against the mechanics. The field was taken to demonstrate the power of knowledge: a frequent trope was that it could give one man the power of many, whether to move ships or overcome great armies. Unlike mythological figures, whose feats were surrounded by the aura of divine power, Archimedes showed the power of unassisted human ingenuity. The role of devices in imperial processions and displays attests to the continuing role of this discipline as emblematic of social power, not power over nature. By undercutting the argument for the unfathomability of natural changes and the unanalysable creation of powers in natural things, it could be seen to place human creative powers on the same plane as those of the divine. Those who rejected the machine analogy focused on its threat to the immateriality of the human mind; they reasserted this by affirming the power of human capacity to design machines. The line separating human from divine was under reconsideration.

The impact of ancient mechanics on Greek philosophical thought after Aristotle has been little studied, at least partly because of some misconceptions. The evidence I have presented shows that ancient mechanics took their art to contribute to natural philosophy; that natural philosophers took account of work in mechanics; and that some figures, at least, considered the possibility that the world might 'work like that'.

Appendix: Ancient mechanics and the mechanical in the seventeenth century

It is only in the seventeenth century that the term 'mechanical' came into common use to describe a way of doing natural philosophy. This appendix draws on the results of recent scholarly work on this period in disentangling different threads in the complex history of the term 'mechanical'. There are several reasons for attempting to trace the reception of the ancient Greek tradition of mechanics in the seventeenth century. One is to show why twentieth-century usage, based as it is on an opposition that was formulated in the early modern period, is so multifaceted. A second is to justify my rejection of a scholarly commonplace that a view of mechanics Galileo rejects goes back to antiquity. The third is to indicate that the sense in which I have been writing of a 'mechanical hypothesis' in late antiquity is similar to the sense in which that phrase came to be used in the seventeenth century.[1] Comparisons between the ancient and modern reception of mechanics are most often made by experts in the latter period; I hope it does not seem unduly hubristic to trace that reception from a different perspective. This is not of course intended as a complete account of the meanings of 'mechanical' in the seventeenth century but rather focuses on the reception of 'mechanics' in the ancient Greek sense. Because modern categories are shaped by seventeenth-century usage, attention to the shaping of those categories is a task that scholars of ancient Greek thought cannot avoid.

---

[1] I develop this argument in a paper, 'Ancient Atomism and the Mechanical Philosophers', in preparation.

I shall first indicate how 'mechanical philosophy' came to be so-called because of its appropriation of the traditional discipline of mechanics: the work of Galileo, Descartes and Boyle in particular shows this derivation. A second sense of 'mechanical' was also in use at the beginning of the seventeenth century, one with only a spurious connection to the ancient discipline of mechanics. Although this second use played a role in the ideas of the New Science, particularly in Bacon's elevation of the manual arts, it does not seem to be as central as the connection to ancient mechanics in shaping the sense of the term 'mechanical'. The third and fourth senses of the term that emerged in the seventeenth century – referring to a particular form of materialism, and to the mathematization of natural philosophy respectively – both depend on the connection to ancient mechanics. The sense in which the 'mechanical philosophy' came to be called 'mechanical' seems to depend primarily upon its perceived use of ideas from the mechanical tradition inherited from antiquity.

THE DISCIPLINE OF MECHANICS AND THE 'MECHANIZATION' OF PHILOSOPHY

The seventeenth century saw a number of philosophies that look to one particular field for inspiration as to the governing principles of the natural world. The 'Hermetical Philosophers',[2] with their 'Chymical Hypothesis'[3] or 'Chymists Philosophy'[4] tried to explain all phenomena from the interactions of three fundamental substances, each with its own unique powers. The 'Magnetique Philosophy'[5] took inspiration from the fact that, in Gilbert's work, a clear parallel had been drawn between the earth and the magnet, offering hope that all forces of attraction and repulsion in the natural world could be explained from a single principle. Henry More even refers, in his correspondence of 1678, to 'Elastick

---

[2] E.g. Charleton (1966), p. 267.
[3] Boyle (1999), vol. VIII, p. 318.   [4] Boyle (1999), vol. II, p. 327.
[5] E.g. Charleton (1966), p. 401. I owe the reference to Cabeo's 1629 work, *Philosophia magnetica*, to Craig Martin.

Philosophers'.[6] The Mechanical Philosophy was so characterized because it appealed to mechanics.[7]

There were, of course, changes in the discipline of mechanics between antiquity and the seventeenth century.[8] Nonetheless, the understanding of its scope, purpose and methods at the beginning of the seventeenth century was essentially continuous with that found in antiquity. Many of the ancient texts themselves received new attention in the sixteenth and early seventeenth centuries, after a period of relative obscurity.[9] Latin translations in the early sixteenth century brought the work to a larger audience.[10] In the same period the *Pneumatica* and *Automata* of Hero of Alexandria were translated; much of Archimedes' work was published in Latin; Vitruvius' *de Architectura*, with its compendium of ancient mechanical devices, became immensely popular, especially in sixteenth-century Italy.[11]

There was some debate at the time as to whether the Aristotelian *Mechanica* still provided the basis for the theory of mechanics, or whether it had been superseded by more abstract, mathematical treatments in the tradition of Archimedes.[12] The Aristotelian text was still regarded as an important source at the University of Padua in the late sixteenth century, and it was taught as part of the

[6] Cited by Shapin and Schaffer (1985), p. 214.

[7] See Menn (1998), pp. 72–3, on the tendency to take some new discovery as a model for a new philosophy. Gabbey (1982) notes More's penchant for coinage, and also the possibly derogatory sense of such neologisms.

[8] For an overview of changes in mechanics, see Moody and Clagett (1952); Clagett (1959); Knorr (1982); E. Grant (1996).

[9] Rose and Drake (1971); Bottecchia Dehò (2000). The Aristotelian *Mechanica* came into circulation in the sixteenth century after it was included in the Greek Aldine edition of 1495–8, the first printed edition of Aristotle's works.

[10] Rose and Drake (1971), pp. 81–8; Laird (1986).

[11] Rose and Drake (1971); Micheli (1995), pp. 136ff.

[12] Rose and Drake (1971); Laird (1986). Pappus is sometimes thought to be superimposing the different traditions originated by the Aristotelian text and by Archimedes: e.g. Roux (1996), p. 12. However, Archimedes seems to have adopted some central ideas from the Aristotelian approach, and there is evidence that, even before Pappus, the two traditions were not seen as competing so much as complementary. See Knorr (1982), pp. 115ff.; Micheli (1995), p. 118; and Russo (2004), p. 352 for the idea that the division of ancient mechanics into two competing approaches only originated with modern scholars.

curriculum by professors of mathematics, including Galileo.[13] Wallace
has argued that the Jesuits of the Collegio Romano – important influ-
ences on the early work of Galileo – regarded the Aristotelian *Mechanica*
as a legitimate approach to the study of motion.[14] Galileo wrote an early
work on mechanics, as it was traditionally conceived; his mature work
still drew on the Aristotelian *Mechanica*.[15] Whatever 'mechanics' later
came to mean, at the dawn of the seventeenth century it was still
recognizably the discipline inherited from antiquity. The ancient
Greek classifications of the subfields of mechanics are still maintained
in the work of, for example, Barrow and Boyle.[16]

A number of scholars have noted the importance of the methods
of the tradition of mechanics in the new science of motion.[17]
Westfall noted how the new programme to develop a quantified,
mathematical science of motion originated in an attempt at extension of the law of the lever.[18] Of the techniques of the new physics
drawn from the discipline of mechanics, the most important was that
of measuring the nebulous notion of power or force by assessing the
amount of weight required to keep a system in equilibrium. In the
Two New Sciences, for example, Salviati measures the 'force of

---

[13] Rose and Drake (1971), pp. 92ff.; Laird (1986), pp. 58ff.; Bottecchia Dehò (2000),
pp. 17–25.

[14] Wallace (1984), p. 202; see below.

[15] Rose and Drake (1971), pp. 95–6; de Gandt (2003), p. 341. There are explicit
references to the *Mechanica* in *Two New Sciences*: Galilei (1974), pp. 109–10; 123;
131–3; 257.

[16] See Gabbey (1992b), pp. 311–14. Boyle (1999), vol. VI, p. 455, lists the branches of
mechanics to include not only statics but also fields such as 'Centrobaricks' that
echo the Greek tradition: this is Archimedes' term for centres of weight, and is used
in Proclus' list of the branches of mechanics.

[17] Duhem (1991), p. 182; Dijksterhuis (1955); Westfall (1971); Ferrari (1984);
Gabbey (1992a), p. 311; Crombie (1994), pp. 567–72; Machamer (1998); See
Mahoney (1998); Garber (2000), p. 198; De Groot (2000); Festa and Roux
(2001); Meli (2006).

[18] Westfall (1971), pp. 18–19. Westfall argues that the development of the theory of
motion and its causes between the times of Galileo and Newton was a process of
freeing the theory of motion from the misconceptions acquired along with the
model of the lever, especially the use of speed rather than vertical displacement as
the appropriate parameter.

the vacuum' by finding the weight that is just sufficient to overcome it and move a load that had been suspended.[19] This technique assumes that a weight just sufficient to cause movement in a system can be used as an approximate measure of the force required to keep it in equilibrium.

Since the *Mechanica* was thought to be Aristotle's work, the use of techniques from mechanics in the investigation of natural philosophy need not be perceived as a rejection of Aristotelian science. Mersenne in particular stressed the continuity of Galileo's work on mechanics with the Aristotelian *Mechanica*.[20] Aristotle had classified mechanics as one of several fields – along with optics, astronomy and harmonics – that occupied a position intermediate between mathematical principles and natural philosophy. Mersenne did not initially regard Galileo's programme as a radical break from the Aristotelian tradition, since they both rejected the idea that the purely mathematical approach to mechanics was preferable to the Aristotelian treatise's engagement with causal questions.[21] Some contemporary scholars indeed argue that Galileo's new science of motion was formulated in the spirit of Aristotle's classification of the intermediate sciences, inasmuch as it legitimated the mathematical study of a particular subject without addressing foundational questions of natural philosophy.[22]

---

[19] Galilei (1974), pp. 22–4. See also Kuhn (1977), p. 45, for his demonstration of the limits of *horror vacui*. Machamer argues that Galileo's principal analytic technique is based on the model of a balance: Machamer (1998), p. 60; Machamer and Woody (1994), pp. 216–17. See also Clavelin (1974), p. 122.

[20] An English version might have been transmitted by Hobbes: see Crombie (1994), vol. II, pp. 867, 1450–1 n. 94, 1458 n. 185. On Lenoble's view that Mersenne was the originator of mechanism, see Roux (1996), pp. 739–47.

[21] Dear (1988), p. 127. On Mersenne's use of a mechanical analogy, see Dugas (1958), p. 92. Only later did Mersenne come to adopt Beeckman's more radical ideal of a new 'physico-mathematical' science: Dear (1995), pp. 163ff. On Beeckman's influence on Descartes, see Dugas (1958), pp. 116ff.; Garber (1992).

[22] Machamer (1978); Weisheipl (1985); Lennox (1986). Laird (1997) argues that the Aristotelian view of the intermediate sciences is nonetheless inadequate for Galileo's purposes. See Garber (2000), p. 197, on the relationship of 'physico-mathematical science' to the methods of the *mathematica mixta*.

Descartes – often described as 'Mechanick' by his English contemporaries[23] – claimed that 'my whole physics is nothing but
mechanics'.[24] One reason for his interest in mechanics is that it
seems to reveal its causes.[25] Mechanical devices are not only said to
operate in the same ways as natural bodies but – inasmuch as they
are large enough to be perceived – visibly to exemplify the principles governing both.[26] Moreover, they provide a context in which
the forces at work can be quantified.[27] Boyle shared with Descartes
the view that mechanics, traditionally conceived, is a paradigm of
intelligibility. He described practical mechanics as useful to the
imagination of the investigator by suggesting, writ large, the kinds
of means to be found in natural things. This view that mechanical
demonstrations are perspicuous did not go undisputed: in challenging Boyle's claim to produce a vacuum with his air pump, Hobbes
points to the inability of the experimental results to prove one
theory over another.[28] Although not immune to challenge, the
belief in the intelligibility of the devices used in mechanics does
seem to be a central feature of the *reception* of mechanical devices in
the history of natural philosophy. This idea has roots in antiquity,
as I have argued.

Mechanical devices also seem to have been taken to bolster
'bottom-up' analysis of the properties of complex wholes. This
is because machinery offers a context in which the functions of
complexes are readily understood to be produced by structural

---

[23] More refers to Descartes as a 'Sublime and Subtil Mechanick' in his *Democritus
    Platonissans*: see Gabbey (1982). Charleton (1966), p. 152, accuses Descartes of
    'Solving all the Operations of Sense by Mechanick Principles'. Glanvill (1978),
    p. 38, refers to Descartes as 'Master of Mechanicks'.
[24] Descartes (1964), vol. II, p. 542; cited by Menn (1998), p. 73.
[25] Descartes (1985), vol. I, pp. 33–4; pp. 288–9; cf. Laudan (1981) for a different
    reading of the clock analogy in Descartes.
[26] Descartes (1985), vol. I, pp. 288–9, 198–200.
[27] On the difficulties in determining exactly what parameters were at issue, see Dugas
    (1958), esp. pp. 133–47.
[28] Shapin and Schaffer (1985), pp. 82–91; Hobbes (1839), vol. I, pp. 420–5; 519–21.

arrangements of material parts.[29] As Mahoney puts it, machines are 'quintessentially analytic: one understands their workings by taking them apart and seeing how the parts go together'.[30] This idea that the properties of the parts together, given their arrangement, are sufficient to account for the properties of the whole directly challenged the Aristotelian tradition's insistence on the need for explanatorily irreducible form in addition to material components. Some degree of reconceptualization seems to be an inevitable result of the attempt to generalize one field and apply it to a broader domain.[31] Still, the central part of traditional mechanics, the 'science of determining the amount of force to be applied in order to produce a certain effect',[32] provided an important theoretical inspiration for a new approach to the study of motion.

The building of sophisticated 'working artifacts' in the modern world doubtless also fostered the heuristic role of the discipline, since they suggested the extent to which complex, self-moving and self-regulating systems could be designed to work without – apparently – needing ongoing intelligent direction. The presence of complex working artifacts such as clocks in the public sphere has been credited with fostering the spread of 'mechanistic' conceptions of the natural world, from Kepler's comparison between the heavenly bodies and clockwork to Descartes' animal machines. However, we should not overlook the extent to which the rediscovery and publication of ancient collections of mechanical devices inspired modern works. Salomon de Caus, for example, acknowledges his debt to the work of Hero of Alexandria and Archimedes on the frontispiece of his treatise on devices.[33] Some of the devices constructed and on

---

[29] On the importance of Zabarella's method of analysis and the machine analogy, see J. H. Randall (1940); Dijksterhuis (1961); McMullin (1978); Wallace (1984), pp. 122ff.; Mikkeli (1992), (1997); Laird (1997).

[30] Mahoney (1998), p. 744.

[31] On the reasons why the discipline of mechanics is not *more* evident in Descartes' work, see Gabbey (1993b), pp. 318–20; Garber (2002).

[32] Weisheipl (1985), p. 36.

[33] Caus (1624); Bredekamp (1995), p. 50. On Philo's reception, see Prager (1974), pp. 28–31.

public display in the early modern period owed much to ancient treatises.[34] Some credit clockwork in particular – rather than the kinds of devices available in antiquity – with inspiring 'mechanical' conceptions of the natural world.[35] It is certainly true that technological innovations such as the spring vastly increased the complexity of wind-up devices over those of antiquity, and the length of time for which they could be left to run unassisted.[36] But the simpler wind-up devices of antiquity seem to have elicited a similar reaction, although the time scale of their independent motions is much less. I suggest that the difference is one of degree, not of kind.

Pneumatic technology is also prominent in some of the classic articulations of the potential of mechanics for illuminating the workings of nature. Consider Descartes' famous use of the machine analogy in his treatise *On Man*:

> I suppose the body to be nothing but a statue or machine made of earth, which God forms with the explicit intention of making it as much as possible like us. Thus God not only gives it externally the colours and shapes of all the parts of our bodies, but also places inside it all the parts required to make it walk, eat, breathe, and indeed to imitate all those of our functions which can be imagined to proceed from matter and to depend solely on the disposition of our organs. We see clocks, artificial fountains, mills, and other such machines which, although only man-made, have the power to move of their own accord in many different ways.[37]

Although the leading comparison here is also to clockwork, the devices most critical in sustaining the idea that organisms might be replicated by technological devices are really the fountains. A central problem in physiology, addressed by the analogy, is to account for breathing and the 'flow of spirits'. For this, Descartes turns to 'pneumatics', a field that had been part of the discipline of mechanics since antiquity and was still so regarded.[38] It concerns the building of

---

[34] Bredekamp (1995), p. 50. The 'owl-and-birds' described by Montaigne (1929), p. 165, for example, is straight out of Hero's *Pneumatica*; cf. Bedini (1964), p. 26.

[35] E.g. Mayr (1986); see also Rossi (1970), pp. 36ff.

[36] Cf. 'spring' (*ressort*) in Descartes (1985), vol. I, p. 100.

[37] Descartes (1985), vol. I, p. 99.

[38] Boyle (1999), vol V, p. 351; Boyle (1999), vol. XI, p. 148.

devices that produce effects by the motion of fluids and includes composites of pipes, siphons, pumps, whistles, and the like.[39]

The idea that this use of a governing analogy amounts to a 'Mechanick Philosophy' first appears in Henry More's 1659 work, *The Immortality of the Soul*.[40] More is citing and perhaps labelling an objection that others have brought against his own theory:

> As for the Spirit of Nature, the greatest exceptions are, that I have introduced an obscure Principle for Ignorance and Sloth to take sanctuary in, and so to enervate or foreslack the useful endeavours of curious Wits, and hinder that expected progress that may be made in the Mechanick Philosophy; and this, to aggravate the crime, before a competent search be made what the Mechanical powers of Matter can doe. For what Mechanical solutions the present or foregoing Ages could not light upon, the succeeding may; and therefore it is as yet unseasonable to bring in any such Principle into Natural Philosophy.[41]

More is criticizing advocates of a hypothesis that 'mechanical principles' alone could constitute a natural philosophy. His own philosophy acknowledges these in their proper sphere but denies that they are the only forces operating in the natural world.[42] In *An Antidote to Atheism* More again takes issue with Descartes, 'the great Master of this Mechanical Hypothesis': his concern is whether the laws of mechanics are sufficient to explain all natural phenomena.[43]

When Boyle embraces the term 'mechanical philosophy' in 1661,[44] he makes clear that he also thinks a 'mechanical philosophy' derives its name from its use of the principles at work in the discipline of

---

[39] Des Chene (2001).

[40] Although Boyle is generally regarded as popularizing the idea of a mechanical philosophy, Anstey (2000), p. 12 n. 2, notes that this passage predates Boyle's first use of the term in print. I thank Alan Gabbey for noting, in correspondence, that Boyle's earliest use of the term appears in a treatise written some years before it was published.

[41] More (1978), p. 11.   [42] More (1978), pp. 197–9.

[43] More denies this, citing gravity and 'Fuga Vacui' as counter-evidence: More (1978), p. 43. These passages from book 2, chapter 2.7–13, are not found in the first (1653) edition. On More, see Breteau (1997); Cottingham (1997); Gabbey (1982), (1990), (1992a), (1993c); A. R. Hall (1990); J. Henry (1990).

[44] Boyle (1999), vol. II, pp. 83–91. The index to Hunter and Davis' edition indicates that the earliest citation in the Correspondence dates from 1665.

mechanics. Although he sometimes gives this term a particular fixed meaning – that it uses explanations based on 'matter and motion' – he repeatedly clarifies that explanation by 'matter and motion' is 'mechanical' *because* these are the factors at work in mechanical devices.[45] 'Motion, Size, Figure, and Contrivance of their own Parts' are called 'Mechanical Affections ... because to Them men willingly Referre the various Operations of Mechanical Engines.'[46] Boyle even insists on this open-ended, comparative sense, rather than identifying 'mechanical' with a certain kind of materialism. Henry More objects that Boyle would be unable to give mechanical causes of certain phenomena such as gravity, taking 'mechanical causes' to mean those that depend on local motion, size and shape.[47] Boyle's reply is that his work deserves to be called mechanical not because he can explain the causes of gravity in a certain way, but because he follows *accepted practice in the field of mechanics*, by treating the heaviness of bodies as a given.[48] He insists that the heuristic role of mechanics is definitive of a mechanical philosophy.

An attempt to apply the principles of mechanics to the natural world could take different forms, especially as the field of mechanics was quite heterogeneous, including many areas other than merely the study of simple machines.[49] There are certain features that seem to be particularly prominent in these seventeenth-century attempts to make such an application. First, mechanics presented a field in which the relationships between various parameters were understood to stand in quantified co-varying proportions and offered the possibility that the conditions for motion more generally could be understood in mathematical terms. Notions of force and active cause of motion were understood to be commensurate with the weight that could be kept in balance by a given force; when the amount of action required to move a weight was taken to be approximately – only slightly more than – that measured at equilibrium, this offered the

[45] Anstey (2000), p. 4.
[46] Boyle (1999), vol. v, p. 302; also Boyle (1999), vol. viii, p. 331.
[47] Boyle (1999), vol. vii, pp. 148, 158; cf. also More (1978), pp. 12–13. See Crombie (1994), vol. i, pp. 666–7.
[48] Boyle (1999), vol. vii, p. 148.   [49] Meli (2006), pp. 20, 42.

possibility of studying the causes of motion in quantified terms. Second, insofar as the devices in the mechanics tradition show us how certain functions can be imitated in artificial devices, the application of mechanics to the natural world also suggests that we should look for material causes, acting by contact, and accounted for by their structural arrangements rather than their qualitative features. Third, because the causes at work in mechanical devices were taken to be perspicuous, the appeal to mechanics lent credence to materialism and the search for perceptible, contact-action causes. If a device works solely because of the properties of the material parts arranged into a certain structure, this suggests a methodology for investigation and undercuts the need to turn to substantial forms or other 'top-down' explanatory devices.[50] Only certain parameters – those that are thought to co-vary with one another – are treated as relevant. Another possible implication of the machine analogy is to allow the possibility of design and a designer, thus accommodating a particular kind of analysis to theological concerns.

THE MECHANICAL ARTS AND THE 'MECHANIZATION' OF PHILOSOPHY

As mentioned before, there is a second sense of the term 'mechanics' in the seventeenth century that is only tenuously connected to ancient mechanics. In the Middle Ages the label 'mechanical arts' came to be applied to the entire range of productive arts.[51] Hugh of St Victor initiated a practice of referring to all fields of human production as 'mechanical', on the grounds that they imitate nature. This is not because the discipline of mechanics was so understood, but because – following a mistaken ninth-century etymology – he takes the Greek word *mēchanē* to be derived from *moichus* or *moechus*, adulterer.[52] Hugh's source, Martin of Laon, interprets the

---

[50] For the idea that 'mechanical explanation' refers to *structural* explanation, see McMullin (1978).
[51] See below.
[52] Hugh of St Victor, *Didascalion* 1.9; J. Taylor (1961), p. 191 n. 64; Sternagel (1966).

association with adultery to mean that the 'mechanical' is that which is clever and escapes detection in its operation by means of this ingenuity.[53] Thus calling arts rather generally 'mechanical' was understood to imply that they are deceptive imitations of nature. Hugh's influential schema lists seven 'mechanical arts' to parallel the traditional liberal arts;[54] he includes agriculture, navigation and cloth-making, but no branch of what the Greeks would have called mechanics. This gave rise to a very broad sense of the term in early modern Europe.[55] It is unfortunately close enough to the first to encourage confusion.[56] It seems to be because of this medieval usage and not the Greek tradition that the term 'mechanical' often carried nuances of the crude, lowly and manual in the sixteenth and seventeenth centuries.[57]

It is a commonplace that the view of the arts and of human creation changed considerably in the Renaissance.[58] Rather than treating art as a poor imitation of nature, the suggestion was raised in sixteenth-century discussions that art and nature working together might even be superior to nature alone.[59] Historians and sociologists of science have stressed the importance of the 'maker's knowledge' tradition, dating to Nicholas of Cusa and Petrus Ramus, which Bacon popularized in early seventeenth-century England.[60] This is sometimes taken to represent a radical break from the reception of

---

[53] J. Taylor (1961), p. 191, citing Laistner.
[54] Hugh of St Victor, *Didascalion* 3.1; E. Grant (1996), pp. 49–50; Weisheipl (1985), p. 213.
[55] See Gabbey (2002), (2004).
[56] Gomperz (1943), p. 166, is unusual in taking the word 'mechanical', as applied to antiquity, to mean 'assimilated to a procedure used in the crafts'. Pappus' remark that the manual part of mechanics includes metal-working and carpentry and building and painting may also seem to allow this sense of 'mechanical' in the Greek tradition: Gabbey (1992b), p. 319, cites Pappus 8.1 on this point. But Pappus lists crafts that are ancillary to architecture, and not all manual arts.
[57] Gabbey (2002), (2004).
[58] E.g. Hooykaas (1963); Crombie (1975), p. 197; Whitney (1990); Pérez-Ramos (1993).
[59] Mikkeli (1992), pp. 107–30.
[60] On Bacon's importance for seventeenth-century science, see, e.g., Merton (1970); Kuhn (1977); Perez-Ramos (1996b); Peltonen (1996).

mechanics in antiquity.[61] Bacon's call for a new programme of inquiry included the study of the 'mechanical arts' and of nature's 'wonders' as evidence of what was physically possible.[62] Since the genre of wonders in the period included biological abnormalities, this category is sometimes seen as standing in contrast to the Aristotelian view of biological abnormalities, which were not ascribed to *phuseis*, the species' natures that are responsible for the regular development of organisms.[63]

Doubtless this second sense of 'mechanical', in common use in the early seventeenth century, was easily conflated with the first.[64] Certainly there are traces of this second sense in, say, Boyle's usage, even though he foregrounds his commitment to take the discipline of mechanics as a point of reference. Alan Gabbey notes the presence of this second sense of the term in Descartes' letter of 1637, responding to Froidmont's derogatory comments about the 'gross and mechanical' crudeness of Descartes' approach.[65]

Still, when Descartes claims to restrict explanation to shape, size and motion, these seem to be features employed in the Greek sense of the term 'mechanical' rather than the medieval.[66] It is difficult to see how this second sense of the term 'mechanical' – the manual arts, that came to be called 'mechanical' by courtesy of the fact that they were once thought to be deceptive imitations of nature – could have given rise to a reductive materialism, or to the programme for a mathematical science of motion. Those who stress the importance of Bacon to seventeenth-century natural philosophy sometimes suggest

[61] Kuhn (1977); Hooykaas (1963); Perez-Ramos (1988), (1996b); Bredekamp (1995), p. 26; Daston and Park (1998); Solomon (1998); Des Chene (2001); Newman (2004), p. 299.

[62] On the interest in wonders and the relationship between technology and nature, see Bredekamp (1995); Daston and Park (1998); Newman (2004).

[63] Daston and Park (1998), pp. 220–31; see Newman (2004), pp. 256ff.; Bredekamp (1995), p. 66; Pérez-Ramos (1996a).

[64] Pérez-Ramos (1988), p. 129, takes it to be paradoxical that Bacon, who lauds the 'mechanical arts', contributed little to the 'mechanization of the world picture'. Recognizing the different meanings of mechanical makes the paradox disappear.

[65] Gabbey (1993b), p. 314; (2004), p. 19.

[66] Descartes (1964), vol. I, pp. 420–1; cited in Gabbey (1993b), p. 314.

that the popularity of corpuscularian theories can be explained by the experimental programme of drawing on the manual arts to discover the properties of nature. Pérez-Ramos, for example, traces to Bacon the notion that science needs no metaphysical commitments other than the investigation of nature by means of 'motion, bulk and figure'.[67] However, Bacon himself does not seem to be emphasizing these three properties in particular: in describing gold, for example, he talks of its 'simple natures', including 'tawny colour, weight, ductility, stability, melting, solution, and so on'.[68] Arts such as metallurgy, glass-making and agriculture hardly tend to suggest the view that matter is passive, pure extension: these might equally be the arts inspiring chemical or hermetical philosophy, or – in the case of agriculture – substantial forms.

Scholars studying the seventeenth century have shown that there are four ways in which the term 'mechanical' is used: of a method of understanding other fields by appeal to the discipline of mechanics inherited from antiquity; of the manual arts more broadly; of a particular kind of materialism; and of a mathematical science of motion. It seems that the third and fourth senses came to be called 'mechanical' *because* certain laws of motion, or a certain view of the properties of matter, were understood to arise in applying mechanics to natural philosophy. As such, the reasons for quantifying the causes producing motion, or for taking matter to have some properties rather than others, are closely tied to a commitment to view the natural world as 'like mechanics'. Although the second sense of the term 'mechanical' – as purely manual and menial – is doubtless present in seventeenth-century discussions, this does not undermine the claim that the connection with the discipline of mechanics received from antiquity was crucial to the baptism of the 'mechanical philosophy'. The sense in which I write of a 'mechanical hypothesis' is the sense in which the phrase is used in the seventeenth century.

[67] Pérez-Ramos (1996b), pp. 316ff.   [68] Bacon (2000), p. 105.

Bibliography

Algra, Keimpe (1999) 'The Beginnings of Cosmology', in A. A. Long (ed.), *The Cambridge Companion to Early Greek Philosophy*, Cambridge: 45–65.

American School of Classical Studies at Athens (1976) *The Athenian Agora: a Guide to the Excavation and Museum*, Athens.

Anstey, Peter (2000) *The Philosophy of Robert Boyle*, London and New York.

Argoud, Gilbert (1998) 'Héron d'Alexandrie et les *Pneumatiques*', in G. Argoud and J.-Y. Guillaumin (eds.), *Sciences exactes et sciences appliquées à Alexandrie*, Saint-Étienne: 127–45.

Asmis, Elizabeth (1990) 'Free Action and the Swerve: Review of Walter G. Englert, *Epicurus on the Swerve and Voluntary Action*', *Oxford Studies in Ancient Philosophy* 8: 275–91.

Asper, Marcus (unpublished) 'Syllogistic Structures in *Probl. mech.* and Aristotelian syllogistics'.

Aujac, Germaine (1979) *Autolycos de Pitane: La sphère en mouvement; Levers et couchers héliques; Testimonia*, texte établi et traduit, avec la collaboration de Jean-Pierre Burnet et Robert Nadal, Paris.

Bacon, Francis (2000) *The New Organon*, ed. Lisa Jardine and Michael Silverthorne, Cambridge.

Balme, David (1939) 'Greek Science and Mechanism I. Aristotle on Nature and Chance', *Classical Quarterly* 33: 129–38.

(1941) 'Greek Science and Mechanism II. The Atomists', *Classical Quarterly* 35: 23–8.

Barnes, Jonathan (1982) *The Presocratic Philosophers*, rev. edn., London and New York.

(ed.) (1984) *The Complete Works of Aristotle. The Revised Oxford Translation*, 2 vols., Princeton.

Bedini, Silvio A. (1964) 'The Role of Automata in the History of Technology', *Technology and Culture* 5: 24–42.

Berggren, J. L. (1991) 'The Relation of Greek Spherics to Early Greek Astronomy', in A. C. Bowen (ed.), *Science and Philosophy in Classical Greece*, New York and London: 227–48.

(unpublished) 'Greek Natural Philosophy and the Origins of Spherics'.

Bernal, Martin (2001) 'Was There a Greek Scientific Miracle? A Reply to Robert Palter', in D. C. Moore (ed.), *Black Athena Writes Back: Martin Bernal Responds to his Critics*, Durham and London: 249–68.

Berryman, Sylvia (1997) '*Horror Vacui* in the Third Century BCE: When Is a Theory Not a Theory?', in R. Sorabji (ed.), *Aristotle and After, Bulletin of the Institute of Classical Studies*, Suppl. 68: 147–57.

(1998) 'Euclid and the Sceptic: a Paper on Vision, Doubt, Geometry, Light and Drunkenness', *Phronesis* 43: 176–96.

(2002a) 'Aristotle on *pneuma* and Animal Self-Motion', *Oxford Studies in Ancient Philosophy* 23: 85–97.

(2002b) 'Continuity and Coherence in Natural Things', in W. W. Fortenbaugh and I. Bodnár (eds.), *Eudemus of Rhodes*, Brunswick, NJ: 157–69.

(2002c) 'Democritus and the Explanatory Power of the Void', in V. Caston and D. Graham (eds.), *Presocratic Philosophy: Essays in Honour of Alexander Mourelatos*, London: 183–91.

(2002d) 'Galen and the Mechanical Philosophy,' *Apeiron: a Journal for Ancient Philosophy and Science* 35: 235–53.

(2002e) 'The Sweetness of Honey: Philoponus against the Doctors on Supervenient Qualities', in C. Leijenhorst, C. Lüthy and J. M. M. H. Thijssen (eds.), *The Dynamics of Aristotelian Natural Philosophy from Antiquity to the Seventeenth Century*, Leiden: 65–79.

(2003) 'Ancient Automata and Mechanical Explanation', *Phronesis* 48: 344–69.

(2005) 'Necessitation and Explanation in Philoponus' Aristotelian Physics', in R. Salles (ed.), *Metaphysics, Soul, and Ethics: Themes from the Work of Richard Sorabji*, Oxford: 65–79.

(2007a) 'The Imitation of Life in Ancient Technology', in J. Riskin (ed.), *Genesis Redux*, Chicago: 85–97.

(2007b) 'Teleology without Tears: Aristotle and the Role of Mechanistic Conceptions of Organisms', *Canadian Journal of Philosophy* 37: 357–70.

(forthcoming 1) 'The Evidence for Strato of Lampsacus in Hero of Alexandria's *Pneumatica*', in W. W. Fortenbaugh (ed.), *Strato of Lampsacus*, Rutgers University Studies in Classical Humanities.

(forthcoming 2) 'Rainbows, Mirrors and Light: Can Aristotle's Theory of Vision be Saved?', in M. Martin and M. Stone (eds.), *Problems of Perception and Vision*, London Studies in the History of Philosophy.

Bobzien, Suzanne (2000) 'Did Epicurus Discover the Free Will Problem?', *Oxford Studies in Ancient Philosophy* 19: 287–337.

Bodnár, István M. (2004) 'The Mechanical Principles of Animal Motion', in A. Laks and M. Rashed (eds.), *Aristote et le mouvement des animaux: dix études sur le* De motu animalium, Villeneuve d'Ascq: 137–47.

Boegehold, Alan L. (1995) *The Athenian Agora*, vol. XXVIII: *The Lawcourts at Athens, Sites, Buildings, Equipment, Procedure, and Testimonia*, Princeton.

Borger, Theo (1980) 'Proklos Diadochos Über die Vorsehung, das Schicksal und den freien Willen an Theodoros, den Ingenieur (Mechaniker)', trans. Michael Erler, *Beiträge zur klassischen Philologie* 121: 1–150.

Bossier, Fernand and Jozef Brams (eds.) (1990) *Aristoteles Latinus VII.I Fasciculus secundus: Physica Translatio Vetus*, Leiden.

Bottecchia Dehò, Maria Elisabetta (2000) *Aristotele, Problemi meccanici: Introductione, testo greco, traduzione italiana, note*, Studia Aristotelica, Catanzaro.

Bowen, Alan C. (1983) 'Menaechmus *versus* the Platonists: Two Theories of Science in the Early Academy', *Ancient Philosophy* 3: 12–29.

(2001) 'La scienza del cielo nel periodo pretolemaico', in S. Petroccioli (ed.), *Storia della scienza*, vol. I: *La scienza greco-romana*, Rome: 806–39.

(2002a) 'The Art of the Commander and the Emergence of Predictive Astronomy', in C. J. Tuplin and T. E. Rihll (eds.), *Science and Mathematics in Ancient Greek Culture*, New York: 76–111.

(2002b) 'Simplicius and the Early History of Greek Planetary Theory', *Perspectives on Science* 10: 155–67.

Bowen, Alan C. and Robert B. Todd (2004) *Cleomedes' Lectures on Astronomy: a Translation of* The Heavens, Berkeley.

Boyle, Robert (1999) *The Works of Robert Boyle*, ed. Michael Hunter and Edward B. Davis, 14 vols., London.

Boys-Stones, G. R. (2001) *Post-Hellenic Philosophy: a Study of its Development from the Stoics to Origen*, Oxford.

Bredekamp, Horst (1995) *The Lure of Antiquity and the Cult of the Machine*, trans. Allison Brown, Princeton.

Bréguet, Esther (1980) *Cicéron: La République*, vol. I, Paris.

Breteau, Jean-Louis (1997) ' "La Nature est un art". Le vitalisme de Cudworth et de More', in G. A. J. Rogers, J. M. Vienne and Y. C. Zarka (eds.), *The Cambridge Platonists in Philosophical Context: Politics, Metaphysics and Religion*, Dordrecht: 145–58.

Bruce, J. D. (1913) 'Human Automata in Classical Tradition and Mediaeval Romance', *Modern Philology* 10: 1–16.

Brumbaugh, Robert S. (1961) 'Plato and the History of Science', *Studium Generale* 9: 520–27.

(1964) *The Philosophers of Greece*, New York.

(1966) *Ancient Greek Gadgets and Machines*, New York.

Burford, Alison (1972) *Craftsmen in Greek and Roman Society*, Ithaca, NY.

Burnyeat, M. F. (1992) 'How Much Happens When Aristotle Sees Red and Hears Middle C? Remarks on *De Anima* 2.7–8', in M. C. Nussbaum and A. O. Rorty (eds.), *Essays on Aristotle's* De Anima, Oxford: 421–34.

Busse, A. (1898) *Philoponi in Aristotelis categoria commentarium*, Commentaria in Aristotelem Graeca 13.1, Berlin.

Cambiano, Guiseppe (1998) 'Archimede Meccanico e la meccanica de Archita', *Elenchos* 19: 291–324.

Carteron, Henri (1975) 'Does Aristotle Have a Mechanics?', in J. Barnes, M. Schofield and R. Sorabji (eds.), *Articles on Aristotle*, vol. 1: *Science*, London: 161–74.

Caston, Victor (1999) 'Aristotle's Two Intellects: a Modest Proposal,' *Phronesis* 44: 199–227.

Caus, Salomon de (1624) *Les raisons des forces mouuantes, auec diuerses machines tant vtiles que plaisantes*, Paris.

Chapuis, Alfred and Edmond Droz (1958) *Automata: a Historical and Technological Study*, trans. Alec Reid, London.

Charles, David (1988) 'Aristotle on Hypothetical Necessity and Irreducibility', *Pacific Philosophical Quarterly* 69: 1–53.

Charleton, Walter (1966) *Physiologia Epicuro-Gassendo-Charltoniana, or a Fabrick of Science Natural upon the Hypothesis of Atoms*, London: 1654, reprinted New York.

Charlton, W. W. (1970) *Aristotle's Physics I, II*, Oxford.

Cherniss, Harold (1935) *Aristotle's Criticism of Presocratic Philosophy*, Baltimore.

Clagett, Marshall (1957) *Greek Science in Antiquity*, London.

(1959) *The Science of Mechanics in the Middle Ages*, Madison.

Clavelin, Maurice (1974) *The Natural Philosophy of Galileo: Essays on the Origins and Formation of Classical Mechanics*, trans. A. J. Pomerans, Boston.

Close, A. J. (1969) 'Commonplace Theories of Art and Nature in Classical Antiquity and in the Renaissance', *Journal of the History of Ideas* 30: 467–86.

Cohen, Morris R. and I. E. Drabkin (1958) *A Source Book in Greek Science*, Cambridge, MA.

Cooper, John M. (1987) 'Hypothetical Necessity and Natural Teleology', in A. Gotthelf and J. G. Lennox (eds.), *Philosophical Issues in Aristotle's Biology*, Cambridge: 243–74.

(2004) *Knowledge, Nature, and the Good: Essays in Ancient Philosophy*, Princeton.

Copenhaver, Brian (1984) 'Scholastic Philosophy and Renaissance Magic in the *De vita* of Marsilio Ficino', *Renaissance Quarterly* 37: 523–54.

Cornford, F. M. (1937) *Plato's Cosmology: the Timaeus of Plato, Translated with a Running Commentary*, London.

(1957) *From Religion to Philosophy: a Study in the Origins of Western Speculation*, New York.

Cottingham, John (1997) 'Force, Motion and Causality: More's Critique of Descartes', in G. A. J. Rogers, J. M. Vienne and Y. C. Zarka (eds.), *The Cambridge Platonists in Philosophical Context: Politics, Metaphysics and Religion*, Dordrecht: 159–72.

Coulton, J. J. (1974) 'Lifting in Early Greek Architecture', *Journal of Hellenic Studies* 94: 1–19.

(1977) *Ancient Greek Architects at Work: Problems of Structure and Design*, Ithaca, NY.

Couprie, Dirk L., Robert Hahn and Gerard Naddaf (2003) *Anaximander in Context: New Studies in the Origins of Greek Philosophy*, Albany.

Crombie, A. C. (1975) 'Marin Mersenne (1588–1648) and the Seventeenth-Century Problem of Scientific Acceptability', *Physis: Rivista Internazionale de Storia della Scienza* 17: 186–204.

(1994) *Styles of Scientific Thinking in the European Tradition: the History of Argument and Explanation especially in the Mathematical and Biomedical Sciences and Arts*, 3 vols., London.

(1996) *Science, Art and Nature in Medieval and Modern Thought*, London.

Culham, Phyllis (1992) 'Plutarch on the Roman Siege of Syracuse: the Primacy of Science over Technology', in I. Gallo (ed.), *Plutarco e le Scienze: Atti del IV Convengo plutarcheo Genova-Bocca de Magra, 22–25 Aprile 1991*, Genova: 179–98.

Cuomo, S. (2000) *Pappus of Alexandria and the Mathematics of Late Antiquity*, Cambridge.

(2001) *Ancient Mathematics*, London.

(2002) 'The Machine and the City: Hero of Alexandria's *Belopoeica*', in C. J. Tuplin and T. E. Rihll (eds.), *Science and Mathematics in Ancient Greek Culture*, New York: 165–77.

(2007) *Technology and Culture in Greek and Roman Antiquity*, Cambridge.

Dalley, S. and J. P. Oleson (2003) 'Sennacherib, Archimedes, and the Water Screw: the Context of Invention in the Ancient World', in *Technology and Culture* 44.1: 1–26.

Daston, Lorraine and Katherine Park (1998) *Wonders and the Order of Nature*, New York.

Dear, Peter (1988) *Mersenne and the Learning of the Schools*, Ithaca, NY.

(1995) *Discipline and Experience: the Mathematical Way in the Scientific Revolution*, Chicago.

(2001) *Revolutionizing the Sciences: European Knowledge and its Ambitions, 1500–1700*, Basingstoke.

De Camp, L. Sprague (1963) *The Ancient Engineers*, London.

De Groot, J. (2000) 'Aspects of Aristotelian Statics in Galileo's Dynamics', *Studies in the History and Philosophy of Science* 31: 645–64.

(2008) '*Dunamis* and the Science of Mechanics: Aristotle on Animal Motion', *Journal of the History of Philosophy* 46: 43–68.

De Haas, Frans (1997) *John Philoponus' New Definition of Prime Matter*, Leiden.

(1999) 'Mixture in Philoponus. An Encounter with a Third Kind of Potentiality', in J. M. M. H. Thijssen and H. A. G. Braakhuis (eds.), *The Commentary Tradition on* De Generatione et Corruptione*: Ancient, Medieval, and Early Modern*, Turnhout: 21–46.

De Lacy, Phillip (1972) 'Galen's Platonism', *American Journal of Philology* 93: 27–39.

(1992) *Galen On Semen*, edition, translation and commentary, Berlin.

Delcourt, Marie (1982) *Héphaistos ou la légende du magicien*, Paris.

Descartes, René (1964) *Oeuvres de Descartes*, ed. C. Adam and P. Tannery, rev. edn., 12 vols., Paris.

(1985) *The Philosophical Writings of Descartes*, trans. John Cottingham, Robert Stotthoff and Dugald Murdoch, 3 vols., Cambridge.

Des Chene, Dennis (2001) *Spirits and Clocks: Machine and Organism in Descartes*, Ithaca, NY.

DeVoto, James G. (1996) *Philon and Heron: Artillery and Siegecraft in Antiquity*. Greek text, translation and notes, Chicago.

Dicks, D. R. (1970) *Early Greek Astronomy to Aristotle*, Bristol.

Diels, Hermann (1893) 'Über das physikalische System des Straton', *Sitzungsberichte der Preussischen Akademie der Wissenschaften* 12: 101–27.

(1915) 'Über Platons Nachtuhr', *Sitzungsberichte der Preussischen Akademie der Wissenschaften* 47: 824–30.

Dijksterhuis, E. J. (1955) *The Principal Works of Simon Stevin*, vol. i: *General Introduction; Mechanics*, Amsterdam.

(1956) *Archimedes*, Copenhagen.

(1961) *The Mechanization of the World Picture*, trans. C. Dikshoorn, Oxford.

Donini, Pierluigi (1988) 'The History of the Concept of Eclecticism', in J. M. Dillon and A. A. Long (eds.), *The Question of Eclecticism: Studies in Later Greek Philosophy*, Berkeley: 15–33.

Dorandi, Tiziano (1991) *Storia dei Filosofi: Platone e l'Academie* (Pherc. 1021 e 164), edizione, traduzione e commento, Naples.

Dover, K. J. (1978) *Greek Homosexuality*, London.

Drabkin, Israel E. (1938) 'Notes on the Laws of Motion in Aristotle', *The American Journal of Philology* 59: 60–84.

(1950) 'Aristotle's Wheel: Notes on the History of a Paradox', *Osiris* 9: 162–98.

Drachmann, A. G. (1948) *Ktesibios, Philon and Heron: a Study in Ancient Pneumatics*, Copenhagen.

(1951) 'On the Alleged Second Ktesibios', *Centaurus* 2: 1–10.

(1958) 'How Archimedes Expected to Move the Earth', *Centaurus* 5: 278–82.

(1963a) *The Mechanical Technology of Greek and Roman Antiquity. A Study of the Literary Sources*, Copenhagen.

(1963b) 'Fragments from Archimedes in Heron's Mechanics', *Centaurus* 8: 91–146.

(1971) 'Heron's Model of the Universe (*Pneumatics* 2:7)', in *Science et Philosophie Antiquité – Moyen Age – Renaissance*, XIIe Congrès International d'Histoire des Sciences Actes Tome IIIA, Paris: 47–50.

Dugas, René (1958) *Mechanics in the Seventeenth Century (from the Scholastic Antecedents to Classical Thought)*, trans. Freda Jacquot, foreword by Louis de Broglie, Neuchatel.

Duhem, Pierre (1969) *To Save the Phenomena; an Essay on the Idea of Physical Theory from Plato to Galileo*, trans. Edmund Doland and Chaninah Maschler, introduction by Stanley L. Jaki, Chicago.

(1991) *The Origins of Statics*, vol. I, trans. Grant F. Leneaux, Victor N. Vagliete and Guy H. Wagner, foreword by Stanley L. Jaki, Dordrecht.

Dupuis, J. (1892) *Théon de Smyrne, philosophe Platonicien. Exposition des connaissances mathématiques utiles pour la lecture de Platon*, Paris.

Edelstein, Ludwig (1967) *Ancient Medicine: Selected Papers of Ludwig Edelstein*, ed. Owsei Temkin and C. Lilian Temkin, Baltimore.

Elliott, Alison Goddard (1997) 'A Brief Introduction to Medieval Latin Grammar', in K. P. Harrington (ed.), *Medieval Latin*, 2nd edn., revised by Joseph Pucci, Chicago: 1–56.

Engberg-Pedersen, Troels (1990) *The Stoic Theory of Oikeiosis: Moral Development and Social Interaction in Early Stoic Philosophy*, Aarhus.

Espinas, Alfred (1903) 'L'organisation ou la machine vivant en Grèce, au IVe siècle avant J.-C.', *Revue de Métaphysique et de Morale* 11: 703–15.

Evans, James (1998) *The History and Practice of Ancient Astronomy*, New York and Oxford.

Faraone, Christopher A. (1992) *Talismans and Trojan Horses: Guardian Statues in Ancient Greek Myth and Ritual*, Oxford.

Farrington, Benjamin (1961) *Greek Science: Its Meaning for Us*, London.

Ferrari, Gian Arturo (1984) 'Meccanica "allargata"', in G. Giannantoni and M. Vegetti (eds.), *La scienze ellenistica. Atti delle tre giornate di studio tenutesi a Pavia dal 14 al 16 Aprile 1982*, Napoli: 225–96.

Festa, Egidio and Sophie Roux (2001) 'Le "παρα φυσιν" et l'imitation de la natura dans quelques commentaires du prologue des *Questions mécaniques*', in J. Montesinos and C. Silos, *Eurosymposium Galileo 2001*, Fundacion de la Historia de la Cienca, La Orotava: 217–36.

Field, J. V. and M. T. Wright (1985) 'Gears from the Byzantines: a Portable Sundial with Calendrical Gearing', *Annals of Science* 42: 87–138.

Finley, M. I. (1965) 'Technical Innovation and Economic Progress in the Ancient World', *The Economic History Review*, 2nd ser., 18: 29–45.

Fleury, P. (1993) *La mécanique de Vitruve*, Caen.

Forbes, R. J. (1949) 'The Ancients and the Machine', *Archives Internationales d'Histoire des Sciences* 28: 919–33.

Forbes, R. J. and E. J. Dijksterhuis (1963) *A History of Science and Technology*, vol. I: *Ancient Times to the Seventeenth Century*, Baltimore.

Forster, E. S. (1913) *Mechanica*, in W. D. Ross (ed.), *The Works of Aristotle Translated into English*, vol. IV, Oxford.

Francis, James A. (1995) *Subversive Virtue: Asceticism and Authority in the Second-Century Pagan World*, University Park, PA.

Fränkel, Hermann (1960) *Wege und Formen frühgriechischen Denkens*, Munich.

Fraser, P. M. (1972) *Ptolemaic Alexandria*, Oxford.

Frede, Dorothea (1985) 'Aristotle on the Limits of Determinism; Accidental Causes in *Metaphysics* E3', in A. Gotthelf (ed.), *Aristotle on Nature and Living Things*, Bristol: 207–25.

Frede, Michael (1992) 'On Aristotle's Conception of the Soul', in M. C. Nussbaum and A. O. Rorty (eds.), *Essays on Aristotle's*, De Anima, Oxford: 93–107.

Freeland, Cynthia (1991) 'Accidental Causes and Real Explanations', in L. Judson (ed.), *Aristotle's* Physics: *a Collection of Essays*, Oxford: 49–72.

Freeth, T., Y. Bitsakis, X. Moussas *et al.* (2006) 'Decoding the Ancient Greek Astronomical Calculator Known as the Antikythera Mechanism', *Nature* 444.30: 587–652.

Friedlein, G. (1873) *Procli Diadochi in primum Euclidis elementorum librum commentarii*, Leipzig.

Frontisi-Ducroux, Françoise (1975) *Dédale: mythologie de l'artisan en grèce ancienne*, Paris.

Furley, David J. (1955) *Aristotle: On the Cosmos*, London and Cambridge, MA.
  (1987) *The Greek Cosmologists*, vol. I: *The Formation of the Atomic Theory and its Earliest Critics*, Cambridge.
  (1989) *Cosmic Problems: Essays on Greek and Roman Philosophy of Nature*, Cambridge.
  (1996) 'The Earth in Epicureanism and Contemporary Astronomy', in G. Giannantoni and M. Gigante (eds.), *Epicureismo Greco e Romano: Atti del Congresso Internazionale Napoli, 19–26 Maggio 1993*, Naples: 119–25.

Furley, David J. and J. S. Wilkie (1984) *Galen on Respiration and the Arteries. Edition with English Translation and Commentary of* De usu respirationis,

An in arteriis natura sanguis contineatur, De usu pulsuum, *and* De causis respirationis, Princeton.

Gabbey, Alan (1982) 'Philosophia Cartesiana Triumphata: Henry More (1646–1671)', in T. M. Lennon, J. M. Nicholas and J. W. Davis (eds.), *Problems of Cartesianism*, Kingston and Montreal: 171–250.

  (1990) 'Henry More and the Limits of Mechanism', in S. Hutton (ed.), *Henry More (1614–1687): Tercentenary Studies*, Dordrecht: 19–35.

  (1992a) 'Cudworth, More and the Mechanical Analogy', in R. Kroll, R. Ashcraft and P. Zagorin (eds.), *Philosophy, Science, and Religion in England 1640–1700*, Cambridge: 109–27.

  (1992b) 'Newton's *Mathematical Principles of Natural Philosophy*: a treatise on "mechanics"?', in P. M. Harman and A. E. Shapiro, *The Investigation of Difficult Things: Essays on Newton and the History of the Exact Sciences in Honour of D. T. Whiteside*, Cambridge: 305–22.

  (1993a) 'Between *ars* and *philosophia naturalis*: Reflections on the Historiography of Early Modern Mechanics', in J. V. Field and F. A. J. L. James (eds.), *Renaissance and Revolution: Humanists, Scholars, Craftsmen and Natural Philosophers in Early Modern Europe*, Cambridge: 133–45.

  (1993b) 'Descartes's Physics and Descartes's Mechanics: Chicken and Egg?', in S. Voss (ed.), *Essays on the Philosophy and Science of René Descartes*, Oxford: 311–23.

  (1993c) ' "A Disease Incurable": Scepticism and the Cambridge Platonists', in R. H. Popkin and A. Vanderjagt (eds.), *Scepticism and Irreligion in the Seventeenth and Eighteenth Centuries*, Leiden: 71–91.

  (2001) 'Mechanical Philosophies and their Explanations', in C. Lüthy, J. E. Murdoch and W. R. Newman (eds.), *Late Medieval and Early Modern Corpuscular Matter Theories*, Leiden: 441–66.

  (2002) 'Newton, Active Powers, and the Mechanical Philosophy', in I. B. Cohen and G. E. Smith (eds.), *The Cambridge Companion to Newton*, Cambridge: 329–57.

  (2004) 'What Was "Mechanical" about "The Mechanical Philosophy"?', in C. R. Palmerino and J. M. M. H. Thijssen, *The Reception of the Galilean Science of Motion in Seventeenth-Century Europe*, Boston: 11–23.

Gaiser, Konrad (1988) *Philodems Academica: Die Berichte über Platon und die Alte Akademie in zwei herkulanensischen Papyri*, Stuttgart and Bad Cannstatt.

Galilei, Galileo (1960) *On Motion and On Mechanics*, trans. Stillman Drake, Madison, WI.

  (1974) *Two New Sciences including Centers of Gravity and Force of Percussion*, trans., introduction and notes by Stillman Drake, Madison, WI.

(1929–40) *Le opere di Galileo Galilei*, Edizione Nationale VIII, ed. Antonio Favaro, 20 vols., Florence.

Gandt, François de (1982) 'Force et science des machines', in J. Barnes, J. Brunschwig, M. Burnyeat and M. Schofield (eds.), *Science and Speculation: Studies in Hellenistic Theory and Practice*, Cambridge: 96–127.

(2003) 'Technology', in J. Brunschwig and G. E. R. Lloyd (eds.), *The Greek Pursuit of Knowledge*, translated under the direction of Catherine Porter, Cambridge, MA: 335–46.

Garber, Daniel (1992) *Descartes' Metaphysical Physics*, Chicago.

(2000) 'A Different Descartes: Descartes and the Program for a Mathematical Physics in the Correspondence', in S. Gaukroger, J. Schuster and J. Sutton (eds.), *Descartes' Natural Philosophy*, London and New York: 113–30.

(2002) 'Descartes, Mechanics, and the Mechanical Philosophy', in P. French and H. Wettstein (eds.), *Midwest Studies in Philosophy 26: Renaissance and Early Modern Philosophy*, Malden, MA: 185–204.

Garber, Daniel, John Henry, Lynn Joy and Alan Gabbey (1998) 'New Doctrines of Body and its Powers, Place, and Space', in D. Garber and M. Ayers (eds.), *The Cambridge History of Seventeenth-Century Philosophy*, vol. I, Cambridge: 553–623.

Giannantoni, Gabriele (1984) 'Su alcuni problemi circa i rapporti tra scienza e filosofia nell' età ellenistica', in G. Giannantoni and M. Vegetti (eds.), *La scienze ellenistica. Atti delle tre giornate di studio tenutesi a Pavia dal 14 al 16 Aprile 1982*, Napoli: 41–71.

Gill, Mary Louise and James G. Lennox (eds.) (1994) *Self-Motion: From Aristotle to Newton*, Princeton.

Glanvill, Joseph (1978) *Scepsis Scientifica: or, Confest Ignorance, the way to Science; In an Essay of The Vanity of Dogmatizing, and Confident Opinion. With a Reply to the Exception of the Learned Thomas Albius*, London 1665, reprinted New York and London.

Godfrey, R. (1990) 'Democritus and the Impossibility of Collision', *Philosophy* 65: 212–17.

Goe, George (1972) 'Archimedes' Theory of the Lever and Mach's Critique', *Studies in History and Philosophy of Science* 2: 329–45.

Goldstein, Bernard R. (1980) 'The Status of Models in Ancient and Medieval Astronomy', *Centaurus* 24: 132–47.

(1997) 'Saving the Phenomena; the Background to Ptolemy's Planetary Theory', *Journal for the History of Astronomy* 28: 1–12.

Goldstein, Bernard R. and Alan C. Bowen (1983) 'A New View of Early Greek Astronomy', *Isis* 74: 330–40.

Gomperz, H. (1943) 'Problems and Methods of Early Greek Science', *Journal of the History of Ideas* 4: 161–76.

Gomperz, T. (1955) *Greek Thinkers: a History of Ancient Philosophy*, vol. 1, trans. L. Magnus, New York.

Gotthelf, Allan (1976) 'Aristotle's Conception of Final Causality', *Review of Metaphysics* 30: 226–54.

Gottschalk, H. B. (1965) 'Strato of Lampsacus: Some Texts', *Proceedings of the Leeds Philosophical and Literary Society* 11: 95–182.

(1968) 'The *De Audibus* and Peripatetic Acoustics', *Hermes* 96: 435–60.

Granger, Frank (1985) *Vitruvius On Architecture*, 2 vols., Cambridge, MA and London.

Grant, Edward (1981) *Much Ado about Nothing: Theories of Space and Vacuum from the Middle Ages to the Scientific Revolution*, Cambridge.

(1996) *The Foundations of Modern Science in the Middle Ages: Their Religious, Institutional and Intellectual Contexts*, Cambridge.

Grant, Robert M. (1952) *Miracle and Natural Law in Graeco-Roman and Early Christian Thought*, Amsterdam.

Green, Peter (1990) *Alexander to Actium: the Historical Evolution of the Hellenistic Age*, Berkeley.

Greene, Kevin (2000) 'Technological Innovation and Economic Progress in the Ancient World: M. I. Finley Re-Considered', *Economic History Review* n.s. 53.1: 29–59.

(2004) 'Archaeology and Technology', in J. Bintliff (ed.), *A Companion to Archaeology*, Oxford: 155–73.

Grene, Marjorie (1963) *A Portrait of Aristotle*, Chicago.

Gros, Pierre (2006) 'Un problème de la science Hellénistique', in *Vitruve et la tradition des traités d'architecture: fabrica et ratiocinatio*, Rome: 437–46.

Guerra, Adele Tepedino and Luigi Torraca (1996) 'Etica e Astronomia nella polemica epicura contro i Ciziceni', in G. Giannantoni and M. Gigante (eds.), *Epicureismo Greco e Romano: Atti del Congresso Internazionale Napoli, 19–26 Maggio 1993*, Naples: 127–54.

Hahm, David E. (1977) *The Origins of Stoic Cosmology*, Columbus.

Hahn, Robert (2001) *Anaximander and the Architects: the Contributions of Egyptian and Greek Architectural Technologies to the Origins of Greek Philosophy*, Albany.

Hall, A. Rupert (1990) 'Henry More and the Scientific Revolution', in S. Hutton (ed.), *Henry More (1614–1687): Tercentenary Studies*, Dordrecht: 37–54.

Hall, Marie Boas (1981) *The Mechanical Philosophy*, New York.

Hamlyn, D. W. (1976) 'Aristotle's Cartesianism', in George C. Simmons (ed.), *Paideia: Special Aristotle Issue*, Buffalo, NY: 8–15.

Hammerstein, Reinhold (1986) *Macht und Klang: Tönende Automaten als Realität und Fiktion in der alten und mittelalterlichen Welt*, Bern.

Hankinson, R. J. (1989) 'Galen and the Best of All Possible Worlds', *Classical Quarterly* 39: 206–27.

(1996) 'Cicero's Rope', in K. Algra, P. van der Horst and D. Runia (eds.), *Polyhistor: Studies in the History and Historiography of Ancient Philosophy*, Leiden: 185–205.

(1998a) *Cause and Explanation in Ancient Greek Thought*, Oxford.

(1998b) *Galen On Antecedent Causes*, edited with an introduction, translation and commentary, Cambridge.

Harrison, J. E. (1908–9) 'Kouretes and Zeus Kouros: a Study in Prehistoric Sociology', *Annual of the British School at Athens* 15: 308–38.

Hassell, Mark (1979) 'Review of J. Ramin, *La technique minière et métallurgique des anciens*, J. F. Healey, *Mining and Metallurgy in the Greek and Roman World*, J. G. Landels, *Engineering in the Ancient World*', *Journal of Roman Studies* 69: 202–3.

Heath, Thomas (1913) *Aristarchus of Samos: the Ancient Copernicus. A New Greek Text with Translation and Notes*, Oxford.

(1921) *A History of Greek Mathematics*, 2 vols., Oxford.

(1953) *The Works of Archimedes*, edited in modern notation with introductory chapters, with a supplement, 'The Method of Archimedes', New York.

Heidel, William Arthur (1933) *The Heroic Age of Science: the Conception, Ideals, and Methods of Science among the Ancient Greeks*, Baltimore.

Helmreich, George (1909) *Galeni De Usu Partium Libri XVII*, Leipzig.

Henry, Devin (2005) 'Embryological Models in Ancient Philosophy', *Phronesis* 50: 1–42.

Henry, John (1986) 'Occult Qualities and the Experimental Philosophy: Active Principles in Pre-Newtonian Matter Theory', *History of Science* 24: 335–81.

(1990) 'Henry More versus Robert Boyle: the Spirit of Nature and the Nature of Providence', in S. Hutton (ed.), *Henry More (1614–1687): Tercentenary Studies*, Dordrecht: 55–76.

Hesse, Mary (1962) *Forces and Fields: the Concept of Action at a Distance in the History of Physics*, New York.

Hicks, R. D. (1972) *Diogenes Laertius: Lives of Eminent Philosophers*, vol. I, Cambridge, MA.

Hiller, E. (1878) *Theonis Smyrnaei philosophi Platonici expositio rerum mathematicarum ad legendum Platonem utilium*, Leipzig.

Hirsch, Ulrike (1990) 'War Demokrits Weltbild mechanistisch und antiteleologisch?', *Phronesis* 35: 225–44.

Hobbes, Thomas (1839) *The English Works of Thomas Hobbes of Malmesbury*, ed. William Molesworth, London.

Hodges, Henry (1970) *Technology in the Ancient World*, London.

Hooykaas, Reijer (1963) 'Das Verhältnis von Physik und Mechanik in histor-
ischer Hinsicht', *Beiträge zur Geschichte der Wissenschaft und der Technik*,
vol. VI, Wiesbaden.

Hornblower, Simon and Antony Spawforth (2003) *The Oxford Classical
Dictionary*, 3rd edn., rev. Oxford.

Huffman, Carl (2003) 'Archytas,' in E. N. Zalta (ed.), *The Stanford
Encyclopedia of Philosophy* (fall 2003 edn.), http://plato.stanford.edu/
archives/fall2003/entries/archytas/.

(2005) *Archytas of Tarentum: Pythagorean, Philosopher and Mathematician
King*, Cambridge.

Hultsch, Friedrich (1878) *Pappi Alexandrini Collectionis quae supersunt*, vol. III,
Berlin.

Humphrey, John W., John P. Oleson and Andrew N. Sherwood (1998) *Greek
and Roman Technology: a Sourcebook*, London.

Hunter, Graham (forthcoming) 'Cicero's Neglected Argument from Design',
British Journal for the History of Philosophy.

Hussey, Edward (1972) *The Presocratics*, London.

(1991) 'Aristotle's Mathematical Physics: a Reconstruction', in L. Judson
(ed.), *Aristotle's Physics: a Collection of Essays*, Oxford: 213–42.

Hutchison, Keith (1982) 'What Happened to Occult Qualities in the Scientific
Revolution?', *Isis* 73: 233–53.

Irby-Massie, Georgia L. and Paul T. Keyser (2002) *Greek Science of the
Hellenistic Era: a Sourcebook*, London and New York.

Irwin, T. (1988) *Aristotle's First Principles*, Oxford.

Jaeger, Werner (1948) *Aristotle: Fundamentals of the History of his Development*,
2nd edn., trans. R. Robinson, Oxford.

Johnson, Monte Ransome (2005) *Aristotle on Teleology*, Oxford.

Kahn, Charles H. (1960) *Anaximander and the Origins of Greek Cosmology*,
New York.

(1985) 'The Prime Mover and Teleology', in A. Gotthelf (ed.), *Aristotle on
Nature and Living Things*, Bristol: 183–205.

Kaibel, G. (1887) *Athenaei Naucratitae deipnosophistarum libri xv*, 3 vols.,
Leipzig.

Kant, Immanuel (2002) *Metaphysical Foundations of Natural Science*, trans.
Michael Friedman, in H. Allison and P. Heath (eds.), *Theoretical
Philosophy after 1781*, The Cambridge Edition of the Works of
Immanuel Kant, Cambridge: 171–270.

Keyser, Paul T. (1992) 'A New Look at Heron's Steam Engine', *Archive for
History of the Exact Sciences* 44: 107–24.

(1994) 'The Use of Artillery by Philip II and Alexander the Great', *Ancient
World* 25: 27–59.

(1998) 'Orreries, the Date of [Plato] *Letter* 11, and Eudoros of Alexandria', *Archiv für Geschichte der Philosophie* 80: 241–67.

(forthcoming) '*Peri Kosmou*', in Thomas P. Hockey (ed.), *Biographical Encyclopedia of Astronomers*.

Kirk, G. S., J. E. Raven and M. Schofield (1983) *The Presocratic Philosophers: a Critical History with a Selection of Texts*, 2nd edn., Cambridge.

Kline, A. D. and C. A. Matheson (1987) 'The Logical Impossibility of Collision', *Philosophy* 62: 509–15.

Knorr, W. R. (1982) *Ancient Sources of the Medieval Tradition of Mechanics: Greek, Arabic and Latin Studies of the Balance*, Florence.

(1989) *Textual Studies in Ancient and Medieval Geometry*, Boston.

(1990) 'Plato and Eudoxus on the Planetary Motions', *Journal for the History of Astronomy* 15: 315–29.

Konstan, David (1979) 'Problems in Epicurean Physics', *Isis* 70: 394–418.

(1982) 'Atomism and its Heritage: Minimal Parts', *Ancient Philosophy* 2: 60–75.

Koyré, Alexandre (1961) *Études d'histoire de la pensée philosophique*, Paris.

Krafft, Fritz (1970a) *Dynamische und Statische Betrachtungsweise in der Antike Mechanik*, Wiesbaden.

(1970b) 'Die Stellung der Technik zur Naturwissenschaft in Antike und Neuzeit', *Technik Geschichte* 37: 189–209.

(1972) 'Heron von Alexandria', in K. Fassmann *et al.* (eds.), *Die Grossen der Weltgeschichte*, vol. II: *Cäsar bis Karl der Große*, Zurich: 333–79.

Kuhn, Thomas (1957) *The Copernican Revolution: Planetary Astronomy in the Development of Western Thought*, Cambridge, MA.

(1977) *The Essential Tension: Selected Studies in Scientific Tradition and Change*, Chicago.

Laird, W. R. (1986) 'The Scope of Renaissance Mechanics', *Osiris*, 2nd ser., 2: 43–68.

(1997) 'Galileo and the Mixed Sciences', in D. A. Di Liscia, E. Kessler and C. Methuen (eds.), *Method and Order in Renaissance Philosophy of Nature; The Aristotle Commentary Tradition*, Aldershot: 253–70.

Landels, J. G. (1978) *Engineering in the Ancient World*, London.

Laudan, Larry (1981) 'The Clock Metaphor and Hypotheses: the Impact of Descartes on English Methodological Thought, 1650–1670', in *Science and Hypothesis: Historical Essays on Scientific Methodology*, Dordrecht: 27–58.

Lehoux, Daryn (1999) 'All Voids Great and Small, Being a Discussion of Place and Void in Strato of Lampsacus's Matter Theory', *Apeiron: a Journal for Ancient Philosophy and Science* 32: 1–36.

Lennox, James G. (1986) 'Aristotle, Galileo, and "Mixed Sciences"', in W. A. Wallace (ed.), *Reinterpreting Galileo*, Studies in Philosophy and the History of Philosophy, vol. XV, Washington, DC: 29–51.

Liddell, Henry George and Robert Scott (1996) *A Greek–English Lexicon*, 9th edn., rev. Henry Stuart Jones, Oxford.

Lindberg, David C. (1992) *The Beginnings of Western Science: the European Scientific Tradition in Philosophical, Religious, and Institutional Context, 600 BC to AD 1450*, Chicago.

Lloyd, A. C. (1976) 'The Principle that the Cause Is Greater than its Effect', *Phronesis* 21: 146–56.

Lloyd, G. E. R. (1966) *Polarity and Analogy: Two Types of Argumentation in Early Greek thought*, Cambridge.

(1970) *Early Greek Science: Thales to Aristotle*, New York.

(1973) *Greek Science after Aristotle*, New York.

(1979) *Magic, Reason and Experience: Studies in the Origins and Development of Greek Science*, London.

(1987) *Revolutions of Wisdom: Studies in the Claims and Practice of Ancient Greek Science*, Berkeley.

(1991) *Methods and Problems in Greek Science*, Cambridge.

Long, A. A. and D. N. Sedley (1987) *The Hellenistic Philosophers*, 2 vols., Cambridge.

Longrigg, J. (1993) *Greek Rational Medicine: Philosophy and Medicine from Alcmaeon to the Alexandrians*, London.

Lonie, I. M. (1973) 'The Paradoxical Text "On the Heart"', *Medical History* 17: 1–15, 136–53.

(1981a) *The Hippocratic Treatises 'On Generation', 'On the Nature of the Child', 'Diseases IV': a Commentary*, Berlin.

(1981b) 'Hippocrates the Iatromechanist', *Medical History* 25: 113–50.

Lorimer, W. L. (1933) *Aristotelis qui fertur libellus de mundo*, Paris.

Louis, P. (1964–9) *Aristote. Histoire des animaux*, vols. I–III, Paris.

Mach, Ernst *The Science of Mechanics: a Critical and Historical Account of its Development*, 3rd edn., trans. Thomas J. McCormack, Chicago.

Machamer, Peter (1978) 'Galileo and the Causes', in R. E. Butts and J. C. Pitt, *New Perspectives on Galileo*, Dordrecht: 161–80.

(1998) 'Galileo's Machines, his Mathematics, and his Experiments', in P. Machamer (ed.), *The Cambridge Companion to Galileo*, Cambridge: 53–79.

Machamer, Peter and Andrea Woody (1994) 'A Model of Intelligibility in Science: Using Galileo's Balance as a Model for Understanding the Motion of Bodies', *Science and Education* 3: 215–44.

Macierowski, E. M. and R. F. Hassing (1988) 'John Philoponus on Aristotle's Definition of Nature', *Ancient Philosophy* 8: 73–100.

Maggiòlo, P. M. (ed.) (1954) *S. Thomae Aquinatis Doctoris Angelici In octo libros Physicorum Aristotelis expositio*, Rome.

Mahoney, Michael (1998) 'The Mathematical Realm of Nature', in D. Garber and M. Ayers (eds.), *The Cambridge History of Seventeenth-Century Philosophy*, vol. i, Cambridge: 702–55.

Makin, Stephen (1993) *Indifference Arguments*, Oxford.

Manitius, C. (1909) *Procli Diadochi hypotyposis astronomicarum positionum*, Leipzig.

Mansfeld, Jaap (1992) 'PERI KOSMOU: a Note on the History of the Title', *Vigiliae Christianae* 46: 391–411.

Marcovich, Miroslav (ed.) (1999) *Diogenis Laertii Vitae Philosophorum*, vol. i, Stuttgart and Leipzig.

Marsden, E. W. (1969) *Greek and Roman Artillery: Historical Development*, Oxford.

  (1971) *Greek and Roman Artillery: Technical Treatises*, Oxford.

Marshall, C. W. (2003) 'Sophocles' *Nauplius* and Heron of Alexandria's "Mechanical Theatre"', in A. H. Sommerstein (ed.), *Shards from Kolonos: Studies in Sophoclean Fragments*, Bari: 261–79.

Matthen, Mohan (1989) 'The Four Causes in Aristotle's Embryology', in R. Kraut and T. Penner (eds.), *Nature, Knowledge and Virtue: Essays in Memory of Joan Kung. Apeiron* Special Issue 22: 159–80.

Maurice, Klaus and Otto Mayr (1980) *The Clockwork Universe: German Clocks and Automata 1550–1650*, Washington, DC.

May, Margaret Talmadge (1968) *Galen On the Usefulness of the Parts of the Body, Translated from the Greek with an Introduction and Commentary*, Ithaca, NY.

Mayr, Otto (1970) *The Origins of Feedback Control*, Cambridge, MA.

  (1986) *Authority, Liberty and Automatic Machinery in Early Modern Europe*, Baltimore.

McEwen, Indra Kagis (2003) *Vitruvius: Writing the Body of Architecture*, Cambridge, MA.

McKirahan, Jr., Richard D. (1994) *Philosophy before Socrates: an Introduction with Texts and Commentary*, Indianapolis.

McMullin, Ernan (1978) 'Structural Explanation', *American Philosophical Quarterly* 15: 139–47.

McNicoll, A. W. (1997) *Hellenistic Fortifications from the Aegean to the Euphrates*, with revisions and an additional chapter by N. P. Milner, Oxford.

McPherran, Mark L. (1996) *The Religion of Socrates*, University Park, PA.

Meli, Domenico Bertoloni (2006) *Thinking with Objects: the Transformation of Mechanics in the Seventeenth Century*, Baltimore.

Mendell, Henry (2000) 'The Trouble with Eudoxus', in P. Suppes, J. M. Moravcsik and H. Mendell (eds.), *Ancient and Medieval Traditions in the Exact Sciences: Essays in Memory of Wilbur Knorr*, Stanford: 59–138.

Menn, Stephen (1990) 'Descartes and Some Predecessors on the Divine Conservation of Motion', *Synthese* 83: 215–38.

(1998) 'The Intellectual Setting', in D. Garber and M. Ayers (eds.), *The Cambridge History of Seventeenth-Century Philosophy*, vol. I, Cambridge: 33–86.

(2002) 'Aristotle's Definition of Soul and the Programme of the *De anima*', *Oxford Studies in Ancient Philosophy* 22: 83–140.

(in preparation) 'Anaxagoras, Empedocles, Leucippus'.

Merton, Robert K. (1970) *Science, Technology and Society in Seventeenth Century England*, New York.

Micheli, Gianni (1995) *Le origini del concetto di macchina*, Firenze.

Mikkeli, Heikki (1992) *An Aristotelian Response to Renaissance Humanism: Jacopo Zabarella on the Nature of Arts and Sciences*, Helsinki.

(1997) 'The Foundations of an Autonomous Natural Philosophy; Zabarella on the Classification of Arts and Sciences', in D. A. Di Liscia, E. Kessler and C. Methuen (eds.), *Method and Order in Renaissance Philosophy of Nature; the Aristotle Commentary Tradition*, Aldershot: 211–28.

Montaigne, Michel de (1929) *The Diary of Montaigne's Journey to Italy in 1580 and 1581*, translated with introduction and notes by E. J. Trechmann, New York.

Moody, Ernest A. and Marshall Clagett (1952) *The Medieval Science of Weights (Scientia de ponderibus)*, Madison.

More, Henry (1978) *A Collection of Several Philosophical Writings*, New York.

Moritz, L. A. (1958) *Grain-Mills and Flour in Classical Antiquity*, Oxford.

Morris, Sarah P. (1992) *Daidalos and the Origins of Greek Art*, Princeton.

Morrow, Glenn R. (1970) *Proclus: a Commentary on the First Book of Euclid's Elements*, translated with introduction and notes, Princeton.

Mourelatos, A. P. D. (1967) 'Aristotle's "Powers" and Modern Empiricism', *Ratio* 9: 97–104.

(1981) 'Astronomy and Kinematics in Plato's Project of Rationalist Explanation', *Studies in History and Philosophy of Science* 12: 1–32.

(1984) 'Democritus: Philosopher of Form', in *Proceedings of the 1st International Congress on Democritus*, Xanthi: 109–19.

(1991) 'Plato's Science – His View and Ours of His', in A. C. Bowen (ed.), *Science and Philosophy in Classical Greece*, New York and London: 11–30.

Mumford, Lewis (1934) *Technics and Civilization*, New York.

Murdoch, John E. (2001) 'The Medieval and Renaissance Tradition of *Minima Naturalia*', in C. Lüthy, J. E. Murdoch and W. R. Newman (eds.), *Late Medieval and Early Modern Corpuscular Matter Theories*, Leiden: 91–132.

Murphy, Susan (1995) 'Heron of Alexandria's *On Automaton-Making*', *History of Technology* 17: 1–44.

Mutschmann, H. (1914) *Sexti Empirici opera*, vol. II, Leipzig.

Nadler, Steven (1998) 'Doctrines of Explanation in Late Scholasticism and in the Mechanical Philosophy', in D. Garber and M. Ayers (eds.), *The Cambridge History of Seventeenth-Century Philosophy*, vol. I, Cambridge: 513–52.

Needham, Joseph (1934) *A History of Embryology*, Cambridge.

Netz, Reviel (1999) *The Shaping of Deduction in Greek Mathematics: a Study in Cognitive History*, Cambridge.

(2000) 'The Origins of Mathematical Physics: New Light on an Old Question', *Physics Today* 53: 31–6.

Neugebauer, Otto (1975) *A History of Ancient Mathematical Astronomy*, 3 vols., New York.

Newman, William R. (2004) *Promethean Ambitions: Alchemy and the Quest to Perfect Nature*, Chicago.

Newton, Isaac (1995) *The Principia*, trans. Andrew Motte, New York.

Noble, Joseph V. and Derek J. de Solla Price (1968) 'The Water Clock in the Tower of the Winds', *American Journal of Archaeology* 72: 345–55.

Nussbaum, Martha C. (1978) *Aristotle's* De Motu Animalium: *Text with Translation, Commentary, and Interpretive Essays*, Princeton.

Nutton, Vivian (2004) *Ancient Medicine*, London and New York.

Oleson, John Peter (1984) *Greek and Roman Mechanical Water-Lifting Devices: the History of a Technology*, Toronto.

Owen, G. E. L. (1986) 'Aristotelian Mechanics', in M. Nussbaum (ed.), *Logic, Science and Dialectic: Collected Papers in Greek Philosophy*, London: 315–33.

Owens, Joseph (1991) 'The Aristotelian Conception of the Pure and Applied Sciences', in A. C. Bowen (ed.), *Science and Philosophy in Classical Greece*, New York and London: 31–42.

Papalexandrou, Nassos (1998) *Warriors, Youths, and Tripods: the Visual Poetics of Power in Geometric and Early Archaic Greece*, PhD dissertation, Princeton.

Patterson, Richard (1985) *Image and Reality in Plato's Metaphysics*, Indianapolis.

Peltonen, Markku (ed.) (1996) *The Cambridge Companion to Bacon*, Cambridge.

Pérez-Ramos, Antonio (1988) *Francis Bacon's Idea of Science and the Maker's Knowledge Tradition*, Oxford.

(1993) 'Francis Bacon and Man's Two-Faced Kingdom', in G. H. R. Parkinson (ed.), *Routledge History of Philosophy*, vol. IV: *The Renaissance and Seventeenth Century Rationalism*, London and New York: 140–66.

(1996a) 'Bacon's Forms and the Maker's Knowledge Tradition', in M. Peltonen (ed.), *The Cambridge Companion to Bacon*, Cambridge: 99–120.

(1996b) 'Bacon's Legacy', in M. Peltonen (ed.), *The Cambridge Companion to Bacon*, Cambridge: 311–34.

Pleket, H. W. (1973) 'Technology in the Greco-Roman World: a General Report', *TALANTA* 5: 6–47.

Pollitt, J. J. (1974) *The Ancient View of Greek Art: Criticism, History and Terminology*, New Haven.

(1990) *The Art of Ancient Greece: Sources and Documents*, Cambridge.

Prager, Frank David (1974) *Philo of Byzantium Pneumatica. The First Treatise on Experimental Physics: Western Version and Eastern Version*, Wiesbaden.

Price, Derek J. de Solla (1964) 'Automata and the Origins of Mechanism and Mechanistic Philosophy', *Technology and Culture* 5: 9–23.

(1975) *Gears from the Greeks: the Antikythera Mechanism – a Calendar Computer from ca. 80 BC*, New York.

Pyle, Andrew (1997) *Atomism and its Critics: From Democritus to Newton*, Bristol.

Rackham, H. (1968) *Pliny Natural History IX, Books XXXIII–XXXV*, London.

Randall, J. H. (1940) 'The Development of Scientific Method in the School of Padua', *Journal of the History of Ideas* 1: 177–206.

Randall, John Herman Jr. (1960) *Aristotle*, New York.

Rehm, A. (1937) 'Antike "Automobile"', *Philologus* 92: 317–30.

Repici, Luciana (1988) *La natura e l'anima: saggi su Stratone de Lampsaco*, Torino.

Rice, E. E. (1983) *The Grand Procession of Ptolemy Philadelphus*, Oxford.

Robinson, John Mansley (1968) *An Introduction to Early Greek Philosophy: the Chief Fragments and Ancient Testimony, with Connecting Commentary*, Boston.

Rochefort, G. (1960) *Saloustios. Des dieux et du monde*, Paris.

Rose, Paul Lawrence and Stillman Drake (1971) 'The Pseudo-Aristotelian *Questions of Mechanics* in Renaissance Culture', *Studies in the Renaissance* 18: 65–104.

Ross, W. D. (1923) *Aristotle*, London.

(1936) *Aristotle's Physics: a Revised Text with Introduction and Commentary*, Oxford.

Rossi, Paolo (1970) *Philosophy, Technology, and the Arts in the Early Modern Era*, trans. Salvator Attanasio, ed. Benjamin Nelson, New York, Evanston and London.

Roth, Catharine P. (1993) *St Gregory of Nyssa: the Soul and the Resurrection*, Crestwood, NY.

Roux, Sophie (1996) *La philosophie mécanique (1630–1690)*, PhD dissertation, Paris.

Russo, Lucio (2004) *The Forgotten Revolution: How Science Was Born in 300 BC and Why It Had to Be Reborn*, trans. and with the collaboration of Silvio Levy, Berlin.

Salmon, Wesley (1984) *Scientific Explanation and the Causal Structure of the World*, Princeton.

Sambursky, S. (1956) *The Physical World of the Greeks*, trans. Merton Dagut, London.

(1959) *Physics of the Stoics*, Princeton.

(1962) *The Physical World of Late Antiquity*, London.

(1963) 'Conceptual Developments and Modes of Explanation in Later Greek Scientific Thought', in A. C. Crombie (ed.), *Scientific Change: Historical Studies in the Intellectual, Social and Technical Conditions for Scientific Discovery and Technical Invention, from Antiquity to the Present*, New York: 61–78.

Savage-Smith, Emilie (1985) *Islamicate Celestial Globes; their History, Construction, and Use*, Washington, DC.

Schiaparelli, Giovanni (1997) 'Le sfere omocentriche di Eudosso di Callippo e di Aristotele', *Scritti sulla storia della astronomica antica*, vol. II, Rome: 5–112.

Schiefsky, Mark J. (2005) 'Technical Terminology in Greco-Roman Treatises on Artillery Construction', in T. Fögen (ed.), *Antike Fachtexte; Ancient Technical Texts*, Berlin: 253–70.

(2007a) 'Art and Nature in Ancient Mechanics', in B. Bensaude-Vincent and W. Newman (eds.), *The Artificial and the Natural: an Evolving Polarity*, Cambridge, MA: 67–108.

(2007b) 'Galen's Teleology and Functional Explanation', *Oxford Studies in Ancient Philosophy* 33: 369–400.

(forthcoming) 'Theory and Practice in Heron's *Mechanics*', in S. Roux and W. R. Laird (eds.), *Mechanics and Natural Philosophy before the Scientific Revolution*.

Schmidt, Wilhelm (1899) *Heronis Alexandrini opera quae supersunt omnia*, Leipzig.

Schuhl, P.-M. (1947) *Machinisme et philosophie*, 2nd rev. edn., Paris.

Sedley, David (1976) 'Epicurus and the Mathematicians of Cyzicus', *Cronache Ercolanesi* 6: 23–54.

(1987) 'Philoponus' Conception of Space', in R. Sorabji (ed.), *Philoponus and the Rejection of Aristotelian Science*, London: 140–153.

(1988) 'Epicurean Anti-Reductionism', in J. Barnes and M. Mignucci (eds.), *Matter and Metaphysics: Fourth Symposium Hellenisticum*, Naples: 297–327.

(1998) *Lucretius and the Transformation of Greek Wisdom*, Cambridge.

Seymour, Thomas Day (1908) *Life in the Homeric Age*, New York.

Shapin, Steven and Simon Schaffer (1985) *Leviathan and the Air-Pump: Hobbes, Boyle, and the Experimental Life*, Princeton.

Simms, D. L. (1995) 'Archimedes the Engineer', *History of Technology* 17: 45–111.

Simpson, J. A. and E. S. C. Weiner (eds.) (1989) *The Oxford English Dictionary*, 2nd edn., Oxford.

Singer, P. N. (1997) *Galen: Selected Works*, translated with an introduction and notes, Oxford.

Siorvanes, Lucas (1996) *Proclus: Neo-Platonic Philosophy and Science*, Edinburgh.

Snell, Bruno (1953) *The Discovery of the Mind: the Greek Origins of European Thought*, trans. T. G. Rosenmeyer, Oxford.

Solmsen, Friedrich (1960) *Aristotle's System of the Physical World: a Comparison with his Predecessors*, Ithaca, NY.

Solomon, Julie Robin (1998) *Objectivity in the Making: Francis Bacon and the Politics of Inquiry*, Baltimore and London.

Sorabji, Richard R. K. (1983) *Time, Creation and the Continuum: Theories in Antiquity and the Early Middle Ages*, London and Ithaca, NY.

(ed.) (1987) *Philoponus and the Rejection of Aristotelian Science*, London.

(ed.) (1990) *Aristotle Transformed*, London.

(2002) 'Latitude of Forms in Ancient Philosophy', in C. Leijenhorst, C. Lüthy and J. M. M. H. Thijssen (eds.), *The Dynamics of Aristotelian Natural Philosophy from Antiquity to the Seventeenth Century*, Leiden: 57–63.

Staden, Heinrich von (1975) 'Experiment and Experience in Hellenistic medicine', *Bulletin of the Institute of Classical Studies* 22: 178–99.

(1989) *Herophilus: the Art of Medicine in Early Alexandria*, Cambridge.

(1996) 'Body and Machine: Interactions between Medicine, Mechanics, and Philosophy in Early Alexandria', in J. Walsh and T. F. Reese (eds.), *Alexandria and Alexandrianism*, Malibu: 85–106.

(1997) 'Teleology and Mechanism: Aristotelian Biology and Early Hellenistic Medicine', in W. Kullmann and S. Föllinger (eds.), *Aristotelische Biologie: Intentionen, Methoden, Ergebnisse*, Stuttgart: 183–208.

(1998) 'Andréas de Caryste et Philon de Byzance: médecine et mécanique à Alexandrie', in G. Argoud and J.-Y. Guillaumin (eds.), *Sciences exactes et sciences appliquées à Alexandrie*, Saint-Étienne: 147–72.

Steel, Carlos (2007) *Proclus On Providence*, Ithaca, NY.

Stern, Jacob (1996) *Palaephatus On Unbelievable Tales*, Wauconda, IL.

Sternagel, Peter (1966) *Die Artes Mechanicae im Mittelalter: Begriffs- und Bedeutungsgeschichte bis zum Ende des 13. Jahrhunderts*, Kallmünz.

Taub, Liba Chaia (1993) *Ptolemy's Universe: the Natural Philosophical and Ethical Foundations of Ptolemy's Astronomy*, Chicago and Lasalle, IL.

Taylor, C. C. W. (1999) 'The Atomists', in A. A. Long (ed.), *The Cambridge Companion to Early Greek Philosophy*, Cambridge: 181–204.

Taylor, Jerome (1961) *The* Didascalicon *of Hugh of St Victor*, translated from the Latin with introduction and notes, New York and London.

Thomas, Ivor (1951) *Selections Illustrating the History of Greek Mathematics*, 2 vols., Cambridge.

Thompson, Homer A. and R. E. Wycherley (1972) *The Athenian Agora*, vol. XIV: *The Agora of Athens*, Princeton.

Thorndike, Lynn (1929) *A History of Magic and Experimental Science during the First Thirteen Centuries of Our Era*, vol. I, New York.

Todd, R. B. (1972) '*Epitêdeiotês* in Philosophical Literature: Towards an Analysis', *Acta Classica* 15: 25–35.

  (1976) 'Galenic Medical Ideas in the Greek Aristotelian Commentators', *Symbolae Osloenses* 52: 117–34.

  (1984) 'Philosophy and Medicine in John Philoponus' Commentary on Aristotle's *De Anima*', *Dumbarton Oaks Papers* 38: 103–10.

Toomey, G. J. (1984) *Ptolemy's Almagest*, translated and annotated, New York.

Tybjerg, Karin (2003) 'Wonder-making and Philosophical Wonder in Hero of Alexandria', *Studies in History and Philosophy of Science* 34: 443–66.

  (2004) 'Hero of Alexandria's Mechanical Geometry', in P. Lang (ed.), *Re-Inventions: Essays on Hellenistic and Early Roman Science*, *Apeiron* 37.4: 29–56.

  (2005) 'Hero of Alexandria's Mechanical Treatises: Between Theory and Practice', in A. Schürmann (ed.), *Physik/Mechanik: Geschichte der Mathematik und der Naturwissenschaften in der Antike*, Stuttgart: 204–26.

Ugaglia, Monica (2004) *Modelli idrostatici del moto da Aristotele a Galileo*, Rome.

Vallance, J. T. (1990) *The Lost Theory of Asclepiades of Bithynia*, Oxford.

Van Der Waerden, B. L. (1961) *Science Awakening*, trans. Arnold Dresden, Groningen.

Vaux, Carra de (1893) '*Les mécaniques* ou *L'élévateur* de Héron d'Alexandrie, publiées pour la première fois sur la version arabe de Qostâ Ibn Lûqâ', *Journal Asiatique* 9th ser., 1: vol. I, 386–472; vol. II, 152–269; 420–514.

  (1903) '*Les pneumatiques* de Philon de Byzance', *Notes et extraits des MSS de la Bibliothèque Nationale* 39: 27–229.

Vegetti, Mario (1993) 'I nervi dell' anima', in J. Kollesch and D. Nickel (eds.), *Galen und das Hellenistische Erbe: Verhandlungen des IV. Internationalen Galen-Symposiums*, Stuttgart: 63–77.

  (1998) 'Between Knowledge and Practice: Hellenistic Medicine', in M. D. Grmek (ed.), *Western Medical Thought from Antiquity to the Middle Ages*, trans. Antony Shugaar, Cambridge, MA: 72–103.

Ver Eecke, Paul (1933) *Pappus d'Alexandrie: La Collection Mathématique*, 2 vols., Paris.

Vernant, Jean Pierre (1983) *Myth and Thought among the Greeks*, London.

Vlastos, Gregory (1971) 'Reasons and Causes in the *Phaedo*', in Vlastos (ed.), *Plato: a Collection of Critical Essays*, vol. I, Notre Dame, IN: 132–66.

(1975) *Plato's Universe*, Seattle.

Wallace, William A. (1984) *Galileo and his Sources: the Heritage of the Collegio Romano in Galileo's Science*, Princeton.

Wardy, Robert (1990) *The Chain of Change: a Study of Aristotle's* Physics *VII*, Cambridge.

Waterlow, Sarah (1982) *Nature, Change, and Agency in Aristotle's Physics: a Philosophical Study*, Oxford.

Wehrli, Fritz (1951) *Die Schule des Aristoteles*, vol. V, Basel.

Weisheipl, James A. (1985) *Nature and Motion in the Middle Ages*, ed. William E. Carroll, Washington, DC.

Weiss, Rosalyn (1990) 'Hedonism in the *Protagoras* and the Sophist's Guarantee', *Ancient Philosophy* 10: 17–23.

Weitzmann, Kurt (1959) *Ancient Book Illumination: Martin Classical Lectures*, vol. XVI, Cambridge, MA.

(1971) 'The Greek Sources of Islamic Scientific Illustrations', in H. L. Kessler (ed.), *Studies in Classical and Byzantine Manuscript Illumination*, Chicago: 20–44.

Westfall, Richard S. (1971) *The Construction of Modern Science: Mechanisms and Mechanics*, New York.

White, K. D. (1984) *Greek and Roman Technology*, Ithaca, NY.

White, Steven (2002) 'Thales and the Stars', in V. Caston and D. Graham (eds.), *Presocratic Philosophy: Essays in Honour of Alexander Mourelatos*, London: 3–18.

Whitehead, David and P. H. Blyth (2004) *Athenaeus Mechanicus*, On Machines, translated with introduction and commentary, Stuttgart.

Whitney, Elspeth (1990) *Paradise Restored: the Mechanical Arts from Antiquity through the Thirteenth Century*, Transactions of the American Philosophical Society 80.1.

Wieland, W. (1975) 'The Problem of Teleology', in J. Barnes, M. Schofield and R. Sorabji (eds.), *Articles on Aristotle*, vol. I: *Science*, London: 141–60.

Wolff, Michael (1987) 'Philoponus and the Rise of Preclassical Dynamics', in R. Sorabji (ed.), *Philoponus and the Rejection of Aristotelian Science*, London: 84–120.

(1988) 'Hipparchus and the Stoic Theory of Motion', in J. Barnes and M. Mignucci (eds.), *Matter and Metaphysics*, Naples: 471–545.

Woodcroft, Bennet (1851) *The Pneumatics of Hero of Alexandria*, London.

Wright, M. R. (1995) *Cosmology in Antiquity*, London.

Zachhuber, Johannes (2000) *Human Nature in Gregory of Nyssa: Philosophical Background and Theological Significance*, Leiden.

Zhmud, Leonid (2006) *The Origin of the History of Science in Classical Antiquity*, trans. Alexander Chernoglazov, Berlin and New York.

Ziegler, K. (1968) *Plutarchi vitae parallelae*, vol. II.2, 2nd edn., Leipzig.

   (2001) 'Theodoros Mechaniker', *Der Neue Pauly: Enzyklopädie der Antike*, vol. XII, Stuttgart: 692–3.

Index of passages

General index

CPSIA information can be obtained
at www.ICGtesting.com
Printed in the USA
LVHW081454240719
624999LV00027B/457/P